Youth Violence

Theory, Prevention, and Intervention

About the Author

Kathryn Seifert received her PhD from the University of Maryland, Baltimore Campus, in 1995. She is a Fellow and Past President for the Maryland Psychological Association and advocates for the highest quality services for all children needing mental health treatment.

Dr. Seifert has more than 30 years experience in mental health, addictions, and criminal justice work. In addition to creating the Juvenile *CARE2* (*Chronic Violent Behavior Risk and Needs Assessment*, 2nd Edition), she has authored articles and lectured nationally and internationally on family violence and suicide prevention and trauma. She founded Eastern Shore Psychological Services, a multidisciplinary private practice that specializes in working with high-risk youth and their families. Her first book was *How Children Become Violent: Keeping Your Kids Out of Gangs, Terrorist Organizations and Cults.* You can find it at her Web site: www. DrKathySeifert.com

Dr. Seifert is a regular lecturer for PESI.com, an organization providing continuing education credits for professionals. She is a regular contributor to Americanchronicle.com, an online international news and opinion magazine. She has appeared on EBRU TV's *Bullying in America*, Fox News Radio, CNN, and the Discovery Channel TV program *Investigation Discovery.*

Youth Violence

Theory, Prevention, and Intervention

Kathryn Seifert, PhD

With Chapters by

Karen Ray, PhD, Coordinator of Psychology Department, ESPS, LLC
Robert Schmidt, MS, LCPC, Talbot County Board of Education

SPRINGER PUBLISHING COMPANY
NEW YORK

Springer Publishing Company, LLC
11 West 42nd Street
New York, NY 10036
www.springerpub.com

Acquisitions Editor: Jennifer Perillo
Composition: Newgen Imaging

ISBN: 978-0-8261-0740-4
E-book ISBN: 978-0-8261-0741-1

11 12 13/5 4 3 2 1

The author and the publisher of this Work have made every effort to use sources believed to be reliable to provide information that is accurate and compatible with the standards generally accepted at the time of publication. The author and publisher shall not be liable for any special, consequential, or exemplary damages resulting, in whole or in part, from the readers' use of, or reliance on, the information contained in this book. The publisher has no responsibility for the persistence or accuracy of URLs for external or third-party Internet Web sites referred to in this publication and does not guarantee that any content on such Web sites is, or will remain, accurate or appropriate.

CIP data is available from the Library of Congress

Special discounts on bulk quantities of our books are available to corporations, professional associations, pharmaceutical companies, health care organizations, and other qualifying groups.

If you are interested in a custom book, including chapters from more than one of our titles, we can provide that service as well.

For details, please contact:
Special Sales Department, Springer Publishing Company, LLC
11 West 42nd Street, 15th Floor, New York, NY 10036-8002
Phone: 877-687-7476 or 212-431-4370; Fax: 212-941-7842
Email: sales@springerpub.com

Printed in the United States of America by Gasch Printing

*This book is dedicated with love to my parents,
Maurice and Jean Lewis, and grandparents,
Maurice and Mary Lewis, who made me who I am.*

Contents

Contributors

Karen Ray, PhD, Coordinator of Psychology Department, Eastern Shore Psychological Services, Salisbury, MD

Robert Schmidt, MS, Talbot County Board of Education, Easton, MD

Kathryn Seifert, PhD, CEO, Eastern Shore Psychological Services and CARE2, LLC, Salisbury, MD

Foreword

On April 20, 1999, two high school seniors, Dylan Klebold and Eric Harris, perpetrated what was to become one of the boldest and bloodiest assaults on a student body in American high school history. When the mayhem was over, 14 students, including the two perpetrators, along with a teacher were dead. That assault sparked much anger and soul searching as to how these adolescents could consider mass murder as an expression of whatever problems they had with anyone, including those at the school. There were subsequent events since that time that to this day highlight the difficulties of youth violence.

Mental health practitioners, health care professionals, the courts, and many questioning citizens continue to wonder how we got to this point, and whether the ongoing "war" to curb youth violence will ever be won. While there aren't any easy answers, Dr. Seifert's enlightening elaboration on youth violence issues in this book sheds refreshing light on an old discussion. By walking us through the physical, cognitive, and psychosocial aspects of youth violence, we are able to gain an updated perspective on the underpinnings of violence, and what could and should be done to understand and indeed curb such difficulties in our communities.

Kathryn Seifert has followed all protocols in this book, *Youth Violence: Theory, Prevention, and Intervention*, but the reality of her research is nonetheless dramatic, alarming, and an insistent "emergency alert" to professionals and lay citizens alike who must respond if our nation is to avoid a social meltdown, not from terrorists abroad but from our own hurting and desperate children who see violence as the only escape from their miserable, cornered, nothing-to-lose existence.

As her research indicates, youth violence is systemic to and predominant in our American culture. From infancy we idolize "action" in comic books, electronic games, Wild West movies, girl gangs, contact sports, and confrontational domestic relationships. Our language exudes, exalts, and glorifies violent phrases "smash the opposition," "take down," "wipe out," and "floored." For generations our folklore heroes were those who took no prisoners, slammed the opponents, and cheered those who won by any means necessary. "The Avengers" and "Girl Bratz" are role models. Our children get the message. Violence is respected. Violence works, until it gets out of hand.

As it has, all across America, here, now, with tragic frequency and heartbreak, youth violence has reached epidemic proportions among all segments of our society. The time has long passed for us to recognize and begin to address this danger to our children and our country.

Nearly two decades ago, The American Institute for Urban Psychological Studies, Inc., of which I am founder, hosted two conferences on "Grief and Loss" and "Young People and Violence." Our speakers included first responders, child advocates, law enforcement, and mental health professionals. One of the most poignant observations by the then Baltimore City Prosecutor was that more children had been victims of violent murders in the first months of that year in Baltimore than the total of war victims of the just-concluded military action in Iraq.

"Our children are living in a state of emergency," she stated, referring to the street violence that resulted in children attending more funerals for their peers than for their grandparents.

Among other jurisdictions within Maryland and indeed throughout the country during that same period, there were documented growing problems of junior repeat offenders, which alerted law enforcement agencies of the growing trend toward "bubble-gum criminals" as the challenge for the courts and our society. Few seemed to listen.

Today, child criminals have become so commonplace that many have become bored or fatigued with the issue, until an incident in an unexpected (nice) community awakens them to the reality that youth violence knows no boundaries, no class, and no gender. It is a prevalent, pervasive fact of life, or death, in our 21st-century landscape.

This work by Dr. Seifert is not an exposé of parents, educators, social workers, politicians, or any one group or culture. Rather than seeking villains responsible for the culture in which youth violence gestates, she charts the genesis for and subsequent interlocking forces that lead to teachers being afraid of students in their classrooms, motorists being intimidated by squeegee kids, bicyclists hesitant to venture on unfamiliar trails, elderly shoppers fearful of carrying their groceries to the car, students having bullying experiences in school bathrooms, and even juvenile facilities staff squeamish that they may be "gang banged" as they go about their duties. She provides the information and recommendations to understand and come to grips with where we are.

This book is about a time bomb that already has, and, unless we find and utilize methods to defuse, contain, and redirect its energy, will continue to explode within our homes, schools, workplaces, institutions, and self-denying culture.

Dr. Seifert painstakingly provides the statistics to support what the newspapers and police reports have already enumerated in cities and towns across our nation: More and more American children are increasingly violent at alarmingly younger ages and with greater severity than in any other developed nation and devoid of the survival urgency found among so-called "child soldiers" in war-ravaged third-world countries.

Informational, fact-filled, and with eye-opening, albeit familiar approaches to child development, this book deserves permanent placement on the office desk or nearby reachable reference library of every school principal, foster parent, child welfare worker, juvenile court judge, juvenile facility administrator, child advocate, mental health provider, psychologist, or psychiatrist, whether specializing in children or working with families in which crime or fear of crime is a presenting problem. This book probably will not answer all your questions about why so many of our young people are involved in or victims of violent behaviors. It may simply lead you to further research or to a new, more enlightened frame of reference. It may influence your conversations and your management of children under your guidance. However it affects you, I am sure it will be a positive addition to your library. In short, I recommend it to you and your associates as a valuable tool to enrich your perspective on youth violence in today's society.

Grady Dale, Jr., EdD
President
American Institute for Urban Psychological Studies
Baltimore, MD

Preface

This book investigates the existing evidence-based and promising practices for assessment, prevention, and intervention with youth at risk for violent behaviors and shows ways that programs for such youth can improve.

I have worked with these youth for over 30 years and I have cheered at their successes and cried when they fell down. Some succeeded after a lot of hard work and some are still a work in progress. My motto is, "Never give up on a kid." I have seen youth so damaged by horrible abuse and neglect that it hurts to hear their stories. "There but for the grace of God, go I." However, the hopeful news is that in my experience, many if not all youth can rise above their beginnings. I have written this book to share the stories and insights that will help show violence as a public health problem and treat it as such.

Chapter 1 describes the prevalence and trends in youth violence. Some of the statistics are staggering: The estimated cost of gun violence in the United States is $100 billion per year. In addition, the United States has one of the highest violence rates in non–third world countries and incarcerates more people than most industrialized nations. The rate of serious violent crimes in schools is 4 per thousand, while the rate away from school is twice that. The United States has approximately 1 million gang members and gangs are found in every state. A third of students report being bullied in school.

In Chapter 2, I describe some of the demographic factors that impact youth violence, including gender, race/ethnicity, and socioeconomic status.

Chapter 3 describes the different classifications of violence. Hot violence is reactive and situational. It can result from an extreme or ongoing stressor. Relationship violence happens between people who know each other, such as romantic partners, schoolmates, siblings, and parents. Predatory or psychopathic violence is "cold" violence and fortunately rare. Instrumental violence is to gain an object, position, sex, or power. Youth who engage in this behavior believe that the violent means justifies the end.

Chapter 4 offers various theoretical perspectives on the causes of violent behavior. One theory proposes that there are two life courses for violent youth. Youngsters that show severe aggressive traits between the ages of 3 and 12 are more likely, without effective treatment, to have a lifelong course of violence that may decrease around age 60. Youth who show no aggressive traits until their teen years are often not violent past age 25. That tells us that if we want to pull the roots of violence, we must start our prevention efforts between the ages of 0 and 10.

The other theories of violence presented here include social learning, intergenerational transmission of violence, social exchange, subculture, and social structure theories. Drawing from these one- and two-dimensional theories, one can derive a more complex theory that looks at the interactions among a person's biology, development, psychological makeup, social environment, physical environment, strengths, and stressors.

There are individual and environmental factors that influence the course of youth violence. Chapter 5 will describe the individual factors associated with youth violence, such as physiology, cognition, and psychological makeup. Every factor can be further broken down into risk and resiliency items. For example, being psychologically healthy can be a resiliency factor, while past trauma can be a risk factor. However, overcoming and healing from trauma can become a resiliency factor if a youth gains strengths and skills in the process of prevailing over adversity. Both risk and resiliency factors can have an impact on individual development.

There are also environmental risk and resiliency factors: family, peers, school, community, and media. These are discussed in Chapter 6. It is ultimately the unique combination of risk and resiliency factors that determines whether a young person will become violent or nonviolent.

Bullying is universal; yet only recently have we begun to realize that bullying is not a normal part of growing up, but a behavior that harms others. The estimates of the extent of bullying in the United States have a wide range (17–77% of samples tested). Being the victim of bullying can be associated with internalizing symptoms, such as depression, and externalizing behaviors, such as bullying others, as well as school problems and suicide. It appears that many bullies lack empathy and that is a potential area for working with bullies. This is discussed in Chapter 7.

Chapter 8 deals with violence turned inward: suicide. The risk and resiliency factors and warning signs for suicide are discussed, as well as effective programs, such as "Yellow Ribbon."

Research has identified programs that work and are promising and those that don't work. Chapters 9 to 11 describe evidence-based assessment, prevention, and interventions. Some assessments are more effective than others for particular reasons. It is important to use the assessment and intervention that matches the needs of the youth and his family.

Finally, there are many system issues in working with violent youth (Chapter 12). Most, if not all, violent youth have been abused, neglected, or exposed to home or community violence. Agencies that serve children, youth, and families must certainly coordinate their efforts better than is presently being done. Finally, we must find ways to make neighborhoods safer and provide young people with pro-social avenues to success. Mental health services must also be readily available.

I end this introduction with a personal story. Several people in my family have been abused, neglected, and/or exposed to domestic violence. I, fortunately, was not. I have seen the struggles of one relative, in particular, as she worked to overcome the influence of abuse, neglect, and the criminal behavior of her adult caregivers. I have tried to help her and ours has not been an easy path. When I thought I could not stand her behaviors another minute, she gained a significant insight. When I went to the jail to pick her up one more time and she swore it was a mistake, I wanted to believe her, but I knew I could not. When I wanted to hug her and cry, she was too angry to listen. But that was the past. Our young heroine is in college, working, and going to church. Hallelujah! She went to Capitol Hill with me to advocate for mental health services and told her story to congressmen's aides. Much of what I learned, I learned from her. It was wonderful. It can happen for others, but it is a lot of work. I will share what I have learned in this book.

Acknowledgments

I have lots of people to thank. The list is long and I am sure I will miss someone. I am grateful to everyone who helped me along my path. I thank Dr. Grady Dale for his friendship and kind listening ear for the struggles and triumphs of "my kids." His thoughtful foreword touched my heart. As for Judy Howell, my "BFF," I am grateful for her eagle eye and finding all my typos and dangling participles. Judy, and her family, the Richardsons, were very important to my development in my formative years and I thank them all. I am in debt forever to Sarah Hooper, also my "BFF," whose thousands of hours making ESPS run smoothly can never be fully repaid. Her mother, Peg Phillips, is an ongoing proofreader for all my work and someone I cannot do without. Lynn Gavigan, who is a great friend and I am appreciative for her dedication and commitment to ESPS and the many tasks I have put before her. I want to thank my husband, Rick, for his enormous patience while I spent endless hours on this book. I am grateful to Jordan Wright, my granddaughter and my sunshine, for her joy, support, love, and valuable lessons. Ken Maton has been my academic support since college, for which I am grateful. I thank the ESPS staff for infinite hours of hard work and what they have taught me about the mental health field. I especially thank clients who have taught me so much and without whom this book could not be written. You know who you are. I also thank colleagues who encouraged and supported me through this seemingly endless process. I am indebted to Dr. Karen Ray and Rob Schmidt for writing chapters of this book as a labor of love in addition to their day jobs.

I am forever grateful for my son, John Wright, and his family, Melissa, Jordan, Max, and Grace, whom I love with all my heart, for their patience while I worked such long hours and spent little time with them. There are teachers galore that shaped my identity and career. I can't begin to remember them all. I will surely forget to mention some. So, to all of my teachers, I say thanks with all my heart. My sisters Cindy, Linda, Nancy, and Marcia are a source of strength and solace. I can call them any time I need to talk. My parents, grandparents, and "aunts and uncles" from my youth shaped my character and gave me a work ethic along with a mix of creativity, rebel, and rule boundedness. I know I will forget someone, but they were Bill and Nancy Spicer, who sat up all night when I had my tonsils out; Teddy and Ann Malkus, who would pile us in the back of a farm truck to go to Ocean City; and Barton and Becky Spicer, who sang "You are My Sunshine" when we cooked a big pot of crabs. Thanks to everyone who helped shape my life.

Introduction

ONE

Youth Violence: Prevalence and Trends

...the moral test of government is how that government treats those who are in the dawn of life, the children; those who are in the twilight of life, the elderly; those who are in the shadows of life; the sick, the needy, and the handicapped.

—Hubert H. Humphrey

The World Health Organization (2002, p. 5) defines *violence* as "the intentional use of physical force or power, threatened or actual, against oneself, another person, or against a group or community, that either results in or has a high likelihood of resulting in injury, death, psychological harm, mal-development, or deprivation."

The Centers for Disease Control and Prevention (CDC) broadly defines the issue of *youth violence* as: "harmful behaviors that can start early and continue into young adulthood. The young person can be a victim, an offender, or a witness to the violence" (2010a, p. 1). This is the framework that will be used within this book. It will examine the impact of violence on victims, the motives of perpetrators, and the impact on bystanders who witness it.

Violence can be categorized in terms of chronicity, severity, and type. Violence can occur in a single act, or it may repeat intermittently or chronically over a lifetime. Many children are victims of multiple forms of violence. The term *polyvictimization* is used to include a wide variety of violent acts against children: "violent and property crimes (e.g., assault, sexual assault, theft, burglary), (2) child welfare violations (child abuse, family abduction), (3) the violence of warfare and civil disturbances, and (4) bullying victimization. It includes

3

acts that would be considered crimes if committed between adults, although not necessarily considered criminal when occurring among children (e.g., hitting by peers and siblings)" (Finkelhor, Ormrod, & Turner, 2007, p. 11). The complicated interplay of these various forms of violence—and their cumulative effect upon children—is still being studied. However, it is becoming clear that children need to be assessed for multiple forms of violence.

The physical impact of violence can range from little to none (as in the case of emotional or psychological bullying) all the way to severe injury and/or death.

Tolan and Guerra (1994) identify four types of violence: situational, relationship, predatory, and psychopathological. *Situational violence* refers to violence that occurs in response to certain situational factors, such as (but not limited to) the availability of weapons, use of alcohol or other drugs, or other setting or occasion-specific incidents. *Relationship violence* arises from interpersonal disputes between individuals. *Predatory violence* includes acts that are perpetrated for gain (i.e., violence that occurs during a robbery). *Psychopathological violence*, a relatively rare form, arises from an underlying pathological condition in the offender. Cornell et al. (1996) define *instrumental violence* as violence used to achieve a goal; as opposed to *reactive violence*, which arises in response to a situation or provocation. Violence can be perpetrated against an individual, a group or community, or (in the case of self-injury or suicide) the self. Chapter 3 will examine various types of youth violence in more detail.

What causes a child or adolescent to be violent, under what circumstances, and for what reasons? Can youth violence be predicted and/or prevented? These are questions that this book will address to the extent of what is presently known.

PREVALENCE OF YOUTH VIOLENCE

The CDC (2010a) characterizes youth violence as a public health crisis. According to the Bureau of Justice Statistics (2009), teens and young adults experience the highest rates of violent crime out of all age groups (see Figure 1.1).

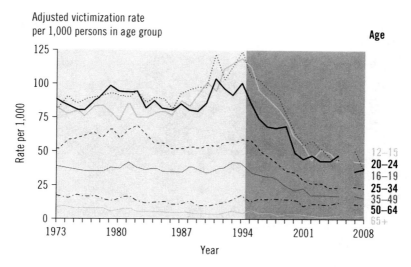

Adjusted victimization rate
per 1,000 persons in age group

Age

FIGURE 1.1 Violent crime rates by age of victim. *Source:* Bureau of Justice Statistics. (2009). *Criminal victimization, 2009*. Retrieved from http://bjs.ojp. usdoj.gov/content/glance/vage.cfm

Over the next sections I will present a small sampling of statistics regarding homicides, sexual assault, other violent crimes, school violence, gang violence, dating violence, bullying, and suicide among youth in the United States. (These data show overall rates; trends by age, sex, race/ethnicity, and other factors will be discussed in more detail in Chapter 2.)

Youth as Victims of Homicide

In September, 2009, Derrion Albert, 16, a high school honor roll student from the South Side of Chicago, was brutally beaten and killed after he accidentally walked into the middle of a fight between two rival groups of adolescents. The incident, which was videotaped by a bystander, led to a public outcry over the level of violence in Chicago schools. (Fitzsimmons, 2009)

According to the CDC (2010a), in 2007, 5,764 young people aged 10 to 24 years were murdered—an average of 16 each day. That same year, homicide was the fourth leading cause of death among children aged 1 to 14 years and the second leading cause of death among adults aged 15 to 24 years (CDC, 2010b).

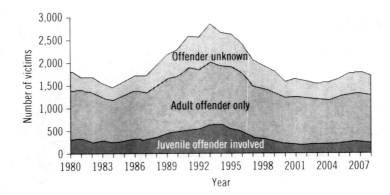

FIGURE 1.2   Juvenile homicide victims, 1980–2008. *Source:* OJJDP. *Statistical Briefing Book.* Retrieved December 21, 2010, from http://www.ojjdp.gov/ojstatbb/victims/qa02304.asp?qaDate=2008

Puzzanchera (2009) reports the following:

- In 2008, 11% of all murder victims were younger than 18 years.
- More than one-third (38%) of all juvenile murder victims were younger than 5 years (this proportion varied widely across demographic groups; see Chapter 2 for a more detailed discussion of demographic variables).

Figure 1.2 shows the rise and fall in rates of juvenile homicide victims over nearly three decades.

Youth as Perpetrators of Homicide

On January 27, 2001, two popular professors from Dartmouth College were found stabbed to death in their home in Hanover, New Hampshire. The killers, Robert Tulloch, 18, and James Parker, 17, admitted that they killed their victims for money; they were bored with their hometown and wanted $10,000 for a trip to Australia. (Butterfield, 2002)

In 2008, the juvenile murder arrest rate was 3.8 arrests per 100,000 juveniles aged 10 to 17 years. The proportion of homicides attributed to juveniles has held relatively constant in recent years, ranging between 5% and 6% (Puzzanchera, 2009).

The juvenile arrest rate for murder increased sharply beginning in the mid-1980s, hitting a peak in 1993. It then began to decline and continued to drop through the mid-2000s. In 2004, it began to grow

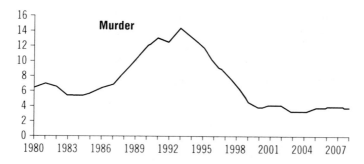

FIGURE 1.3 Juvenile arrest rates for murder, 1980–2008. *Source:* Office of Juvenile Justice and Delinquency Prevention. *Statistical Briefing Book.* Retrieved from http://www.ojjdp.gov/ojstatbb

again; however, that increase was interrupted in 2008 (Puzzanchera, 2009). Figure 1.3 graphically represents arrest rates during this period. However, it is important to note that arrest rates may not present a comprehensive picture, since many offenses by juveniles go unreported, and/or do not involve arrest.

Experts suggest several reasons for the overall decline, including decreasing gang violence, more effective community-oriented law enforcement efforts, and evidence-based school and community-based violence prevention programs.

How do youth homicide rates in the United States compare with other countries? According to the *World Report on Violence and Health* (World Health Organization, 2002), the rate stands at roughly 11.0 per 100,000 in the United States. The countries/territories with highest rates include Colombia (84.4 per 100,000), Puerto Rico (41.8 per 100,000), the Russian Federation (18 per 100,000), and Albania (28.2 per 100,000). Most of the other countries with rates above 10.0 per 100,000 are either developing countries or those experiencing rapid social and economic changes. At the other end of the spectrum, countries with low rates of youth homicide include France (0.6 per 100,000), Germany (0.8 per 100,000), the UK (0.9 per 100,000), and Japan (0.4 per 100,000).

Sexual Assault

Nineteen boys and men, ranging in age from 14 to 27 years, were charged in connection with the gang rape of an 11-year-old girl in

Cleveland, Texas. According to police, the girl was raped on six separate occasions between September and December, 2010, before it was finally reported to the authorities. The crime has shaken and disgusted community members, family, and friends, who wonder how it could have gone unnoticed and unreported for so long. (McKinley & Goode, 2011)

A significant portion of sexual violence in the United States is perpetrated by juveniles. According to the FBI's Uniform Crime Report (2001), in 2000, 16.4% of arrests for forcible rape and 18.6% of arrests for other sexual offenses were of individuals under the age of 18 years. Furthermore, 6.4% of arrests for forcible rape and 9.7% of arrests for other sexual offenses were of individuals under the age of 15 years.... Despite fluctuating rates of sexual violence, juveniles consistently account for almost 20% of arrests for rape and other sex offenses. (Becker & Hicks, 2003, p. 398)

Other Violent Crimes

In a shocking attack in a Baltimore area McDonald's, a transgender woman was beaten by two teenage girls; one was 14 years old, the other 18 years old. One McDonald's employee videotaped the assault; others could be heard laughing and encouraging the attackers. "They just seemed like they wanted to pick a fight that night, they really did. And come to find out that girl was only 14 years old. I was shocked," the victim said. "They kicked me in my face; they really hurt me really bad and I'm just afraid to go outside now because of stuff like this." (Martinez, 2011)

According to Puzzanchera (2009), juveniles accounted for 16% of all violent crime arrests in 2008. In that year, 3,340 juveniles were arrested for forcible rape and 56,000 for aggravated assault. Between 1999 and 2008, the number of arrests in most offense categories declined for juveniles: forcible rape declined 27%, aggravated assault declined 21%, weapons law violations decreased 2%, and drug abuse violations decreased 7%. Robbery increased 25% and the arrest rate for simple assault was unchanged (Puzzanchera, 2009).

In 2008, more than 656,000 young people aged 10 to 24 years were treated in emergency departments for injuries sustained from violence (CDC, 2010a).

Child Maltreatment

A recent tragedy in which three young children died highlights the issues facing mothers who cannot cope with parenthood, and the sometimes

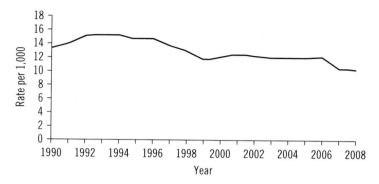

FIGURE 1.4   Maltreatment victimization rate per 1,000 children aged 0 to 17 years, 1999–2008. *Source*: U.S. Department of Justice Office of Juvenile Justice and Delinquency Prevention. *Statistical Briefing Book*. Retrieved from online at http://www.ojjdp.gov/ojstatbb/

heartbreaking results. In April 2011, 25-year-old LaShanda Armstrong drove her minivan containing her four children into the Hudson River in upstate New York. Three of her children—ages 5 years, 2 years, and 11 months—perished, as did Armstrong. Only her 10-year-old son was able to escape the car, swim to safety, and survive. No one is certain of her motives, but the surviving son says that LaShanda was fighting with his stepfather shortly before the incident, and reports say the two had a rocky relationship made more difficult by the stresses of trying to care for four children on meager means. (Barron, 2011)

Tragically, a significant portion of all crimes against children are committed by their parents or caregivers. *Child maltreatment* is broadly defined as physical abuse, psychological abuse, sexual abuse, and/or neglect that is committed by a parent or caretaker. Many children are victims of more than one kind of abuse.

In 2009, an estimated 700,000 children were victims of some form of maltreatment (U.S. Department of Health and Human Services, 2009); this number has been decreasing over recent years (see Figure 1.4).

Of all the outcomes of maltreatment, child fatalities are the most tragic and often the most widely publicized in the media. It is estimated that 1,770 children died from abuse and neglect in 2009 (U.S. Department of Health and Human Services, 2009). Of the reported fatalities

- 80.8% involved children who were younger than 4 years
- 35.8% were attributed to neglect exclusively

- 36.7% were caused by multiple maltreatment types (U.S. Department of Health and Human Services, 2009)

The assessment, treatment, and (above all) prevention of child abuse and neglect are incredibly important in ending the cycle of violence. Research suggests that children who are abused or neglected have a much higher risk of becoming offenders themselves. "Being abused or neglected as a child increased the likelihood of arrest as a juvenile by 59 percent, as an adult by 28 percent, and for a violent crime by 30 percent" (Widom & Maxfield, 2001).

School Violence

On April 16, 2007, Seung-Hui Cho—a student with a long history of mental health issues and a propensity to write about violence—killed 32 people on the Virginia Tech campus before killing himself. The massacre is considered one of the deadliest shooting incidents by a single gunman in U.S. history. (Urbina & Fernandez, 2007)

Terrifying, high-profile school shootings, such as those that occurred at Columbine and Virginia Tech, remain relatively rare. According to the National Center for Education Statistics (2010):

- Among youth aged 5 to 18 years, there were 38 school-associated violent deaths among students, staff, and nonschool personnel between 2008 and 2009 (24 were homicides and 14 were suicides).
- During the school year 2007–2008, there were 1,701 homicides among school-age youth aged 5 to 18 years.
- During the 2007 calendar year, there were 1,231 suicides of youth aged 5 to 18 years.

Interestingly, perpetrators of school-associated homicides were nine times as likely as victims to have exhibited some form of suicidal behavior before the event and were more than twice as likely as victims to have been bullied by their peers. Furthermore, more than half of the incidents during 1992–1999 were preceded by some signal, such as threats, notes, or journal entries, that indicated the potential for the coming event (Anderson et al., 2001). Such was the case with Seung-Hui Cho, whose violent plays and other writings concerned his teachers and classmates.

Incidents of nonfatal school violence are much more prevalent (National Center for Education Statistics, 2010):

- In 2008, students aged 12 to 18 years were victims of about 1.2 million nonfatal crimes (theft plus violent crime) at school.
- The rates for serious violent crimes were lower at school than away from school in 2008; students aged 12 to 18 years were victims of four serious violent crimes per 1,000 students at school and eight serious violent crimes per 1,000 students away from school.
- Eight percent of students in grades 9 to 12 reported being threatened or injured by someone with a weapon, such as a gun, knife, or club, on school property in 2009.
- Twenty percent of public schools reported that gang activities had occurred within their schools during 2007–2008.

In a 2009 nationally representative sample of youth in grades 9 to 12 (CDC, 2010c):

- 31.5% reported being in a physical fight in the 12 months preceding the survey.
- 17.5% reported carrying a weapon (gun, knife, or club) on one or more days in the 30 days preceding the survey.
- 7.7% reported being threatened or injured by someone with a weapon on school property one or more times in the 12 months preceding the survey.
- 11.1% reported being in a physical fight on school property in the 12 months preceding the survey.
- 5% did not go to school on one or more days in the 30 days preceding the survey because they felt unsafe at school or on their way to or from school.

Gang Violence

After his 17-year-old nephew, Emilio, was killed in a neighborhood dispute, Martin Torres was intent on revenge. Nicknamed "Pacman" because he always carried a gun, Torres, the head of a small gang, quickly identified his nephew's murderer and planned to kill him after Emilio's funeral. He received a phone call from a fellow former gang member, Zale Hoddenbach, and assumed Hoddenbach was going to help him. Instead, to his surprise, Hoddenbach successfully talked him out of committing any further acts of violence. Hoddenbach was working on behalf of an organization called CeaseFire, which features "violence interrupters"—former gang members and offenders themselves—who now use their knowledge of the streets to attempt to defuse gang violence. (Kotlowitz, 2008)

Approximately 1 million gang members—belonging to more than 20,000 different gangs—were criminally active in the United States as of September 2008. Nearly 58% of state and local law enforcement agencies reported that criminal gangs were active in their jurisdictions in 2008, an increase of 13% over 2004 (National Gang Intelligence Center, 2009).

Gangs are no longer a strictly urban phenomenon. According to the National Gang Intelligence Center (2009), gangs are migrating to suburban and rural communities, and these communities are experiencing increasing gang-related crime and violence as a result.

Dating Violence

In 2009, when pop singer Rihanna was beaten by her then-boyfriend, singer Chris Brown, many teachers and parents seized upon the incident as a chance to discuss the issues of domestic violence with children. They were dismayed to hear many teenagers—including teenage girls— suggest that Rihanna must have done something to deserve her injuries, or express sympathy for Brown's actions. (Hoffman, 2009)

Intimate partner violence is typically thought of as an adult concern, but adolescents also report experiencing violence within their dating relationships. Like its adult counterpart, teen dating violence can take physical, emotional, verbal, and/or sexual forms.

According to the CDC (2010d), one in four adolescents report some form of abuse from a dating partner each year, and approximately 10% of students nationwide report being physically hurt by a boyfriend or girlfriend in the past 12 months.

Bullying

Margarite, an eighth-grader in Olympia, Washington, texted a nude picture of herself to her boyfriend, Isaiah, also an eighth-grader. The two later broke up. Shortly thereafter, Isaiah forwarded the photo to another girl—who then forwarded it to all of her contacts with the following message: "Ho Alert! If you think this girl is a whore, then text this to all your friends." Within days, hundreds, and possibly thousands of students in Margarite's school, as well as neighboring schools and communities, had received the text. (Hoffman, 2011)

Cases like Margarite's have emphasized the extreme consequences of bullying and its newest variant, cyberbullying, which are increasingly impacting students of all ages:

- An estimated 20% of high school students reported being bullied on school property in 2009 (CDC, 2010a).
- During the 2007–2008 school year, 25% of public schools reported that bullying occurred among students on a daily or weekly basis (National Center for Education Statistics, 2010).
- In 2007, 32% of students aged 12 to 18 years reported having been bullied at school during the school year. Twenty-one percent said that they had made fun of; 18% reported being the subject of rumors; 11% said that they were pushed, shoved, tripped, or spit on; 6% said they were threatened with harm; 5% said they were deliberately excluded from activities; 4% said that someone tried to make them do things they did not want to do; and 4% said that their property was destroyed on purpose (National Center for Education Statistics, 2010).

Bullying is a particular concern with lesbian, gay, bisexual, and transgender (LGBT) teens. According to a national survey of more than 7,000 LGBT youth:

- Nearly 9 out of 10 reported being verbally harassed at school.
- More than 60% said they felt unsafe at school because of their sexual orientation.
- Nearly 45% reported being physically harassed in school.
- Nearly one-third said they had missed a day of school in the past month because of feeling unsafe (the Gay, Lesbian and Straight Education Network, 2010).

Cyberbullying is a relatively new and growing concern, as the case of Margarite illustrates. Some researchers suggest that between 9% and 33% of youth aged 10 to 18 years experience cyberbullying (Wolak, Mitchell, & Finkelhor, 2007; Ybarra, Mitchell, Finkelhor, & Wolak,

2007). According to "Cyberbullying 2010: What the Research Tells Us," a study by the Pew Research Center, Washington, DC, 32% of teens surveyed experienced one of the following forms of online harassment:

- 15% had private material (such as texts) forwarded without their permission.
- 13% received threatening messages.
- 13% had rumors about themselves spread online.
- 6% had someone post an embarrassing picture of them online without permission (Lenhart, 2010).

Suicide

> Phoebe Prince, 15, a freshman at South Hadley High School in western Massachusetts, hanged herself after enduring months of ridicule and harassment from fellow students. The resulting legal case, in which six teenagers were charged with various felony counts, also raised numerous issues about the roles of teachers and school staff in identifying and taking action against bullying. (Eckholm & Zezima, 2010)

Suicide is the third leading cause of death in youth; each year, approximately 2,000 adolescents in the United States aged 13 to 19 years commit suicide (Worhcel & Gearing, 2009). (Suicide in children younger than 10 years are extremely rare.) Some studies suggest that nearly 10% of adolescents report attempting suicide, and nearly 30% thought about committing suicide at some point (Worhcel & Gearing, 2009).

COSTS OF YOUTH VIOLENCE

Youth violence is expensive both financially and in terms of the immeasurable pain and suffering it causes youth, their families, peers, and communities. It was projected that violence in the United States costs $425 billion, both directly and indirectly, in 1998. Cook and Ludwig (2002) estimated the cost of gun violence in the United States to be $100 billion. Catalano (2006) estimated the average cost of violent crime per victim to be $221.

The direct cost of child abuse and neglect in the United States (including law enforcement, judicial system, child welfare, and health care costs) totals more than $33 billion annually. When factoring in indirect costs (special education, mental health care, juvenile delinquency, lost productivity, and adult criminality), the figure rises to more than $103 billion annually (Wang & Holton, 2007).

Approximately 93,000 youth are held in residential juvenile justice facilities in the United States (Sickmund, Sladky, Kang, & Puzzanchera, 2008) at an average cost of $241 per day. Recidivism rates are higher (50%–90%) for these youth than for those who are treated in the community (30%) (Justice Policy Institute, 2009). Thirty-six percent of juvenile facilities are at or over capacity and thus overcrowded. Several states (California, Texas, and Maryland) have been sued for poor conditions in their facilities (Justice Policy Institute, 2009).

In contrast, community programs, such as Functional Family Therapy and Multisystemic Therapy, are highly effective and are known to yield $13 public safety dollars for every dollar spent (Justice Policy Institute, 2009). The key is to choose the correct level of care for the safety of the youth and the community. Millions of dollars could be saved if nondangerous youth were treated in the community. Missouri is the model for residential care for youth in conflict with the law. This state uses smaller facilities geared for education and rehabilitation. The recidivism rate is 8.7% (Justice Policy Institute, 2009). To the contrary, research over the past decade has shown that for states that increased the incarceration rates of youth, there has not been an equivalent drop in the crime rate (Justice Policy Institute, 2009).

REFERENCES

Anderson, M., Kaufman, J., Simon, T. R., Barrios, L., Paulozzi, L., Ryan, G., et al. (2001). School-associated violent deaths in the United States, 1994–1999. *Journal of the American Medical Association, 286*(21), 2695–2702.

Barron, J. (2011). Woman tells of boy's plea for help after 4 drownings. *New York Times*, April 13, 2011. Retrieved from http://www.nytimes.com/2011/04/14/nyregion/14newburgh.html?ref=lashandaarmstrong

Becker, J. V., & Hicks, S. J. (2003). Juvenile sexual offenders: Characteristics, interventions, and policy issues. *Annals of the New York Academy of Science, 989*, 397–410.

Bureau of Justice Statistics. (2009). *Criminal victimization, 2009*. Retrieved from http://bjs.ojp.usdoj.gov/index.cfm?ty=pbdetail&iid=2217

Butterfield, F. (2002). Teenagers are sentenced for killing two professors. *New York Times*, April 5, 2002. Retrieved from www.nytimes.com/2002/04/05/us/teenagers-are-sentenced-for-killing-two-professors.html

Catalano, S. M. (2006). *Criminal victimization, 2005*. Washington, DC: U.S. Department of Justice, Bureau of Justice Statistics.

Centers for Disease Control and Prevention. (2010a). *Understanding youth violence*. Retrieved from www.cdc.gov/violenceprevention/pdf/YV-FactSheet-a.pdf

Centers for Disease Control and Prevention. (2010b). *Health, United States, 2010*. Retrieved from www.cdc.gov/nchs/data/hus/hus10.pdf

Centers for Disease Control and Prevention. (2010c). Youth risk behavioral surveillance—United States, 2009. *MMWR Surveillance Summaries*, 59(No. SS–5). Retrieved from www.cdc.gov/mmwr/pdf/ss/ss5905.pdf

Centers for Disease Control and Prevention. (2010d). *Understanding teen dating violence*. Retrieved from http://www.cdc.gov/violenceprevention/pdf/TeenDatingViolence_2010-a.pdf

Cook, P. J., & Ludwig, J. (2002). *Gun violence: The real costs*. Oxford, UK: Oxford University Press.

Cornell, D. G., Warren, J., Hawk, G., Stafford, E., Oram, G., & Pine, D. (1996). Psychopathy in instrumental and reactive violent offenders. *Journal of Consulting and Clinical Psychology, 64*(4), 783–790.

Eckholm, E., & Zezima, K. 6 Teenagers are charged after classmate's suicide. *New York Times*. March 29, 2010. Retrieved from http://www.nytimes.com/2010/03/30/us/30bully.html

Finkelhor, D., Ormrod, R. K., & Turner, H. A. (2007). Poly-victimization: A neglected component in child victimization. *Child Abuse & Neglect, 31*, 7–26.

Fitzsimmons, E. G. (2009). 4 Teenagers charged in youth's beating death. *New York Times*, September 28, 2009. Retrieved from http://www.nytimes.com/2009/09/29/us/29fight.html

Gay, Lesbian and Straight Education Network. (2010). *2009 National School Climate Survey*. Retrieved from www.glsen.org/cgibin/iowa/all/library/record/2624.html?state=research&type=research

Hoffman, J. (2009). Teenage girls stand by their man. *New York Times*, March 18, 2009. Retrieved from www.nytimes.com/2009/03/19/fashion/19brown.html

Hoffman, J. (2011). A girl's nude photo, and altered lives. *New York Times*, March 26, 2011. Retrieved from www.nytimes.com/2011/03/27/us/27sexting.html

Justice Policy Institute. (2009). *The costs of confinement: Why good juvenile justice policies make good fiscal sense.* Washington, DC: Author.

Kotlowitz, A. (2008). Blocking the transmission of violence. *New York Times,* May 4, 2008. Retrieved from http://www.nytimes.com/2008/05/04/magazine/04health-t.html

Lenhart, A. (2010). *Cyberbullying 2010: What the research tells us.* Pew Research Center. May 6, 2010. Retrieved from http://www.pewinternet.org/Presentations/2010/May/Cyberbullying-2010.aspx

Martinez, E. (2011). *Transgender woman Chrissy Lee Polis calls Md. McDonald's attack hate crime.* Retrieved from http://www.cbsnews.com/8301–504083_162–20057042-504083.html

McKinley, J., & Goode, E. (2011). 3-Month nightmare emerges in rape inquiry. *New York Times.* March 28, 2011. Retrieved from www.nytimes.com/2011/03/29/us/29texas.html

National Center for Education Statistics. (2010). *Indicators of school crime and safety: 2010.* Retrieved from http://nces.ed.gov/programs/crimeindicators/crimeindicators2010

National Gang Intelligence Center. (2009). *National gang threat assessment.* Retrieved from www.fbi.gov/stats-services/publications/national-gang-threat-assessment-2009-pdf

Office of Juvenile Justice and Delinquency Prevention (OJJDP). (2010). *Statistical Briefing Book.* Retrieved from http://www.ojjdp.gov/ojstatbb/victims/qa02304.asp?qaDate=2008

Puzzanchera, C. (2009). *Juvenile arrests 2008. Juvenile Justice Bulletin.* Washington, DC: Office of Juvenile Justice and Delinquency Prevention. Retrieved from www.ncjrs.gov/pdffiles1/ojjdp/228479.pdf

Sickmund, M., Sladky, T. J., Kang, W., & Puzzanchera, C. (2008). *Easy access to the census of juveniles in residential.* Washington, DC: Office of Juvenile Justice and Delinquency Prevention.

Tolan, P. H., & Guerra, N. G. (1994). Prevention of delinquency: Current status and issues. *Journal of Applied and Preventive Psychology, 3*(4), 251–274.

U.S. Department of Health and Human Services. (2009). *Child maltreatment 2009.* Retrieved from http://www.acf.hhs.gov/programs/cb/pubs/cm09/cm09.pdf

Urbina, I., & Fernandez, M. (2007). University explains the return of troubled student. *New York Times.* Retrieved from www.nytimes.com/2007/04/20/us/20virginia.html

Wang, C.-T., & Holton, J. (2007). *Total estimated cost of child abuse and neglect in the United States.* Washington, DC: Prevent Child Abuse America. Retrieved from http://www.preventchildabuse.org/about_us/media_releases/pcaa_pew_economic_impact_study_final.pdf

Widom, C. S., & Maxfield, M. G. (2001). *An update on the "Cycle of Violence."* Retrieved from http://www.ncjrs.gov/pdffiles1/nij/184894.pdf

Wolak, J., Mitchell, K., & Finkelhor, D. (2007). Unwanted and wanted exposure to online pornography in a national sample of youth Internet users. *Pediatrics, 119*(2), 247–257.

Worhcel, D., & Gearing, R. (2010). *Suicide assessment and treatment: Empirical and evidence-based practices.* New York, NY: Springer Publishing Company.

World Health Organization. (2002). *World report on violence and health.* Geneva, Switzerland: World Health Organization. Retrieved from http://whqlibdoc.who.int/publications/2002/9241545615_chap1_eng.pdf

Ybarra, M., Mitchell, K., Finkelhor, D., & Wolak, J. (2007). Internet prevention messages: Targeting the right online behaviors. *Archives of Pediatric and Adolescent Medicine, 161*, 138–145.

TWO

Demographic Factors in Youth Violence

Chapter 1 offered a brief overview of the prevalence of various forms of youth violence in the United States. However, those rates vary greatly by age, gender, race, ethnicity, and socioeconomic status (SES). A child's likelihood of being a perpetrator and/or victim of violence is impacted heavily by all of these factors, and often they influence each other in complex ways. This chapter will offer a broad overview to the demographic factors that impact youth violence.

An in-depth discussion of the research findings and practice implications of any one of the variables discussed here could easily fill an entire volume. To keep the chapter to a reasonable length, most sections include a brief discussion of the demographic variable as it relates to perpetrators, followed by a section on victims. Victimization by maltreatment, homicide, sexual assault, and suicide are all examined separately when possible.

AGE

"Shawn" killed a woman when he was less than 14 years old. He had shown aggressive tendencies toward his peers, and had demonstrated school behavior problems, since kindergarten. Although given therapy, his aggression persisted and escalated throughout his childhood.

Age of Child Perpetrators of Violent Crimes

As might be expected, violent crimes committed by children younger than 10 years are relatively rare; for most violent offenses, crime rates

19

TABLE 2.1   Number of Arrests for Selected Violent Offenses by Age, 2009

Offense	Under 10	10–12	13–14	15	16	17	18
Murder and non-negligent manslaughter	2	11	74	149	290	416	690
Forcible rape	10	170	586	460	512	647	819
Aggravated assault	344	3,035	8,567	7,455	9,451	10,615	12,563
Carrying or possessing weapons	404	2,127	5,768	4,812	6,154	7,566	8,801
Sex offenses (except forcible rape and prostitution)	209	1,377	3,481	1,785	1,757	1,958	2,384
Violent Crime Percent Distribution	*.1*	*.8*	*2.9*	*2.9*	*3.8*	*4.4*	*5.1*

Source: Excerpted from U.S. Department of Justice, 2009.

increase along with age. Table 2.1 summarizes the number of children and adolescents arrested for selected violent crimes in 2009. The data are taken from the Uniform Crime Reporting Program of the Federal Bureau of Investigation (FBI), which tallies nationwide arrest data. It should be noted that arrest rates do not capture all violent activity by children, since many offenses may go unreported or may not lead to an arrest.

Figure 2.1 shows arrest rates for juveniles who committed homicide by age. Note how rates across all age ranges follow a very similar pattern; a peak around 1993, followed by a steep decline, and then a smaller increase in recent years, which appears to be falling off, according to the most recent data available.

Age of Child Victims of Violent Crimes

Maltreatment. The youngest children are the most vulnerable to maltreatment; rates decrease as children age. See Figure 2.2, which

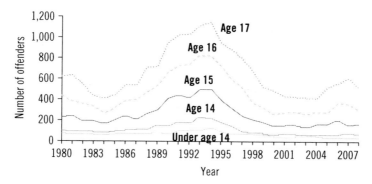

FIGURE 2.1   Known juvenile homicide offenders by age, 1980–2008. *Source:* U.S. Department of Justice Office of Juvenile Justice and Delinquency Prevention.

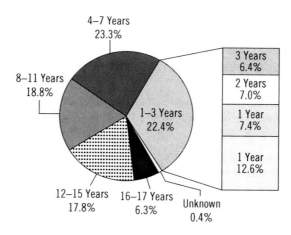

FIGURE 2.2   Child Maltreatment Victims by Age, 2009. *Source:* America's Children: Key National Indicators of Well-Being, 2011. Excerpted from http://www. childstats.gov/americaschildren/famsoc7.asp

shows data for 2009; these rates have remained fairly stable in recent years.

Homicide. Murder rates are highest among the oldest and the youngest children. In 2008, 39% of juvenile murder victims were younger than 6 years; a substantial portion were victims of family violence, as discussed earlier. Forty-six percent of juvenile murder victims were aged 15 to 17 years.

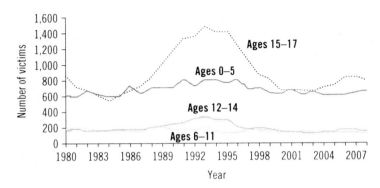

FIGURE 2.3   Juvenile homicide victims by age, 1980–2008. *Source*: U.S. Department of Justice Office of Juvenile Justice and Delinquency Prevention.

Figure 2.3 shows juvenile homicide victims by year. Note that the rates for older adolescents (aged 15–17 years) follow the familiar pattern seen in Chapter 1; rates begin to climb in the mid-1980s, peak around 1993, and decrease significantly thereafter. Rates for all other age groups do not vary nearly as much (U.S. Department of Justice, 2009).

Assault. Sexual assault (which includes any forced or inappropriate sexual activity, including rape, sexual abuse, molestation, and incest) also appears to rise slightly with age among adolescents. According to the Department of Justice, recent annual rates of sexual assault per 1,000 persons (male and female) were 0.9 for ages 12 through 15 years, 0.6 for ages 16 through 19 years, 0.8 for ages 20 through 24 years, and 0.8 for ages 24 through 29 years (Truman & Rand, 2010). Table 2.2, from the Bureau of Justice Statistics, shows a similar trend and offers a breakdown by types of sexual assault.

"Roger," age 7, was accused of showing his 6-year-old female playmate his "pee-pee." His parents and teachers were unsure how to handle the incident: Was this normal sexual exploration between peers or a sexual offense? Our legal systems struggle to define "normal" versus "illegal" sexual behavior among children.

Suicide. The rate of completed suicide also rises with age. Suicide among children younger than 10 years is an extremely rare phenomenon. For children aged 10 to 14 years, the rate increases to 1.3 per 100,000. For children aged 15 to 19 years, the rate jumps to 8.2 per 100,000 (Worchel & Gearing, 2010).

TABLE 2.2 Age Profile of the Victims of Sexual Assault

Victim age	All sexual assault	Forcible rape	Forcible sodomy	Sexual assault with object	Forcible fondling
Total	100.0%	100.0%	100.0%	100.0%	100.0%
0 to 5	14.0%	4.3%	24.0%	26.5%	20.2%
6 to 11	20.1	8.0	30.8	23.2	29.3
12 to 17	32.8	33.5	24.0	25.5	34.3
18 to 24	14.2	22.6	8.7	9.7	7.7
25 to 34	11.5	19.6	7.5	8.3	5.0
Above 34	7.4	12.0	5.1	6.8	3.5

Source: Snyder, 2000.

GENDER

Gender of Child Perpetrators of Violent Crimes

With images of "mean girls" dominating reality TV, celebrity culture, and several unfortunate real-life cases of girls assaulting and bullying other children, it is easy to assume that violence perpetrated by girls is on the rise.

However in most cases, recent data do not support this. "One of the most consistent and robust findings in criminology is that, for nearly every offense, females engage in much less crime and juvenile delinquency than males" (U.S. Department of Justice, 2008). The FBI collects crime and arrest data from more than 17,000 city, county, and state law enforcement agencies. According to *Crime in the United States* (U.S. Department of Justice, 2009):

- 25.3% of all arrests made in the United States in 2009 (not including traffic violations) were of females.
- 17% of females arrested were younger than 18 years.
- 4.7% of females arrested were younger than 15 years.

Furthermore, "girls' delinquent acts are typically less chronic and often less serious than those of boys" (Office of Juvenile Justice and Delinquency Prevention, 2010). However, researchers and practitioners caution that girls who commit even minor offenses may be

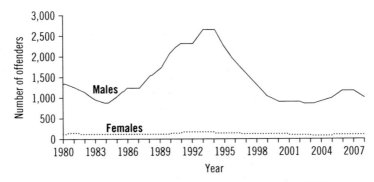

FIGURE 2.4 Known juvenile homicide offenders by sex, 1980–2008. *Source*: U.S. Department of Justice Office of Juvenile Justice and Delinquency Prevention.

experiencing serious problems at home, at school, or both; they may be in desperate need of protection against possible further victimization. This is key, since one of the most significant risk factors in women's criminal behavior is prior victimization, such as physical or sexual abuse by a parent or guardian (Morash, Bynum, & Koons, 1998).

Homicide. Figure 2.4 shows arrest rates for homicide by sex from 1980 to 2008. While the arrest rate for boys shows sharp increases and declines over this period, note that the arrest rate for girls stays low for the entire period.

Sexual Assault. Most studies suggest that adolescent sexual offenders are primarily male, although a few have discussed female perpetrators.

Other Violent Behaviors. According to the Centers for Disease Control and Prevention (CDC, 2009a) Youth Risk Behavior Survey, which surveyed adolescents in 9th to 12th grade, males reported significantly higher behaviors associated with violence:

- 27.1% reported carrying a weapon on at least 1 day in the 30 days prior to the survey (compared with 7.1% for girls)
- 9.6% were threatened or injured by someone with a weapon on school property one or more times in the 12 months prior to the survey (compared with 5.5% for girls)
- 39.3% were in a physical fight one or more times in the 12 months prior to the survey (compared with 22.9% for girls)

Dating Violence. Interestingly, in the CDC survey (2009a), both genders reported roughly equal rates of perpetration of dating violence; 9.3% of girls and 10.3% of boys said that they had hit, slapped, or deliberately physically hurt their boyfriend or girlfriend in the 12 months prior to the survey.

Several other studies find similar results. In one survey of more than 1,300 adolescents in Ohio, researchers found that "More than half of the girls in physically aggressive relationships said both they and their dating partner committed aggressive acts during the relationship. About a third of the girls said they were the sole perpetrators, and 13 percent reported that they were the sole victims" (Mulford & Giordano, 2008). Similar results were found in a study on Long Island, New York (Mulford & Giordano, 2008).

Research into adolescent dating violence is much less advanced than that of violence between adult partners, and the prevalence and dynamics are not yet entirely clear. However, it seems plausible that teenagers "inexperience in communicating and relating to a romantic partner may lead to the use of poor coping strategies, including verbal and physical aggression" (Mulford & Giordano, 2008). Other factors that may influence the use of violence among adolescent couples may be a higher level of unrealistic expectations about relationships, and the influence of peers.

Gender of Child Victims of Violent Crimes

Maltreatment. Maltreatment is split fairly evenly by gender; in 2009, 48.2% of all victims were boys, and 51.1% were girls. This rate has remained fairly stable in recent years (U.S. Department of Health and Human Services, 2010).

Homicide. Males account for the largest share of juvenile homicide victims. See Figure 2.5.

Sexual Assault. According to Snyder (2000, p. 4), "Females were more than six times as likely as males to be the victims of sexual assaults known to law enforcement agencies. More specifically, 86% of all victims of sexual assault were female. The relative proportion of female victims generally increased with age. Sixty-nine percent of victims under age 6 were female, compared with 73% of victims under age 12, and 82% of all juvenile (under age 18) victims. The female proportion of sexual assault victims reached 90% at age 13 years and 95% at age 19."

Of male victims, Snyder (2000, p. 4) states: "Based on the NIBRS data, the year in a male's life when he is most likely to be the victim

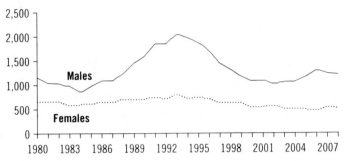

FIGURE 2.5   Juvenile homicide victims by sex, 1980–2008. *Source*: U.S. Department of Justice Office of Juvenile Justice and Delinquency Prevention.

of a sexual assault is age 4.... By age 17 his risk of victimization has been cut by a factor of 5."

In the CDC Youth Risk Behavior Surveillance (YRBS) study (2009a), 10.5% of girls reported ever having been physically forced to have sex, versus 4.5% of boys.

> In Phoenix in 2009, four boys, aged 9 to 14 years, were accused and charged with raping an 8-year-old girl. Community outrage escalated when the girl's father refused to take her back home after the attack. All of the children involved are immigrants from Liberia, where women are often blamed for rape and the "shame" it brings upon the family
>
> Meyers, 2009

Suicide. There are significant gender differences in suicide ideation, attempts, and completion. In the CDC YRBS study (2009a):

- 17.4% of girls reported seriously considering suicide in the 12 months prior to the survey (vs. 10.5% of boys)
- 8.1% of girls attempted suicide once or more in the 12 months prior to the survey (vs. 4.6% of boys).

RACE/ETHNICITY

The racial and ethnic diversity of America's children continues to increase. "In 2008, 56 percent of U.S. children were White, non-Hispanic; 22 percent were Hispanic; 15 percent were Black; 4 percent were Asian; and 5 percent were of other races. The percentage of children who are Hispanic has increased faster than that of any other racial or ethnic group, growing from 9 percent of the child population in 1980 to 22 percent in 2008" (Federal Interagency Forum on Child and Family Statistics, 2009).

Non-White children and adolescents are at significantly higher risk for becoming perpetrators and/or victims of violence, as will be discussed in more detail in the following section. However, the relationship between race/ethnicity and violence is not clear-cut. "Although race, ethnicity, and class may be a risk marker for violence, considered in isolation from other life circumstances, they do not explain a given youth's propensity for violence. . . . Although ethnicity, race, and class have been considered a risk factor for violence in the past, the Surgeon General's Report on Youth Violence clarifies that these variables, by themselves, do not explain a youth's propensity for becoming violent. Other known risk factors must be taken into account" (Center for the Study and Prevention of Violence, 2009, p. 1–2).

These other risk factors include poverty—which will be discussed later in this chapter—as well as community and family structure. Consider, for example, the following research findings as summarized by Hawkins, Laub, Lauritsen, and Cothern (2000, p. 4):

- "High rates of delinquency persisted in certain urban areas regardless of ethnic population composition.
- Rates of delinquency within racial or ethnic subgroups varied across urban communities.
- Rates of delinquency did not increase in areas with less crime as ethnic subgroups migrated to such communities."

Increased urbanization, inequality, and class segregation are also factors correlated with various racial/ethnic groups, and they also play a role. Given all these factors and the interrelations among them, it is extremely difficult to isolate race/ethnicity as one specific variable when examining youth violence.

Race/Ethnicity of Child Perpetrators of Violent Crimes

Homicide. Figure 2.6 shows arrest rates for homicide by juveniles by race from 1980 to 2008. However arrest rates should be interpreted with caution: "If ethnic and racial groups differ in their inclination

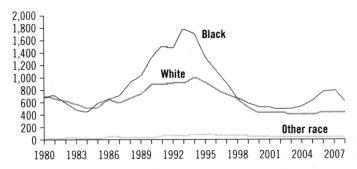

FIGURE 2.6 Known juvenile homicide offenders by race, 1980–2008.
Source: OJJDP Statistical Briefing Book.

to report crime to the authorities, or if crimes committed by certain groups are more likely to result in an arrest, these factors can bias estimates of racial differences in offending rates. Police themselves may be biased in their arrest policies and may handle offenders differently (e.g., arresting rather than warning) depending on the offender's racial or ethnic background" (Hawkins, Laub, et al., 2000, p. 1).

Other Violent Behaviors. The CDC (2009b) Youth Risk Behavior Survey found significant differences between White, Hispanic, and Black students in the 9th to 12th grade. (Other racial and ethnic populations are not included because their numbers were too small to be statistically significant.) See Table 2.3.

Race/Ethnicity of Child Victims of Violent Crimes

Maltreatment. In 2009, child maltreatment victims were primarily White (44.0%), African American (22.3%), and Hispanic (20.7%). However, rates of victimization were highest for African American (15.1 per 1,000), American Indian, or Alaska Native (11.6 per 1,000), and children of multiple racial descent (12.4 per 1,000) (U.S. Department of Health and Human Services, 2010).

Homicide. Black youth accounted for about 16% of the juvenile population between 1980 and 2008 but were the victims in 47% of juvenile homicides during the 29-year period. See Figure 2.7.

TABLE 2.3   Health Risk Behaviors by Race/Ethnicity

	White students	Hispanic students	Black students
Reported being in a physical fight one or more times in the 12 months prior to the survey	27.8%	36.2%	41.1%
Threatened or injured by someone with a weapon on school property one or more times during the 12 months prior to the survey	6.4%	9.1%	9.4%
Did not go to school at least once in the 30 days prior to the survey because they felt unsafe	3.5%	8.1%	6.3%
Reported being bullied on school property	21.6%	18.5%	13.7%
Carried a weapon on at least 1 day during the 30 days prior to the survey	18.6%	17.2%	14.4%
Carried a weapon at school on at least 1 day during the 30 days prior to the survey	5.6%	5.8%	5.3%
Hit, slapped, or deliberately physically hurt a boyfriend or girlfriend in the 12 months prior to the survey	8%	11.5%	14.3%
Attempted suicide one or more times during the 12 months prior to the survey	5%	8.1%	7.9%

Source: Adapted from the Centers for Disease Control and Prevention, 2009b.

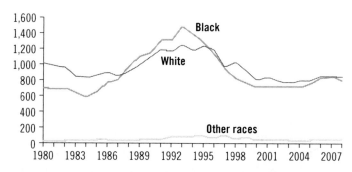

FIGURE 2.7   Juvenile homicide victims by race, 1980–2008. *Source: Statistical Briefing Book*. Retrieved from http://www.ojjdp.gov/ojstatbb/victims/qa02301. asp?qaDate=2008

TABLE 2.4 Rates of Violent Crime, by Gender, Race, Hispanic Origin, and Age of Victim, 2009

Demographic characteristics of victim	Population	Total	Rape/ sexual assault	Robbery	Total assault	Aggravated assault	Simple assault
			Violent victimizations per 1,000 persons aged 12 or older				
Gender							
Male	124,041,190	18.4	0.2^	2.7	15.6	4.3	11.3
Female	130,064,420	15.8	0.8	1.6	13.5	· 2.3	11.2
Race							
White	206,331,920	15.8	0.4	1.6	13.7	2.7	11.0
Black	31,046,560	26.8	1.2	5.6	19.9	6.8	13.0
Other race	13,982,530	9.8	–^	0.5^	9.3	1.9^	7.4
Two or more races	2,744,600	42.1	–^	5.2^	36.9	9.3^	27.5
Hispanic origin							
Hispanic	35,375,280	18.1	0.5^	3.4	14.2	3.2	11.0
Non- Hispanic	218,238,010	17.0	0.5	1.9	14.6	3.3	11.3
Age							
12–15	16,230,740	36.8	0.9^	3.1	32.8	6.9	25.9
16–19	17,203,070	30.3	0.6^	5.2	24.6	5.3	19.3

Source: Excerpted from Criminal Victimization, 2009. ^ Based on 10 or fewer sample cases.

Sexual Assault. In the CDC YRBS survey (2009b), 6.3% of White adolescents in the 9th to 12th grade reported ever being physically forced to have sex, as compared with 8.4% of Hispanic children and 10% of Black children.

Other Violent Crimes. Table 2.4 summarizes rates of violent crime by race, as well as other factors.

Suicide. According to the National Adolescent Health Information Center (2006), among adolescents and young adults, American Indian/Alaskan Native, non-Hispanics have the highest suicide rate. In fact, suicide is the second leading cause of death for adolescent and young adult males in this group. Black non-Hispanic and Hispanic females are least likely to commit suicide. See Figure 2.8.

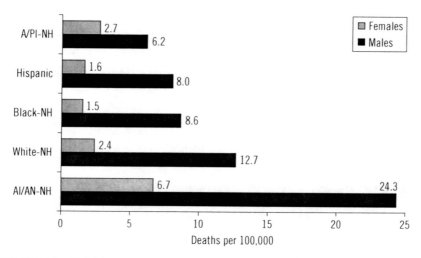

FIGURE 2.8   Suicide rates by race/ethnicity and gender, ages 10–24 years, 2003. *Source:* National Adolescent Health Information Center, 2006.

SOCIOECONOMIC STATUS

As mentioned earlier, low SES is strongly associated with youth violence. Being raised in poverty has been found to contribute to a greater likelihood of involvement in crime and violence. Self-reported felony assault, robbery, teen violence, and convictions for violent offenses have all been found to be correlated with youth living in poverty in various studies (Hawkins et al., 2000a).

The dynamics of youth violence are impacted not only by poverty but also by related community factors. According to Hawkins, Herrenkohl, et al. (2000), the following are community and neighborhood predictors of youth violence:

- Poverty
- Community disorganization (defined as the presence of crime, drugs, gangs, and poor housing within a neighborhood)
- Availability of drugs and firearms
- Neighborhood adults involved in crime
- Exposure to violence and racial prejudice

Many researchers have begun taking a community-level approach to violence, which examines community cultures—rather than individual demographic factors—and their role in encouraging or preventing violence among community members. Chapter 6 will examine these factors in more detail.

REFERENCES

Centers for Disease Control and Prevention. (2009a). *Selected health risk behaviors and health outcomes by sex.* National Youth Risk Behavior Survey: 2009. Retrieved from http://www.cdc.gov/HealthyYouth/yrbs/pdf/us_disparitysex_yrbs.pdf

Centers for Disease Control and Prevention. (2009b). *Selected health risk behaviors and health outcomes by race/ethnicity.* National Youth Risk Behavior Survey: 2009. Retrieved from http://www.cdc.gov/HealthyYouth/yrbs/pdf/us_disparityrace_yrbs.pdf

Center for the Study and Prevention of Violence. (2009). *Ethnicity, race, class and adolescent violence.* Retrieved from http://www.colorado.edu/cspv/publications/factsheets/cspv/FS-003.pdf

Criminal Victimization. (2009). Retrieved from http://bjs.ojp.Criminal Victimizcontent/pub/pdf/cv09.pdf

Federal Interagency Forum on Child and Family Statistics. (2009). *America's Children: Key National Indicators of Well-Being, 2009.* Washington, DC: U.S. Government Printing Office.

Hawkins, D. F., Laub, J. H., Lauritsen, J. L., & Cothern, L. (2000). *Race, ethnicity, and serious and violent juvenile offending.* Office of Juvenile Justice and Delinquency Prevention. Retrieved from http://people.wku.edu/john.faine/soc332/racedel.pdf

Hawkins, J. D., Herrenkohl, T. I., Farrington, D. P., Brewer, D., Catalano, R. F., Harachi, T. W., & Cothern, L. (2000). *Predictors of youth violence.* Office of Juvenile Justice and Delinquency Prevention. Retrieved from http://www.ncjrs.gov/pdffiles1/ojjdp/179065.pdf

Meyers, A. L. (2009). *4 boys accused of raping 8-year-old girl.* Retrieved from http://www.myfoxphoenix.com/dpp/news/local/phoenix/boys_accused_rape_072409

Morash, M., Bynum, T. S., & Koons, B. A. (1998). *Women offenders: programming needs and promising approaches.* Washington, DC: National Institute of Justice.

Mulford, C., & Giordano, P. C. (2008). *Teen dating violence: A closer look at adolescent romantic relationships.* Department of Justice, NIJ Journal

Number 261. Retrieved from http://www.nij.gov/journals/261/teen-dating-violence.htm

National Adolescent Health Information Center. (2006). *Fact sheet on suicide: adolescents & young adults.* San Francisco, CA: Author, University of California.

OJJDP Statistical Briefing Book. Retrieved from http://ojjdp.ncjrs.gov/ojstatbb/offenders/qa03101.asp?qaDate=2008

Snyder, H. N. (2000). *Sexual assault of young children as reported to law enforcement: Victim, incident, and offender characteristics.* U.S. Department of Justice, Office of Justice Programs. Retrieved from http://bjs.ojp.usdoj.gov/content/pub/pdf/saycrle.pdf

Statistical Briefing Book. Retrieved from http://www.ojjdp.gov/ojstatbb/victims/qa02301.asp?qaDate=2008

Truman, J. L. & Rand, M. R. (2010, October). *National Crime Victimization Survey: Criminal Victimization, 2009.* Washington, DC: Bureau of Justice Statistics.

U.S. Department of Health and Human Services, Administration for Children and Families, Administration on Children, Youth and Families, Children's Bureau. (2010). *Child maltreatment 2009.* Retrieved from http://www.acf.hhs.gov/programs/cb/stats_research/index.htm#can

U.S. Department of Justice. (2009). *Crime in the United States.* Retrieved from http://www2.fbi.gov/ucr/cius2009/data/table_38.html

U.S. Department of Justice, Office of Juvenile Justice and Delinquency Prevention. (2010). *Causes and correlates of girls' delinquency.* Retrieved from http://girlsstudygroup.rti.org/docs/GSG_Causes_and_Correlates_Bulletin.pdf

U.S. Department of Justice, Office of Juvenile Justice and Delinquency Prevention. *Statistical briefing book.* Retrieved from http://www.ojjdp.gov/ojstatbb/

U.S. Department of Justice, Office of Justice Programs, Office of Juvenile Justice and Delinquency Prevention. (2008). Girls Study Group. *Understanding and responding to girl's delinquency.* Retrieved from http://www.ncjrs.gov/pdffiles1/ojjdp/218905.pdf

Worhcel, D., & Gearing, R. (2010). *Suicide assessment and treatment: Empirical and evidence-based practices.* New York, NY: Springer Publishing Company.

THREE

Classifications of Youth Violence

Violence can be categorized by purpose, mechanism, and/or target. When categorized by purpose, violence can be instrumental, situational, or predatory.

Instrumental violence is typically planned and used to achieve a goal, such as money, power, or resources (an example might be the violence that occurs during a robbery).

Situational violence occurs more spontaneously, when emotions get out of control. Youth with poor coping skills may become overwhelmed when faced with even minor stressors. Without other means of self-regulation, they may use aggression to vent emotions. It is rare that situational violence occurs without other risk factors being present (see Chapters 5 and 6 for common individual and environmental risk factors for youth violence).

Predatory or psychopathic violence usually has no other goal but to harm another person; typically those who commit this type of violence have goals of domination and control and causing pain and suffering. Psychopathy will be discussed more in Chapter 4.

The World Health Organization divides violence into three general categories, based on the target (World Health Organization, 2002): self-directed, interpersonal, and collective. Self-directed violence includes suicidal behavior (discussed in Chapter 8). Interpersonal violence is against another individual, and can occur within the family or in the community. Collective violence is violence within groups of people. This chapter will focus on interpersonal and collective violence.

INTERPERSONAL VIOLENCE

Interpersonal can be either instrumental, situational, or psychopathic, but always occurs within the context of an ongoing family, intimate, friend, or business relationship. Most teenage violence is within the context of a relationship (Lipsey, 2010; Spencer & Bryant, 2000). Here, we will look at dating violence, family violence, school violence, and youth who commit homicide.

Dating Violence

According to Hanna (2006) one-third of teens experience some form of dating violence.

Girls, aged 16 to 24 years, are most at risk for dating violence (Hanna, 2006). Statistics on the incidence of violence are similar worldwide. About 10% to 20% of teen girls report being physically abused in a romantic relationship, and as many as 25% to 30% report verbal abuse. However, increasingly, both girls and boys may engage in violence in their dating relationships.

Some research suggests that engaging in sex within a dating relationship greatly increases the likelihood of dating violence. The dynamic appears to be an increased commitment to the relationship after sex, which increases the need to control the relationship for both girls and boys. Girls who are sexually active are also at increased risk for entering the juvenile justice system. Interestingly, girls' sexual autonomy may be at the root of the phenomenon (Hanna, 2006). Hanna (2006) suggests that more effective sex education for boys and girls is needed.

Family Violence

Family violence involves children and teens engaged in aggression toward parents, caregivers, grandparents, or siblings. This is likely to be found in homes where adult family members typically use violence to attempt to control the behavior of other family members. This phenomenon can be explained by social learning theory and the intergenerational cycle of violence, both of which will be discussed more in Chapter 4. Children and teens raised in such an atmosphere use force to intimidate other household members, so they can have their way or get what they want.

At the extremes are youth who kill their own mothers (matricide) or fathers (patricide). In these cases, there is usually violence in the home, child abuse or neglect, substance-abusing parents, and significant stressors in the household (Heide & Frei, 2009). Heide and Frei (2009) identified three types of youthful patricide killers: severely abused child, dangerously antisocial child, and the severely mentally ill child. Studies of youth who kill their parents and stepparents indicate that there was abuse, domestic violence, or parental substance abuse or mental illness in the household (Heide, 1999a).

School Violence

According to the National Center for Education Statistics (2010) *Indicators of School Crime and Safety*:

- there were 38 school-associated violent deaths in the 2008 to 2009 school year (24 homicides and 14 suicides)
- there were about 629,800 violent crimes among students aged 12 to 18 years in 2008
- 8% of students reported being threatened or injured by someone with a weapon on school property in 2009
- 75% of public schools recorded one or more violent incidents of crime during the 2007 to 2008 school year
- 25% of public schools reported that bullying occurred among students on a daily or weekly basis during the 2007 to 2008 school year
- 20% of public schools reported that gang activities had happened during 2007 to 2008

There are factors in the school environment that can contribute to school violence.

Lenhardt, Farrell, and Graham (2010) cited problems with school climate in a study of 13 incidents of school violence. Many of the schools in the study lacked sufficient numbers of counselors and support services for the size of the student body. The schools were large and did not foster a strong sense of community among students, teachers, and staff. In 73% of cases, bullying and marginalizing groups of students were not addressed. The authors concluded that the school atmosphere should be one that is welcoming and helpful toward students, with a strong sense of community and action to eliminate mistrust and mistreatment within the school.

The most frightening and extreme incarnation of school violence is the phenomenon of the school shooter, as typified by Eric Harris and Dylan Klebold of Columbine and Seung-Hui Cho of Virginia Tech. The Federal Bureau of Investigation (FBI) has studied school shooters to see if they share common characteristics (O'Toole, 2011). While there is no definitive profile, some commonalities emerge:

- They were predominantly male and Caucasian
- They reported feeling bullied and rejected by peers
- Many were abused and neglected at home as children
- In their homes, discipline was too harsh, too lenient, or inconsistent
- Their families had low warmth and high conflict or domestic violence
- They had poor coping, social, anger management, and problem solving skills
- Many had relationship problems with their parents and/or peers
- They felt like outsiders, disconnected from their peers; they were "different" and didn't fit into the peer culture
- They tended to be rigid and opinionated
- They tended to be racially or religiously intolerant
- They had other behavior problems, a fascination with violence, and had expressed a desire to harm others on film, video, letters, or the Internet, or to friends
- They planned their attack (usually very publicly)
- They had access to firearms and gathered weapons for a long time before taking those weapons to school
- They failed to take responsibility for their actions and blamed their mistakes or misdeeds on others
- They may feel entitled, only concerned about their own needs, and lack empathy toward others. They may feel that they are better than others

Eric Harris and Dylan Klebold, who killed 12 students and a teacher and wounded 23 others before taking their own lives at

Columbine High School, are good examples of the profile. Both felt that they had been bullied and rejected by other students; both were fascinated with violent video games and movies. As early as 1997, Harris posted death threats on his Web site. Klebold had substance-abuse problems, and both he and Harris had been caught stealing. There were signs that they needed significant help, which they obviously did not get.

Seung-Hui Cho was a student at Virginia Tech. He went on a shooting rampage on April 16, 2007 and killed 32 people. His family, and staff at one of the public schools he attended, reportedly recognized that Cho was troubled from a very early age, but he did not receive treatment. Troubling signs continued as he grew older; he spent time at a mental institution in 2005, and he wrote violent stories that an English teacher brought to the attention of the authorities. Unfortunately, the authorities were not universally trained to recognize and react to the threat.

The FBI emphasizes that no one characteristic indicates that a youth will become a school shooter. It takes multiple factors and a sophisticated professional assessment. Factors that place a youth at risk for committing future acts of violence include a history of childhood trauma, school behavior problems, trouble interacting with prosocial peers, history of aggression, delinquency, substance abuse, lack of appropriate parental discipline, high conflict and low warmth within the family, and other behavior problems, especially those that start before the age of 13 years. The greater the number of risk factors, the earlier the problems start, and the fewer resiliency factors that a child has, the greater the risk of major interpersonal problems, such as violence (Lahey, Moffit, & Caspi, 2003; Seifert, 2006). Individual and environmental risk factors will be discussed in more detail in Chapters 5 and 6.

Youth Who Commit Homicide

Certain commonalities emerge when examining youth who commit homicide: a history of family violence, abuse, and neglect; mental illnesses and/or neurological deficits; antisocial behaviors; and/or substance abuse.

Myers, Scott, and Burgess (1995) found that the majority of families of a sample of 25 young people who had killed others were dysfunctional, emotionally abusive, and violent. Busch, Zagar, Hughes, Arbit, and Bussell (1990) found that significantly more of the violent youth came from violent families. In a study by Seifert (2006), 84% (71) of youth who had seriously injured or killed another person had family histories of violence (half of the nonviolent youth had family histories of violence). In the same study, 75% of families (63) of severely violent youth had family members with psychiatric problems, substance abuse, or criminal records. Heide (1999b) reviewed the literature on youth homicide and determined that they had suffered deprivation and maltreatment early in life. King (1975) reported that the nine young homicidal youth whom he studied had suffered from abuse. Sendi (1975) had similar results. In a study by Lewis et al. (1985), seven of the nine youth studied had been severely abused. We can thus conclude that violent and abusive homes distinguish severely violent youth from nonviolent youth.

McKnight (1966) found that 77% of murderers they studied had psychiatric diagnoses; however, this was a group from a hospitalized sample. In the study by Lewis et al. (1985), of nine adolescents who later committed murder, eight had paranoid ideation, all had psychiatric symptoms, and all had a first-degree relative with severe psychiatric disorders. Psychotic symptoms significantly differentiated the group of boys who had murdered from the control group of delinquents ($P < .05$). Wolfgang (1967) found that only 3% of murderers in Philadelphia were insane. Gillies (1976) found that 10% of a Scottish sample of murderers had a psychiatric diagnosis. Of course different percentages over several decades will reflect changes in the field of psychiatry and in diagnostic trends.

Seifert (2006) studied the characteristics of 1031 youth from a variety of settings, including an outpatient mental health clinic, a hospital, residential treatment center, and detention. Eighty-two percent of youth who had injured or killed a victim had psychiatric disorders, 51% had substance-abuse problems, and 46% showed signs of psychosis. By comparison, only 23% of 400 nonassaultive youth had symptoms of psychosis. Similar to severely assaultive youth, 82% of nonassaultive youth in the sample had other psychiatric symptoms.

Several researchers, such as Bailey (1996), have found neurological deficits among young people who have committed homicide. In the Lewis et al. (1985) study, seven of nine had abnormal neurological findings, and two had histories of head injuries with loss of consciousness.

Research about the intelligence of young murderers is mixed (Heide, 1999a), however, they tend to struggle academically. Myers et al. (1995) reported that 70% of adolescent murderers had failed a grade and had learning disabilities. In a study by Seifert (2006) of youth who injured or killed a victim, 63% had learning problems. Only 43% of nonassaultive youth had learning problems.

Skill deficits in anger management and impulse control are also an issue. In the Seifert (2006) study of 1031 youth from a variety of settings spanning 9 years, 99% of youth who had seriously injured or killed a victim and 67% of nonassaultive youth had anger management problems.

The majority of youth who commit homicide have had prior arrests and demonstrated antisocial behavior. Gang participation is also found in high numbers (Heide, 1999a). Busch et al. (1990) also found that significantly more of the youth they studied participated in gangs. Myers et al. (1995) reported that 18 of a sample of 25 youthful murderers (75%) had a prior history of arrests, assaults, and disruptive behaviors. Seventy-nine percent of the Seifert (2006) sample of severely assaultive youth were delinquent, whereas slightly more than 20% of nonassaultive youth were delinquent. Therefore, we conclude that past delinquency, assaults, and disruptive behaviors distinguish severely assaultive and murderous youth from nonviolent young people.

Rates of substance abuse among young murderers vary by study from 25% to 90% (Heide, 1999a). Busch et al. (1990) found that significantly more of the murderers abused alcohol. Seifert (2006) found 51% substance abuse among those who had assaulted victims severely enough to seriously injure or kill them, whereas 15% of nonassaultive youth were substance abusers. In the Seifert sample, more than three times as many severely violent kids have substance-abuse issues than their nonviolent peers.

COLLECTIVE VIOLENCE

In this section, we will briefly examine some forms of collective violence: gang violence, hate crimes, and violence by youth who are involuntarily inducted into military operations.

Gang Violence

The number of gangs, gang membership, and gang activity increased significantly in the United States from 2002 to 2008 (Mahoney, 2010). The estimated number of gang members in the United States in 2008 was 774,000 in 27,900 gangs (Egley, Howell, & Moore, 2010). There was a decline in numbers of gang problems from 1996 to 2001, but then a 28% increase from 2002 to 2008. Forty-one percent of respondents to the National Youth Gang Survey reported increases in gang criminal activity. The greatest increase in gang activity occurred in cities with a population of more than 250,000.

Gangs are primarily male, but there are some female gangs and female members of male gangs. Typical ages range from 12 to 24 years, with a mean age of 17 to 18 years. The more structured the gang, the more likely it is to engage in criminal gang activity, such as selling drugs (Duffy & Gillig, 2004). Mahoney (2010) conjectures that violence is a survival strategy that will not be "cured" by the juvenile justice system alone. Prevention and education is reported to be much more effective than direct gang interventions (Mahoney, 2010).

Spikes in gang activity are seen in times of economic hardship and among youth who are marginalized, have dropped out of school, have been rejected by prosocial peers, and see no opportunities for success; these youth are more likely to join or be recruited by gangs. Family characteristics can be either risk or protective factors against gang membership. Where there are positive role models, organization, and absence of substance abuse and criminality, youth are less likely to join gangs. Schneider (in Duffy & Gillig, 2004) hypothesizes that gangs were an attempt of marginalized youth in poor communities to find affiliation and acceptance (Duffy & Gillig, 2004). In general, gangs appear to be less well organized and entrepreneurial than once thought and, in some cases, span a very large age range as incarcerated gang members return to the community and to the gang. Typical gang composition is not generally equivalent to that of corporations, but much simpler in organizational structure (Coughlin & Venkatesh, 2003).

Hate Crimes

Hate crimes or bias-motivated violence are situations in which a person or persons are targeted for violence because of ethnicity, sexual orientation, religion, class, nationality, age, gender, or disability. The FBI reported more than 9,000 hate crime offenses in 2007, of which 32% were simple assaults and 21% were aggravated assaults (FBI, 2007). Sixty-three percent of hate crime offenders were White and 21% were African American.

There are antifascist and racist skinheads in the United States, including groups such as the Aryan Brotherhood, some of whom are known for extreme violence against minorities (FBI, 2008a). There were 90 chapters of racist skinheads in 2007, an increase of 50% from 2004. According to the FBI, they were responsible for 24 of 38 cases (63%) of violence against others by the "White nationalist extremist movement" from January 1, 2007, to September 30, 2008, including five of seven murders. The racist groups of skin heads often attack in groups and overpower their victims, who are often of minority ethnicity or homosexual, but can also be one of their own or a member of another skinhead group.

Mott (2009) sees a correlation between youth bullying and violence related to hate and bias. Youthful bias aggression may also be associated with attachment problems. The answer to reducing such events is therapy for victims and victimizers who often come from homes with similar attitudes. However, it is also important to address hate and biased attitudes in the home, as well.

Use of Children in the Military

The Coalition to Stop Child Soldiers has reported that the use of children during conflicts has been widespread in many parts of the world. Under the terms of Protocol I of the Geneva Conventions, children younger than 15 years cannot serve in the military, but teens from the age of 15 to 18 years may volunteer to serve in the military. Yet, according to Human Rights Watch (2007), an estimated 200,000 to 300,000 children are serving in the military worldwide. Use of children in the military typically takes three forms: as soldiers, in support roles, and as sexual slaves (Human Rights Watch, 2007).

For example, the recruitment of child soldiers in Sri Lanka during their 25-year war was common, especially by LTTE (Liberation Tigers of Tamil Eelam) and Karuna. Thousands of children were forcibly recruited for hostilities, severely mistreated, and then sent into combat (http://www. hrw.org/news/2007/05/10/sri-lanka-un-security-council-directs-tamil-tigers-karuna-end-use-child-soldiers). Some cases were still reported as late as February 2010. Although recruitment of child soldiers was criminalized by the government of Sri Lanka in 2006, there are no known incidents of investigation or prosecution of child recruitment by the government or militia groups. Reintegration programs of child soldiers being released to the community have begun, however, but often do not meet world standards (Coalition to Stop Child Soldiers, 2010).

Sexual abuse and poor care of children in the Internally Displaced Persons, (IDP) camps following the end of the conflict between the Sri Lanka government and LTTE have been reported. Palestinian factions reportedly use children who "volunteer" for service as suicide bombers. Yassir Arafat was a child soldier who recruited other children into the military (Coalition to Stop Child Soldiers, 2010). Militia units in Chechnya are believed to still use child soldiers for fighting and as suicide bombers (Coalition to Stop Child Soldiers, 2010). One quarter of the Bolivian army is believed to be younger that 16 years (Coalition to Stop Child Soldiers, 2010).

Once released from the military and returned to community reintegration centers, the children often fought with each other and refused school. It has been recommended (Coalition to Stop Child Soldiers, 2010) that reintegration programs last at least 3 years and that they emphasize education. Many tribunals now struggle with deciding the punishment for war crimes by child soldiers.

In the United States, 17-year-olds may enlist in the military, but cannot be sent outside the United States or into combat. In 2003 and 2004, nearly sixty 17-year-olds were sent to fight in Iraq and Afghanistan. When discovered, they were returned to the United States. In 2004, three Afghan children were released from Guantanamo. They were between 13 and 15 years of age when captured.

REFERENCES

Bailey, S. (1996). Adolescents who murder. *Journal of Adolescence*, 129, 19–39.

Busch, K. G., Zagar, R., Hughes, J. R., Arbit, J., & Bussell, R. E. (1990). Adolescents who kill. *Journal of Clinical Psychology*, 46, 472–485.

Coalition to Stop Child Soldiers. (2010, April). *Coalition to Stop Child Soldiers*. Retrieved from http://www.child-soldiers.org/Coalition_report_to_CRC_on_OPAC_implementation_in_Sri_Lanka_-_April_2010.pdf

Coughlin, B. C., & Venkatesh, S. A. (2003). The urban street gang after 1970. *Annual Review of Sociology, 29*, 41–64.

Duffy, M. P., & Gillig, S. E. (2004). *Teen gangs: A global view.* Westport, CT: Greenwood Press.

Egley, A., Howell, J. C., & Moore, J. P. (2010, March). *Highlights of the 2008 national youth gang survey.* Washington, DC: Office of Juvenile Justice and Delinquency Prevention. Retrieved from http://www.ncjrs.gov/pdffiles1/ojjdp/229249.pdf on 5/8/2010

Federal Bureau of Investigation. (2008a). *Rage and racism: Skinhead violence on the far right.* Washington, DC: FBI.

Federal Bureau of Investigation. (2008b). *Crime in the United States.* Washington, DC: FBI. Retrieved from http://www.fbi.gov/about-us/cjis/ucr/ucr on 5/8/2011

Federal Bureau of Investigation. (2007). *Hate crime statistics.* Washington, DC: FBI. Retrieved from http://www.fbi.gov/news/stories/2008/october/hatecrime_102708 on 5/8/2011

Gillies, H. (1976). Homicide in the west of Scotland. *British Journal of Psychiatry, 128*, 106–127.

Hanna, C. (2006). Sex before violence: Girls, dating violence and (perceived) sexual autonomy. *Fordham Urban Law Journal, 33*, 437. Retrieved from SSRN: http://ssrn.com/abstract=1276827

Heide, K. M. (1999a). *Young killers: the challenge of juvenile homicide.* Thousand Oaks, CA: Sage.

Heide, K. M. (1999b). Youth homicide: An integration of psychological, sociological, and biological approaches. *Homicide: A sourcebook of social research.* In: M. D. Smith & M. A. Zahn (eds.). Thousand Oaks, CA: Sage.

Heide, K. M., & Frei, A. (2009). Matricide: a critique of the literature. *Trauma, Violence, and Abuse, 11*(3). Retrieved from http://www.cbsnews.com/stories/2010/04/10/48hours/main6383938.shtml on 5/8/2011

Human Rights Watch. (2007, April). Q & A: *The child soldiers prevention act of 2007.* Retrieved from http://www.hrw.org/news/2007/04/23/q-child-soldiers-prevention-act-2007 on 8/5/2011.

King, C. H. (1975). The ego and the integration of violence in homicidal youth. *American Journal of Orthopsychiatry, 45*(1), 134–145.

Lahey, B. B., Moffit, T. E., & Caspi A. (2003). *Causes of conduct disorder and juvenile delinquency.* New York, NY: Guilford Press.

Lenhardt, A. M. C., Farrell, M., & Graham, L. W. (2010). Providing anchors, reclaiming our troubled youth: Lessons for leaders from a study of 15 targeted school shooters. *The Educational Forum, 74*(2), 104–116.

Lewis, D. O., Moy, E., Jackson, M. A., Aaronson, R., Restifo, N., Serra, S., & Simos, A. (1985). Biopsychosocial characteristics of children who later murder: A prospective study. *American Journal of Psychiatry, 142*(10), 1161–1167.

Lipsey, M. W. (2010). *Improving the effectiveness of juvenile justice programs: A new perspective on evidence-based practice.* Washington, DC: Center for Juvenile Justice Reform.

Mahoney, D. (2010). Teen gangs: Integrated interventions work best. *Clinical Psychiatry News, 38*(10), 1.

McKnight, C. M. (1966). Mental illness and homicide. *Canadian Psychiatric Association Journal, 11*(2), 91–98.

Mott, T. (2009, March). A therapeutic response to youth hate crime offenders and their broken attachments. *Play Therapy,* 22–23. Retrieved from http://www.a4pt.org/download.cfm?ID=27835

Myers, W. C., Scott, K., & Burgess, A. W. (1995). Psychopathology, biopsychosocial factors, crime characteristics, and classification of 25 homicidal youths. *Journal of the American Academy of Child and Adolescent Psychiatry, 34,* 1483–1489.

National Center for Education Statistics. (2010). *Indicators of school crime and safety.* Retrieved from http://nces.ed.gov/pubsearch/pubsinfo.asp?pubid=2011002

O'Toole, M. E. (2011). *The school shooter: A threat assessment perspective.* Quantico, VA: FBI Academy.

Seifert, K. (2006). *How children become violent: Keeping your kids out of gangs, terrorist organizations and cults.* Boston, MA: Acanthus.

Sendi, I. A. (1975). A comparative study of predictive criteria in the predisposition for homicidal adolescents. *American Journal of Psychiatry, 134*(4) 423–427.

Spencer, G. A., & Bryant, S. A. (2000). Dating violence: A comparison of rural, suburban, and urban teens. *Journal of Adolescent Health, 27*(5), 302–305.

Wolfgang, M. E. (1967). *The subculture of violence: Towards an integrated theory of criminology.* New York, NY: Methuen.

World Health Organization. (2002). *World report on violence and health.* Geneva, Switzerland: World Health Organization. Retrieved from http://whqlibdoc.who.int/publications/2002/9241545615_eng.pdf

FOUR

Theoretical Perspectives on Youth Violence

There are many theories from the fields of psychology, criminology, and sociology that attempt to explain the root causes of violence. Many early theories examined a single personal, environmental, or structural precursor of violence in a particular population. What is needed, researchers and practitioners have come to realize, is an overarching theory that incorporates a variety of perspectives—not only individual factors but also community, social, and political dynamics. Most theorists agree that the interaction of individual characteristics, development, and environment influences behavior.

This chapter will briefly discuss many existing theories that attempt to explain the root causes of violent behavior. You will note as you read that some posit psychological factors (i.e., psycopathy), others take a neurobiological approach (i.e., genetic theory), and still others look at broader societal factors (i.e., social structures theory, feminist theory). Toward the end of the chapter, we will examine theories that attempt to integrate all of these various factors.

SOCIAL LEARNING THEORY

Learning would be exceedingly laborious, not to mention hazardous, if people had to rely solely on the effects of their own actions to inform them about what to do. Fortunately, most human behavior is learned observationally through modeling: from observing others, one forms an idea of how new behaviors are performed, and on later occasions this coded information serves as a guide for action.

Bandura, 1977, p. 22

47

As originated in the work of Albert Bandura, a psychologist, *Social Learning Theory* (O'Leary, 1988) proposes that violence is a learned behavior. Social learning theory suggests that people learn how to act through *behavior modeling*—that is, by watching and copying the behaviors of others. Thus, applying the theory to violent behavior, it has been speculated that a person who experiences or witnesses violence (in their childhood home, in their community, and/or through the media) will learn that it is an acceptable strategy and will be more likely to use violence when they grow up (Kaufman & Zigler, 1987; Pagelow, 1981; Straus, Gelles, & Steinmetz, 1980).

In a groundbreaking set of experiments developed by Bandura in the early 1960s, children who watched adults beat a "Bobo" doll were more likely to then beat the doll themselves (numerous videos of the Bobo doll experiment are available on YouTube; see, for example, http://www.youtube.com/watch?v=hHHdovKHDNU). Numerous variations on this study were conducted subsequently, and it also sparked a cascade of research over the potentially harmful effects of allowing children to watch violent content in the media—a debate that still rages to this day.

One criticism of social learning theory is that it completely ignores any unique features of an individual (DNA, brain development, and learning differences) that might impact a person's ability or desire to copy learned behavior. Certainly there are batterers and nonbatterers who do not fit this model.

INTERGENERATIONAL TRANSMISSION OF VIOLENCE

The common thread linking maltreatment, punitive parenting, and exposure to violent parental conflict may reside in their serious disruptions of relationships with caregivers. Such disruptions result in emotion regulation deficits, faulty social information processing, and hostile expectations about the meaning of relationships; these deficits may in turn increase the risk for aggressive behavior in childhood and across the life span.

Ehrensaft et al., 2003, p. 742

Similar to social learning theory, intergenerational transmission of violence postulates that children learn violent behavior patterns from their early home environment—either through witnessing abuse between their adult caregivers, experiencing abuse or extreme physical punishment themselves, or a combination thereof—and then go on to use violent behaviors in their own relationships. Thus, violent behavior patterns may be repeated in subsequent generations (DeKeseredy, 2006).

Many studies have confirmed such a link. "The data are clear; children who are exposed to violence have a significant risk for using violence themselves, becoming delinquent, demonstrating school and behavior problems, and having serious and lifelong mental health problems, including depression, anxiety, and PTSD symptomology" (Walker, 2009, p. 241). In one study involving a sample of more than 500 children, who were followed for 20 years, exposure to violence in childhood was found to be linked to either the perpetration or victimization of intimate partner abuse later in life (Ehrensaft et al., 2003). Another study (Doumas, Margolin, & John, 1994) found that for males, exposure to violence was a predictor of violence across three generations.

The intergenerational transmission theory has strong implications for prevention; children who are exposed to violence at young ages are strong candidates for prevention programs, so they can learn alternate methods of dealing with violence and not repeat the cycle of violence as they themselves become adults.

> "Elizabeth" had been sexually abused and severely brutalized by family members most of her young life. Her grandparents, with whom she often stayed, had a domestically violent relationship. She frequently stayed in her room away from family members, where she started to drink alcohol and experiment with drugs. She abused her first child when she was 15 years old. Her emotional and abuse of children escalated until she was eventually arrested on child abuse charges.

ROUTINE ACTIVITY THEORY

First, we think it inadequate to study "criminality"—the criminal tendencies of persons. As interesting as people might be, it is essential to study what they do. This book focuses on criminal action—who, what, when, where, and how it occurs, and what can be done here and now to prevent it from happening.

Felson and Boba, 2010, p. xi

Routine activity theory (Felson & Boba, 2010), also known as event-centered theory, proposes that the root cause of crime is nothing more than the conjunction of a motivated offender, a suitable target, and a lack of an adequate guardian in the same space and time. In other words, all crime is a crime of opportunity. It suggests that the majority of crimes are petty crimes (theft, vandalism, etc.) that can easily be explained. Although this theory has practical implications, such as the use of appropriate environmental design to reduce crime in a neighborhood (National Institute of Justice, 2002), it underemphasizes violent crimes and how violent offenders are created, and it does not examine the social causes of crime.

SOCIAL EXCHANGE THEORY

A central (and perhaps greatly oversimplified) proposition of an exchange/ social control theory of family violence is that people hit and abuse other family members because they can. In applying the principle of general exchange theory we expect that people will use violence in the family if the costs of being violent do not outweigh the rewards

Gelles, 1983, p. 157

Social exchange theory, which has its roots in psychology, sociology, and economics, suggests that all relationships are based on calculated exchanges: people subtract the relative costs (such as time, money, energy) from the expected benefits (such as money, social status, emotional comfort) of a particular relationship to determine a suitable outcome. People also assume that there will be a reciprocal exchange of rewards within a relationship. As Gelles' quote suggests, people will use violence if they think it will bring them greater rewards than it will cost.

Critics of social exchange theory say that it assumes that people take a purely rational approach to emotional decisions, which may not make it an appropriate theory with which to evaluate highly irrational acts of violence.

Somewhat similarly, according to resource theory (Blood & Wolfe, 1960), the family member with the most resources is able to wield power and control over the family, which may include using violent behavior (Blood & Wolfe, 1960). Dependent members may be helpless to avoid or change this behavior.

PSYCHOPATHY

Kiehl's most memorable [psychopathic patient] was an inmate I'll call George.... George described his criminal past in full detail. He started out committing petty crimes as a child and by seventeen had been convicted of arson. In the early nineties, after serving eighteen months in prison for breaking and entering, he moved back in with his mother. One day, the two had a fight, and his mother picked up the phone to call the cops.... He wrapped the phone cord around his mother's neck and strangled her. "Then I threw her down the basement stairs, but I wasn't sure she was dead, so I got a kitchen knife and stabbed her, and her body made these weird noises, I guess gas escaping, but I wasn't sure, so I grabbed a big propane canister and bashed her brains in." Then he went out and partied for three days.... When he was convicted of manslaughter and sentenced to life imprisonment, George just smiled.

Seabrook, 2008

For at least 200 years, researchers and psychologists have struggled to specifically define and treat a subset of patients, who could be violent, impulsive, insincere, and unreliable, and yet display no empathy for their victims or remorse for their actions. That these patients showed no signs of "insanity" or psychosis, and in fact were usually charming and intelligent, made their behaviors even more difficult to understand. Dr. Hannibal Lecter—the urbane, polite, cultured psychiatrist who just happens to enjoy torture and cannibalism in the 1991 movie *The Silence of the Lambs*—is a classic movie portrayal of a psychopath. Ted Bundy, the handsome and charismatic serial killer who murdered at least 30 women, is a real-life example.

Robert Hare, a psychologist who specializes in psychopathy, has over the course of his career created a number of assessment tools to diagnose the disorder, most famously the *Psychopathy Checklist–Revised* (PCL-R; Hare, 1991). Hare (1991) conceptualized psychopathy as having two components: Factor 1—personality traits and Factor 2—antisocial behaviors.

Hemphill, Hare, and Wong (1998) suggested that psychopathy may be a developmental disorder that begins in childhood. In adulthood, psychopathy is related to violence, poor treatment outcomes, and high rates of recidivism (Hare, 1999; Lahey, Moffit, & Caspi, 2003).

Modern research into psychopathy has attempted to locate a neurobiological basis for the disorder. Many are attempting to determine whether the hallmarks of psychopathy (emotional callousness, antisocial behavior) correspond to abnormalities in the brain. Some studies have found that psychopaths process emotional words (such as "love") only in the "language center" of the brain, and not in the emotional-processing center—suggesting that they cannot feel or understand emotions the way others do. Oliveira-Souza et al. (2008) studied patients with high psychopathy scores and found significant gray matter reductions in the area of the brain associated with moral sensibility and behavior. Clearly, this is an important area for future research.

It is worth noting that use of the term psychopath is controversial; the current edition of the *Diagnostic and Statistical Manual of Mental Disorders (DSM)* does not use it, but rather classifies psychopathic behaviors under the term antisocial personality disorder. Discussions are underway to include "antisocial/psychopathic type" in the upcoming *DSM-V* revision.

It is particularly dangerous to label children or juveniles as psychopaths. The term is highly loaded and stigmatizing, and it may not be clinically accurate to judge child or adolescent behaviors according to such a standard. Although it is highly controversial to apply the label psychopath to young people, characteristics in youth that are associated with later adult psychopathy are impulsivity/conduct problems and callous/unemotional traits. The callous, unemotional trait in youth appears to be associated with lack of empathy and perspective taking, cognitive dysregulation, and superficial charm (Morris, 2007), similar to Dr. Hare's Factor 1. Behaviors might include poor impulse control and delinquency (Frick, O'Brien, Wootton, & McBurnett, 1994) and be similar to Hare's Factor 2. Frick, Bodin, and Barry (2000) discovered a third factor in adolescents and named it the narcissism factor, but this is still undergoing research (Morris, 2007). The incidence of psychopathic traits is estimated to be 21.5% in teens and 15% to 30% in adults (Mizen & Morris, 2007).

The author hypothesizes that childhood and teen psychopathy is comparable to Moffitt's (2001) model of "the early starter," children who follow a lifelong course of antisocial behavior and violence. This will be discussed in more detail later in this chapter.

NEUROBIOLOGICAL THEORIES OF VIOLENCE

When considering potential neurobiological correlates of aggression, it is important to bear in mind that overt behavior is expressed in a complex interaction of biological, psychological, and social determinants.... [A] distinction can be drawn between so-called impulsive-reactive and instrumental, goal-directed dimensions of aggression.... The genetic data presented here...indicate that, whereas both instrumental and impulsive aggression may be present to varying degrees in most violent offenders, the risk imparted by the specific genetic variation studied here contributes to the impulsive dimension of this complex behavior.

Meyer-Lindenberg et al., 2006, p. 6271

Advances in neuroscience have allowed us great insight into the development of the structures of the human brain, and the resulting skills that we acquire in language, thought processing, and emotional control, among many others. From this research, we have learned that early childhood trauma can negatively affect neurotransmitter regulation, brain structures, and brain development (Thompson, 1998) and that these effects can greatly influence a child's behavior—including violent behavior—later in life.

Neurotransmitters are chemicals that communicate information within our bodies: they move from one neuron to another across a synapse. Examples include epinephrine, norepinephrine, dopamine, serotonin, amino acids, and neuroactive peptides. Our nervous systems use these neurochemicals to monitor and react to our environment. For example, the sympathetic nervous system helps us respond to stresses in our environment: possible reactions include dissociation, fight, or flight (Brodal, 2004). In reaction to a severe stressor, some bodily functions slow down, such as our ability for complex thinking; other bodily functions, such as blood flow to the muscles, increase to help us make quick, instinctual action. When the danger is over, neurotransmitters in the parasympathetic nervous system help us return to a restful state called homeostasis.

Severe chronic stressors in childhood can cause the sympathetic and parasympathetic systems to create new "set points" that make it easier to become aroused, and harder to return to homeostasis. Consequently, a youth who grows up in a chronically chaotic, violent, or dangerous home can have his or her "activation point" moved higher so he is constantly "on alert" for danger (Van der Kolk, et al., 1996). Many everyday actions or events may be interpreted by traumatized children and teens as dangerous, even when they are not. Although it is a safety mechanism in reaction to living with a chaotic or violent family, it can become severely maladaptive as the child attempts to interact in the wider world. Children who experience chronic trauma may never feel calm, safe, competent, and confident. Instead, they live in a constant state of anxiety, hypervigilance, anger, and fear. This state interferes with normal development (Van der Kolk, 2005). This can lead to a diagnosis of developmental trauma disorder, which will be discussed in the following section.

Other brain structures are involved in regulation of our behavior. For example, the amygdalae helps manage our emotional reactions to stimuli from the environment. Brain imaging studies have demonstrated that children and adults who were traumatized at a young age have smaller amygdalae than those of nontraumatized controls. There are also indications that these smaller amydalae function in a much less effective way than those of normal size in nontraumatized brains (Weniger, Lange, Sachsse, & Irle, 2009).

Findings in the field of genetics have allowed us to attribute certain traits or behaviors to a single gene or set of genes. Some researchers have postulated that individuals may be genetically hardwired to be predisposed to violence. Recent studies have focused on the *X-linked monoamine oxidase A (MAO-A)* gene. The "L" variant of this gene has been associated with impulsive aggression in animals and humans. In one study (Meyer-Lindenberg et al., 2006) 100 subjects—some with the L-MAOA variation, and some without—were shown pictures with disturbing imagery, such as angry dogs or guns. Those with the "L" (aggression-related) variant of the gene showed increased activity in the amygdala—the brain area that detects danger—but less activity in the cingulate cortex—the brain region that is believed to control aggression. These brain patterns have been linked to impulsive violence.

The link between brain structure, genetics, and violence will be further examined in Chapter 5. However, it would be very simplistic to assign all violent behavior to genetics. Genetic predispositions such as an inclination to use violence can be triggered by certain environmental factors—or, alternately, they can be thwarted by protective aspects of the environment. The current scientific view suggests that virtually all human traits are a result of gene–environment interaction.

DEVELOPMENTAL TRAUMA DISORDER

"Developmental trauma disorder" is predicated on the notion that multiple exposures to interpersonal trauma, such as abandonment, betrayal, physical or sexual assaults or witnessing domestic violence, have consistent and predictable consequences that affect many areas of functioning. These experiences engender 1) intense affects, such as rage, betrayal, fear, resignation, defeat and shame and 2) efforts to ward off the recurrence of those emotions, including the avoidance of experiences that precipitate them or engaging in behaviors that convey a subjective sense of control in the face of potential threats.... These children tend to behaviorally reenact their traumas either as perpetrators, in aggressive or sexual acting out against other children, or in frozen avoidance reactions.... They anticipate and expect the trauma to recur and respond with hyperactivity, aggression, defeat, or freeze responses to minor stresses. All of these problems are expressed in dysfunction in multiple areas of functioning: educational, familial, peer relationships, problems with the legal system, and problems in maintaining jobs.

Van der Kolk, 2005, p. 377

As outlined in the previous section, research suggests that early traumatic experiences in childhood can lead to less than optimal functioning well into adulthood. Children who are exposed to multiple and/or prolonged interpersonal trauma have serious problems regulating their emotions and suffer from dissociation, aggression, lack of impulse control, and poor self-image, among other symptoms.

Pynoos et al. (2008) reported findings from analysis of the National Child Traumatic Stress Network Core Data Set, a national sample of 9,336 children receiving services at NCTSN child trauma centers. More than 70% of these children experienced multiple forms of trauma and adversity, with 48% exhibiting clinically significant behavior problems in the home or community, 41% academic problems, 37% behavior problems in school/daycare, 31% attachment problems, and 11% suicidality.

van der Kolk et al., 2009

Van der Kolk and others (2009) argue that developmental trauma disorder is a different diagnosis than posttraumatic stress disorder, and should be recognized separately within the *DSM* for that reason. However, developmental trauma disorder is not currently included in the *DSM-IV*, and it is unknown if it will be included in the *DSM-V*.

"Jarnell" had a wonderful, infectious smile when he wanted something from you. His mother, though loving, was a drug addict, his brothers were involved in gangs, and his dad was in jail. He himself was running drugs for a gang by age 7 and started drinking and smoking at 9. His brothers taught him how to be tough and protect himself on the streets. Eventually he was expelled from school because he was too often truant, too aggressive with children and teachers, and refused to do any school work.

At age 10, Jarnell was removed from his home to a secure residential placement center. He continued to be quite violent. He escaped from a facility by taking the keys of a staff member and stealing her car, which he subsequently crashed. Once arrested, he was sent to another facility, where he injured another student. Upon release, he got drunk with some older friends, was re-arrested for robbery, and sentenced as an adult.

Jarnell had clearly experienced childhood trauma that severely limited his functioning. When tested, his functioning in various skill domains (such as interpersonal, communication, and adaptive skills) were in the kindergarten range. Using the behavior objective sequence (BOS), a method of teaching skills required for school success, his skill level in all areas was raised to the middle school level. For the first time, he managed well in a structured facility. However, he was still not able to self-manage his behavior in the community, especially when other family members experienced problems and placed strain on family relationships.

Eventually Jarnell was re-arrested, but he managed well within the structure of the jail, as many inmates do. When he is again released into the community, the goal will be to bring his skills to a high school level, so he can operate more independently from his family's strains and stresses and maintain a prosocial lifestyle.

SUBCULTURE OF VIOLENCE THEORY

Like all human behavior, homicide and other violent assaultive crimes must be viewed in terms of the cultural context from which they spring

Wolfgang and Ferracuti, 1967, p. 150

The subculture of violence theory (Wolfgang & Ferracuti, 1967) emerged from the work of Dr. Marvin E. Wolfgang, a renowned criminologist who studied crime in inner-city Philadelphia. The theory suggests that within large societies, subgroups may develop values and attitudes that encourage crime and violence. Wolfgang's original work was focused on Black subculture; however, the theory has since been expanded to include many different subcultures, such as the lower class, gun owners, and street youth, among others. It has particular implications for adolescents, because the theory suggests that if the pattern of delinquent behavior can be understood, practitioners may be able to intervene before a delinquent adolescent becomes an adult criminal. Critics have suggested that, at best, it offers an incomplete theory of violence, and that, at worst, it can be construed as racist.

> Darnell's mother worked long hours to provide a good home for her son. While she worked, his grandmother was his primary caregiver. Although loving and kind, she was also elderly and not able to go with Darnell to ball games, church, and other activities. Darnell was recruited into a local gang at age 9. As part of the gang, he gained protection and could make money delivering drugs. He also witnessed the violence associated with the gang's activities. By age 11, he, too was engaging in violence, which allowed him to participate in the drug trade without fear of injury. At the age of 14, Darnell was arrested for robbery and murder.

FEMINIST THEORY

> Intimate partner violence (IPV), as battering of women, wives, or other intimate relationships is sometimes called, is still considered learned behavior that is used mostly by men to obtain and maintain power and control over a woman.
>
> Walker, 2009, p. 5

Feminism is a widespread movement that aims for equal political, economic, and social rights for women. Feminist theory is concerned with gender and socially constructed roles of men and women, and uses that lens to study a variety of social issues, including violence— particularly that of violence between men and women. Many feminist theorists suggest that male violence against women is a way for men to maintain power and control.

The *gender-based sociobiological theory of violence* discusses the interaction of gender roles and specific environments in determining whether violence will or will not occur in a specific setting. Messerschmidt (1999) theorized that the interactions of gender and gender role challenges, motivations, and opportunities at home and school and on the street determined the development of violent versus nonviolent strategies that are environmentally anchored.

Critics of feminist theories point out that they do not account for violence perpetrated by females, and they do not account for other individual factors that may determine whether someone uses violence. Also, researchers now realize that gender and sexual roles are complex constructs: sexual biology, gender orientation, and sexual orientation are three distinct classifications that need to be considered when analyzing violence.

SOCIAL STRUCTURE THEORIES

High rates of criminal violence are apparently the price of racial and ethnic inequalities. In a society founded on the principle that "all men are created equal" economic inequalities rooted in ascribed positions violate the spirit of democracy and are likely to create alienation, despair, and conflict

Blau and Blau, 1982, p. 126

Social structure theories study the relationships between different groups within a society and suggests that each group has its own role or function. Families, religious groups, economic groups, and so on, are all social structures that contain subgroups. When applied to violence (Blau & Blau, 1982), social structure theory suggests that grievances violating one's sense of justice are the root cause of violence. Lethality is directly related to the social and economic distance between groups; the larger the distance, the greater the lethality of the violence. For example, if a minority group believes that the majority group is blocking their path to obtain their perceived "fair share" of the community's resources, the group can attempt to obtain those resources through violent means (National Institute of Justice, 2002). Communities that are at high risk for conflict can be identified and structures put into place to reduce social distance between "the haves and have nots." Society can pay to assist the underprivileged to obtain abilities needed to allow them to participate effectively in society, or it can pay to punish the violators of rules through structures of control (such as prisons, parole, and probation). Until social distances are reduced, there will be an issue.

STRAIN THEORY

Three sources of strain have been presented: strain as the actual or anticipated failure to achieve positively valued goals, strain as the actual or
anticipated removal of positively valued stimuli, and strain as the actual
or anticipated presentation of negative stimuli.... So, for example, the
insults of a teacher may be experienced as adverse because they (1) interfere with the adolescent's aspirations for academic success, (2) result in
the violation of a distributive justice rule such as equity, and (3) are con-
ditioned negative stimuli and so are experienced as noxious in and of
themselves.... Each type of strain increases the likelihood that individuals will experience one or more of a range of negative emotions.... The
experience of negative affect, especially anger, typically creates a desire
to take corrective steps, with delinquency being one possible response.

Agnew, 1992, p. 60

Like social structures theory, strain theory in its original form suggested that strain could arise when social structures were inadequate
to meet an individual's needs. A later, more robust form (Agnew, 1992)
also took into account the strain that arises from friction between individuals. This new formulation puts less of an emphasis on social class
or cultural variables (as social structures theory does) and more of a
focus on individual interactions. Put simply, it suggests that failure to
achieve one's goals, the removal of positive factors in one's life, and/or
the anticipation of negative factors, all can result in strain. If the strain
is felt strongly enough, an individual may eventually become motivated to engage in crime. According to this theory, a powerful prevention technique would include teaching people how to deal more
positively with strain. Successful coping strategies can moderate the
negative effects of strain or stressors. Increasing an individual's opportunities to succeed can also reduce strain.

CONTROL BALANCE THEORY

[The] amount of control to which people are subject relative to the
amount of control they can exercise affects their general probability of
committing some deviant acts as well as the probability that they will
commit specific types of deviance

Tittle, 1995, p. 42

Control balance theory (Tittle, 1995) proposes that whenever there is an imbalance of control between a person and society, acts of deviance, such as violence, may occur; that is, either when people are much more controlled than controlling (they have no power) or when they are much more controlling than controlled (they have too much power).

SYSTEMS THEORY

As the name suggests, systems theory analyzes the interplay of complex systems. It can be applied to many different disciplines. In terms of psychology, systems theories attempt to explain human behavior and experience as humans partake in various overlapping systems. Family systems theory, for example, suggests that each member of a family plays a role within it; any deviations can cause imbalance and must be addressed so that the old equilibrium is restored, or a new equilibrium is achieved.

In an even broader sense, systems theory can consider all levels of systems in which an individual partakes, including the individual's biological system, family, peers, school, community, racial and ethnic group, socioeconomic class, and culture. All of these systems interplay with each other and impact the individual.

Personal characteristics interact with the environment to influence the development of the individual. The influences of each systemic factor can make a person more or less effective in functioning in the world. The individual can encounter strengths (such as a supportive teacher or school environment) or stressors (such as living in poverty). Every component interacts to support or interfere with a person's healthy development. The balance of strengths and stressors will determine if the behavior of the person will be adaptive or maladaptive to the immediate environment and circumstances at a particular point in time.

Thus, systems theory helps us remember that violent behavior is not typically caused by any one factor, but rather by many factors that amplify each other: high levels of conflict in the family; community and cultural norms that encourage violence; and racial and/or sexual norms that may preclude the individual from participating fully in society.

LIFE COURSE THEORIES

What the life course perspective takes from the criminal career tradition is the idea that it is important to focus on the longitudinal sequencing of offenses and a recognition that the dimensions of criminal careers vary among individuals. What the life course perspective adds to the criminal career tradition is greater recognition of the reciprocal, mutually interacting connections between trajectories in crime and trajectories in other domains of life.... It assumes that trajectories in crime can be better understood if they are viewed within the total context of the individual's life and development.... The life course perspective also is more attuned to the role of history and macrosociological factors in shaping criminal careers and individual life courses.

Benson, 2001, p. 12

Life course theories bring together the dynamics and interactive aspects of biology, psychology, environment, and change over time. Typically, they follow an individual's trajectory through major life events, such as early childhood, school, perhaps college, entry into the workforce, marriage, children, retirement, and older age. Positive and negative influences at any one of these key points can change a person's trajectory.

Furthermore, life course theories consider trajectories in different domains of functioning: biological (i.e., the physical process of growing up), psychological (the growth of emotional maturity), and social (our ability to relate to those around us). All of these domains include significant life events of their own, and often they influence each other. Puberty, for example, is a key point in our biological development, and it has impact on our psychological and social development as well.

As applied to violence, life course theories help us to examine how influences at any point along the path may increase or decrease an individual's risk of becoming a perpetrator or victim of violence. (The intergenerational theory of violence, presented earlier, suggests that children who are exposed to violence early in life are more likely to continue to use violence in their relationships well into adulthood.) They incorporate many of the theories previously discussed here into a complex model involving the dynamic interaction of person and environment, considering also developmental factors over time. When considering violent activity, they will examine age of onset (first time violent activity occurs), as well as frequency, seriousness, and career length (length of time over a life span that the violent activity takes place; Benson, 2001).

Much of the research confirms that certain risk factors in early childhood lead to a greater risk of violence in adulthood. For example, Robbins (1966) found that persons diagnosed with adult antisocial personality disorder frequently had a diagnosis of conduct disorder in their youth, and Loeber (1982) found that children who exhibited severe behavior problems between the ages of 7 and 11 went on to continue their offending behavior into adulthood. White et al. (1990) reported that children who were aggressive at age 3 were more likely to have conduct disorder in middle childhood and be arrested in their early teens.

Terrie Moffitt (2001) studied subjects with a lifelong trajectory of antisocial behaviors (whom she characterized as "early starters") versus those for whom antisocial behavior was limited to adolescence ("late starters"). She emphasizes the interplay of person and environment with differing manifestations of the antisocial behavior over time. In particular, she theorizes that the sometimes provoking behavior of children creates an ongoing, negative cycle—child behavior, negative parental or teacher response, followed by negative child reaction—which forms the basis of interpersonal interactions. Over time, children may act in similar fashion with peers, and well into adulthood.

Age-graded life course theory (Sampson, 2001) contends that there are important events and social environmental conditions that move youth toward or away from an antisocial lifestyle. Social conditions such as poverty, lack of opportunity, and racism can keep youth from identifying with prosocial elements of society (proficiency in a trade, steady employment, and stable interpersonal relationships). On the other hand, a "cumulative cascade" of negative life events, environments, and influences can push a youth to remain in an antisocial lifestyle. They see this process as dynamic and interactive.

RECIPROCAL THEORY OF VIOLENCE

According to the reciprocal theory of violence (Barak, 2003) there are properties of violence that include negative emotional states, such as alienation, shame, denial, and humiliation. There can also be a lack of positive emotional states, such as empathy and compassion. This model suggests that there are nine structural pathways to violence and nine structural pathways to nonviolence. The tensions between pathways to violence and nonviolence can occur across individuals, families, communities, states, or societies. The interaction of the positive and negative emotional states of the individual, family, community, state, and society determine the pathway to violence or nonviolence.

REFERENCES

Agnew, R. (1992). Foundation for a general strain theory of crime and delinquency. *Criminology, 30*(1), 47–87.

Bandura, A. (1977). *Social learning theory.* Englewood Cliffs, NJ: Prentice Hall.

Barak, G. (2003). *Violence and nonviolence: Pathways to understanding.* Thousand Oaks, CA: Sage.

Benson, M. (2001). *Crime and the life course: An introduction.* New York, NY: Oxford University Press.

Blau, J. R., & Blau, P. M. (1982). The cost of inequality: Metropolitan structure and violent crime. *American Sociological Review, 47,* 114–129.

Blood, R. O., & Wolfe, D. M. (1960). *Husbands and wives: The dynamics of married living.* Glencoe, IL: The Free Press.

Brodal, P. (2004). *The central nervous system: Structure and function.* Oxford, UK: Oxford University Press.

DeKeseredy, S. A. (2006). *Advancing critical ciminology: Theory and application.* New York, NY: Lexington Books.

Doumas, D., Margolin, G., & John, R. S. (1994). The intergenerational transmission of aggression across three generations. *Journal of Family Violence, 9*(2), 157–175.

Ehrensaft, M. K., Cohen, P., Brown, J., Smailes, E., Chen, H., & Johnson, J. G. (2003). Intergenerational transmission of partner violence: A 20-year prospective study. *Journal of Consulting and Clinical Psychology, 71*(4), 741–753.

Hare, R. (1991). *The hare psychopathy checklist—revised.* North Tonawanda, NY: Multi-Health Systems.

Felson, M., & Boba, R. L. (2010). *Crime and everyday life* (4th ed.). Thousand Oaks, CA: Sage.

Frick, P. J., Bodin, S. D., & Barry, C. T. (2000). Psychopathic traits and conduct problems in community and clinic-referred samples of children: Further development of the psychopathy screening device. *Psychological Assessment, 12,* 382–393.

Frick, P. J., O'Brien, B. S., Wootton, J. M., & McBurnett, K. (1994). Psychopathy and conduct problems in children. *Journal of Abnormal Psychology, 103,* 700–707.

Gelles, R. (1983). An exchange/social control theory. In D. Finkelhor, R. J. Gelles, G. T. Totaling, & M. A. Straus (Eds.), *The dark side of families: Current family violence research* (pp. 151–165). Thousand Oaks, CA: Sage.

Hare, R. D. (1991). *Manual for the Hare Psychopathy Checklist-Revised.* Toronto, ON: Multi-Health Systems.

Hare, R. (1999). *Without conscience: The disturbing world of psychopaths among us.* New York, NY: Guilford Press.

Hemphill, J. F., Hare, R. D., & Wong, S. (1998). Psychopathy and recidivism: A review. *Legal and Criminological Psychology, 3,* 139–170.

Kaufman, J., & Zigler, E. (1987). Do abused children become abusive parents? *American Journal of Orthopsychiatry, 57,* 316–331.

Lahey, B. B., Moffit, T. E., & Caspi, A. (2003). *Causes of conduct disorder and juvenile delinquency.* New York, NY: Guilford Press.

Loeber, R. (1982). The stability of antisocial and delinquent child behavior: A review. *Child Development, 53,* 1431–1446.

Messerschmidt, J. (1999). *Nine lives: Adolescent masculinities, the body, and violence.* Bolder, CO: Westview.

Meyer-Lindenberg, A., Buckholtz, J. W., Kolachana, B., Hariri, A. R., Pezawas, L., Blasi, G., et al. (2006, April 18). Neural mechanisms of genetic risk for impulsivity and violence in humans. *Proceedings of the National Academy of Sciences of the United States of America, 103*(16), 6269–6274.

Mizen, R., & Morris, M. (Eds.). (2007). *On aggression and violence: An analytic perspective.* New York, NY: Palgrave Macmillan.

Moffitt, T. (2001). Adolescence-limited and life course persistent antisocial behavior: A developmental taxonomy. In A. A. Piquero (Ed.), *Life-course criminology: Contemporary and classic readings.* Belmont, CA: Wadsworth.

Morris, C. M. (2007). *Psychopathic traits and social-cognitive processes in aggressive youth* (Dissertation). Ann Arbor, MI: ProQuest Information and Learning Co.

National Institute of Justice. (2002). *Violence Theory Workshop.* December 10–11

O'Leary, D. K. (1988). Physical aggression between spouses: A social learning theory perspective. In V. B. Van Hasselt (Ed.), *Handbook of family violence* (pp. 31–55). New York, NY: Plenum.

de Oliveira-Souza, R., Hare, R. D., Bramati, I. E., Garrido, G. J., Azevedo Ignácio, F., Tovar-Moll, F., et al. (2008). Psychopathy as a disorder of the moral brain: Fronto-temporo-limbic grey matter reductions demonstrated by voxel-based morphometry. *Neuroimage, 40*(3), 1202–1213.

Pagelow, M. D. (1981). *Women-battering: Victims and their experiences.* Beverly Hills, CA: Sage.

Robbins, L. N. (1966). *Deviant children grown up, a sociological and psychiatric study of sociopathic personality.* Baltimore, MD: Williams/Wilkins Co.

Sampson, R. A. (2001). Crime and deviance in the life course. In A. A. Piquero (Ed.), *Life-course criminology: Contemporary and classic readings.* Belmont, CA: Wadsworth.

Seabrook, J. (2008, November 10). Suffering souls: The search for the roots of psychopathy. *The New Yorker.* Retrieved from http://www.newyorker.com/reporting/2008/11/10/081110fa_fact_seabrook

Straus, M. A., Gelles, R. J., & Steinmetz, S. K. (1980). *Behind closed doors: Violence in the American family.* New York, NY: Anchor.

Thompson, R. A. (1998). Early brain development and social policy. *Policy & Practice of Public Human Services, 56*(2), 67. Retrieved April 19, 2011, from Questia database: http://www.questia.com/PM.qst?a=o&d=5001500947

Tittle, C. R. (1995). *Control balance: Toward a general theory of deviance.* Boulder, CO: Westview.

Van der Kolk, B. A. (2005). Child abuse & victimization. *Psychiatric Annals,* 374–378.

Van der Kolk, B. A., Pynoos, R. S., Cicchetti, D., Cloitre, M., D'Andrea, W., Ford, J. D., et al. (2009). *Proposal to include a developmental trauma disorder diagnosis for children and adolescents in DSM-V.* Retrieved from http://www.traumacenter.org/announcements/DTD_papers_Oct_09.pdf.

Van der Kolk, B. A., McFarlane, A. C., & Weisaeth, L. (1996). *Traumatic stress: The effects of overwhelming experience on mind, body, and society.* New York, NY: Guilford Press.

Walker, L. (2009). *The battered woman syndrome* (3rd ed.). New York, NY: Springer Publishing Company.

Weniger, G., Lange, C., Sachsse, U., & Irle, E. (2009). Reduced amygdala and hippocampus size in trauma-exposed women with borderline personality disorder and without posttraumatic stress disorder. *Journal of Psychiatry & Neuroscience, 34*(5), 383–388. Retrieved from http://goedoc.uni-goettingen.de/goescholar/bitstream/handle/1/5955/irle.pdf?sequence=1.

White, J. L., Moffitt, T. L., Earls, F., Robbins, L., and Silva, P. A. (1990). How early can we tell?: Predictors of childhood conduct disorder and adolescent delinquency. *Criminology. 28*(4), 507–535.

Wolfgang, M. E., & Ferracuti, F. (1967). *The subculture of violence: Towards an intergrated theory of criminology.* New York, NY: Methuen.

Dynamics of Youth Violence

FIVE

Individual Factors That Impact Youth Violence

A s discussed in the previous chapter, the use of violence as a behavior is strongly influenced by both individual (physiological, cognitive, and psychological) and external (social, communal, cultural) factors. This chapter will more closely examine the micro (individual) factors. Chapter 6 will examine the macro (environmental) factors.

The research literature (Borum, 2000; Hahn et al., 2007; Herrenkohl, Maguin, Hill, Hawkins, Abbott, & Catalano, 2000; Mulder, Brand, Bullens, & van Marle, 2011; Seifert, 2006) has identified a number of risk factors, both individual and environmental, often associated with youthful aggressors. These include parental substance abuse (Gabel & Schindledecker, 1991; Seifert, 2006), insecure attachment with mother (Seifert, 2006; Zimmerman, Mohr, & Spangler, 2009), conduct problems (Borum, 2000; Gabel & Schindledecker, 1991; Hahn et al., 2007; Mulder et al., 2011), a lack of empathy (Borum, 2000; Frick et al., 2003; Morris, 2007; Seifert, 2006), cognitive dysregulation (Mezzich et al., 1997; Morris, 2007), dysregulated behaviors (Borum, 2000; Frick et al., 2003; Gabel & Schindledecker, 1991; Hahn et al., 2007; Loeber, 1982; Mulder et al., 2011; Seifert, 2006), belief in the legitimacy of aggression (Borum, 2000; Seifert, 2006; Stickle, Kirkpatrick, & Brush, 2009), childhood trauma (Borum, 2000; Sarchiapone et al., 2009; Seifert, 2006), parent rating of hyperactivity (Herrenkohl et al., 2000), low academic performance and school problems (Borum, 2000; Hahn et al., 2007; Herrenkohl et al., 2000; Seifert, 2006), delinquent peers (Borum, 2000; Herrenkohl et al., 2000; Mulder et al., 2011; Seifert, 2006), availability of drugs (Borum, 2000; Herrenkohl et al., 2000), early initiation of violence, delinquency, or moderate-to-severe behavior problems (Borum, 2000; Hahn et al., 2007; Mulder et al.,

69

2011; Seifert, 2006), and home or family maladjustment (Borum, 2000; Hahn et al., 2007; Mulder et al., 2011; Seifert, 2006). The following sections outline differences by severity of offense, gender, and age. Many of these factors will be examined in this and the next chapter.

The individual factors to be examined here include physiological, cognitive, psychological, and developmental factors. Development proceeds in fairly predictable sequences; the interaction of person and environment can support or interfere with healthy developmental sequences. For example, as discussed in the previous chapter, van Der Kolk (2003) and others have established that complex trauma can interfere with the healthy development of skills needed for coping with every day life.

PHYSIOLOGICAL FACTORS

Various physiological factors impact our development and can play a role in the development of aggression in children and adolescents. This section will briefly summarize findings from genetics and neurology.

Genetics

As discussed in Chapter 3, recent inroads in genetic research have helped us identify genes or groups of genes that may encourage or inhibit the development of certain behaviors. Much research is now focused on understanding, more precisely, how our genetic makeup can be modified by our life experiences (environment). In other words, the debate between "nature" and "nurture" has been reframed: we now certainly know that our behavior is affected by both.

MAO (monoamine oxidase) represents a family of enzymes found in humans. It has two variants, MAO-A and MAO-B. MAO-A has been nicknamed the "warrior gene" because it has been linked with aggressive behavior, although as with many genetic influences on behavior, researchers have found evidence of gene/environment interaction (McDermott, Tingley, Cowden, Frazzetto, & Johnson, 2009). Genetic influences can be triggered, or dampened, depending on environmental influences (Alia-Klein et al., 2008). Recent brain imaging research demonstrates that men with the MAOA-L variant show greater brain reactivity in the amygdala and lower activity in the regulatory prefrontal areas, which explains the link between MAOA-L to impulsive forms of aggression (McDermott et al., 2009).

In addition, the *DRD4-7* allele of the dopamine receptor gene found on chromosome 11 has been related to aggression and problem behaviors in children.

Neurobiology

Chapter 3 explained how many brain structures are associated with aggression, including the amygdalae, hypothalamus, prefrontal cortex, cingulate cortex, and hippocampus. The amygdalae help us form and store memories of emotional events; they play a crucial role in fear conditioning. Abnormalities in the amygdalae have been linked with numerous mental health conditions, including anxiety disorders, obsessive–compulsive disorder (OCD), posttraumatic stress, borderline personality disorder, and psychopathy. The hypothalamus has been linked with "attack behavior" and aggression in many mammals. Malfunction of the prefrontal cortex has been linked with aggressive psychopathology.

Early maltreatment or trauma can severely impact brain development and lead to lifelong consequences in physical, cognitive, social, and emotional development (Child Welfare Information Gateway, 2009):

- Children who are raised in neglectful or abusive environments may eventually grow accustomed to such treatment, because their brains adapt to their circumstances. Later, it may be more difficult for them to respond to nurturance or kindness.
- Chronic activation of the fear response can create permanent memories that shape the child's perception of the environment. Even if the environment improves, the child's reaction to the world may be permanently compromised by early abuse.
- Children exposed to chronic abuse may experience hyperarousal—they overreact to triggers that other children would find nonthreatening.
- Abuse may alter their brain's ability to use serotonin, a neurotransmitter that helps produce feelings of happiness.
- If children are not stimulated appropriately, they may not achieve the usual developmental milestones, such as language or cognitive development.

▪ Maltreated children may retain implicit memories of their abuse, which may produce flashbacks, nightmares, or other uncontrollable reactions well into adulthood.

Finally, infants who are exposed to certain substances in utero may experience changes in brain development, which can place them at greater risk for aggressive behavior later on. Children with histories of fetal alcohol exposure (FAE), for example, show evidence of changes in brain structure and function, as well as a variety of behavioral effects (Archibald et al., 2001). Children with FAE appear to be at increased risk for psychiatric disorders, alcohol abuse, drug abuse, and other maladaptive behaviors (Berman & Hannigan, 2000). They are more likely to be hyperactive, disruptive, and impulsive.

COGNITIVE FACTORS

One of the most enduring controversies in the psychology of crime is the relationship between intelligence, as measured by standardized intelligence quotient (IQ) tests, and violent or criminal behavior. Numerous studies link low IQ to violent and aggressive behavior and crime.... Evidence shows that people who act aggressively in social settings also have lower IQ scores than their peers. Some studies have found a direct IQ-delinquency link among samples of adolescent boys.

Siegel, 2010, p. 106

Cognitive strengths include average or better intelligence quotient (IQ) and the absence of learning disabilities (Seifert, 2007). A child with a lower IQ will have a more difficult time solving problems and learning coping skills; this can lead to frustration and aggression if the child does not learn other behavioral responses. A child with learning disabilities will experience more stress and need additional supports to be successful in school, such as those championed by the Individuals with Disabilities Education Act (IDEA). The IDEA legislation was enacted in 1975 to ensure that every child, regardless of disability, could receive an appropriate education. By the 1999/2000 school year, twice as many (more than 6 million) children were served by IDEA funds than at its inception. The creators of the legislation could not have forseen the huge cost of this endeavor and the ideological debates about methods to accomplish the goals of the legislation. While IDEA funding has helped provide education for millions of children, it has never been adequate to meet the full need of every child needing assistance (Seligman, 2001).

To encourage children's cognitive development, they need

* encouragement of exploration,
* mentoring in basic skills,
* celebration of developmental advances,
* guided rehearsal and extension of new skills,
* protection from inappropriate disapproval, teasing or punishment, and
* a rich and responsive language environment.

Ramey and Ramey, 1998

Verbal IQ measures a person's ability to use and understand language. It will impact a youth's ability to learn and communicate with family, peers, and teachers. Not being able to communicate effectively may lead to frustration and disagreements with family and peers, which can cause difficult interpersonal relationships.

Performance IQ measures the ability to understand nonverbal logic and sequences and the completion of nonverbal tasks. Some studies suggest that maltreated children often have difficulties with logic (Perry, 1998). If a youth has difficulty with logic and reasoning, they may not be able to solve problems as well as their peers. This may cause frustration and outbursts and a more primitive response to getting one's needs met, such as forcefully taking what one needs from others.

PSYCHOLOGICAL FACTORS

In this section, we will discuss three important aspects of psychological makeup: childhood and adolescent development, temperament, and mental health.

Development

Development can include a child's social/emotional, physical, and moral development. If a child's development is delayed, it can make the child more vulnerable to stressors. If the stressor is overcome and skills are built, development can proceed in a healthy manner.

A youth's development proceeds by stage, not age. A child does not enter the next stage until the previous one has been mastered; she crawls before she walks, walks before she runs, and so on. Each new level of maturation brings with it a new set of tasks to master in an ever-widening social context. Mastering necessary skills prepares one to achieve developmental tasks, whereas lack of mastery leaves one vulnerable to being marginalized (Flannery & Huff, 1999).

Infancy

Infants (aged 0–2) need maximum comfort and minimal uncertainty to trust themselves, others, and the environment (Erikson, 1950). The major milestones of early childhood include introduction to language, the development of gross motor skills for walking and grasping, differentiating strangers from caregivers, and bonding to caregivers. This is the stage where trust between child and caregivers develops.

John Bowlby, a British psychologist, defined the connection between infants and caregivers as attachment. From about 6 months to 2 years of age, infants look to caregivers for security and to get their needs met. If a secure relationship is not developed (e.g., because of abuse or neglect), normal social and emotional development will not occur. Children who begin their lives with compromised or disrupted attachment are at risk for aggression and violence later on in their lives (Seifert, 2007).

There are three basic types of attachment bonds: secure, anxious/avoidant, and disorganized/dismissive. When the caregiver adequately meets the child's physical, psychological, and environmental needs, a secure attachment is formed and healthy development is supported (Levy & Orlans, 1998). The child is able to use the primary caregiver as a "safe base" (Ainsworth, Blehar, Waters, & Wall, 1978) and, from there, explore the world and return to the safe base when anxious or frightened. When positive attachment (bonding) experiences occur in infancy, the child's internal model of self, caregiver, and the world is positive. An infant who forms a healthy attachment with a caregiver will accept new relationships as potentially positive and be willing to explore them.

There is a neurobiological component to secure attachment. A caregiver who smiles and coos at a baby, for example, supports the development of mirror neurons in the infant's brain, which are necessary for building the initial relationship with the primary care-giver and later relationships with others. Children who do not have sufficient interaction with nurturing adults do not have sufficiently developed mirror neurons (Hutman & Dapretto, 2009; Rand, 2002). Good attachment bonds in infancy also support the development of the amygdalae in the brain, which manages affect regulation, as discussed in Chapter 3. Perry and Pollard (1998) found that maltreated children have smaller amygdalae than other children.

When the "safe base" is not safe, it becomes the source of anxiety and conflict rather than comfort. In that case, an anxious or avoidant relationship may develop between caregiver and child. If a caregiver is not available or is angry or abusive when the infant needs him or her, an anxious/avoidant attachment bond may develop. Turner (1991) found that insecure attachment was associated with externalizing problems in the preschool years. This is similar to the childhood trauma group with internalizing (anxious, depressed) symptoms described by Weniger, Lange, Sachsse, and Irle (2009).

A second attachment style is disorganized/dismissive. With this type, the caregiver is alternately available and not available, abusive and then nurturing. It causes the child to be extremely confused. Disorganized attachment (Lyons-Ruth, 1996), cluster B personality disorders, and aggression also appear to be related.

The association of certain attachment styles in childhood and adult personality disorders has been studied by Weniger, Lange, Sachsse, and Irle (2009). They found that one childhood trauma group had both externalizing and internalizing symptoms. This group appears to be similar to the youth described as having disorganized attachment styles. Because of disrupted attachment, certain brain structures, skills, and the ability to relate to others do not develop properly.

A neglected child may be indifferent to new relationships. An abused child may approach relationships with fear and confusion. As the child grows, his ability to relate to others and his understanding of relationships becomes more complex. Now all relationships that he sees and experiences can influence his ability to relate to others. Temperament will interact with development, skills, and relationship environment and history to help shape the person's range of interpersonal relatedness on this spectrum.

All children display some aggression in infancy and early childhood. Bridges (1933) reported that instrumental aggression (aggressive behavior used to achieve a goal) in infants begins at about the age of 1 year, appears to peak around 18 to 24 months, and ends at about age 5 years. In one study, Tremblay et al. (1996) found that nearly half of 27-month-old male toddlers hit, bite, or kick occasionally, and about 40% of girl toddlers do. In addition, most studies found no discernable gender differences in the use of aggression in early childhood (Hay in Tremblay, Hartup, & Archer, 2005). Only after 108 months does it fall below 20% of the children studied.

A variety of studies have found that normative aggression in children increases from 9 months to 18 months and then decreases until age 3, where it spikes again and then declines until age 6 (Hay in Tremblay et al., 2005) and that it is both instrumental and reactive in nature.

Longitudinal studies (Tremblay & Nagin in Tremblay et al., 2005) have identified three groups of children whose frequency of aggression is consistently high, moderate, or low throughout childhood, adolescence, and adulthood. However, all three groups show the same relative developmental trajectory. It is hypothesized that some children are much slower to learn the alternatives to aggression, such as delayed gratification, cooperation, and conflict resolution. Those children who are slow to learn alternatives to aggression often live in homes were aggression is common among family members as a way to solve problems (an example of social learning theory, as discussed in Chapter 3). Since early childhood is the optimal time to learn alternatives to aggression, the absence of opportunities to learn those lessons places youth at a distinct disadvantage in terms of behavioral repertoire (Tremblay & Nagin in Tremblay et al., 2005). Parallel play (rather than interactive play, which occurs later) is one way infants begin to learn how to cope with stressors, solve problems, and interact with the world appropriately. A child who has not learned alternatives to aggression in relationships will not get a sufficient number of opportunities to practice social skills and may remain in parallel play and not progress to interactive play.

Toddlers

The toddler (early childhood stage, aged 3–4 years) works to explore and master his physical environment (Erikson, 1950). The toddler's major social context is still primarily his family, although it may expand to include extended family, babysitters, or day care. Reciprocity (the beginning of sharing and social exchange) begins at this stage but is not fully formed.

Normative instrumental and reactive aggression appears to peak at age 3 or 4 years. Erikson (1950) explains this stage as autonomy versus shame and doubt. Parents are still a safe base from which children can begin to explore the world. The child becomes better coordinated in this stage. Language develops quickly when exposed to communication. The child is still self-centered. She seeks the approval of parents, caregivers, and teachers and obeys rules to avoid punishment. A child with adequate interpersonal skill development can engage in cooperative play at this time.

Another development that begins in infancy and expands throughout early childhood is the ability to understand social interactions from another person's perspective. This ability is referred to as "theory of mind (ToM)" (Espelage & Swearer, 2003). If trauma occurs early enough in the life span, a child may fail to develop a "theory of mind" or be able to see things from another person's perspective.

The ToM hypothesizes that people first develop an understanding that they have a reasoning mind with knowledge and intentions (Leslie, 1987). The next level of development is recognizing that other people have a mind that is different from one's own. This stage is necessary for perspective and empathy to develop, as well as understanding the intentions of others. Some autistic children and severely maltreated children do not appear to have developed an adequate ToM (Espelage & Swearer, 2003). Understanding this concept is important when developing treatment modalities for these youth.

Early School Years

A child in the early school years (ages 5–6 years) is learning to adapt to a larger social context and separate from her parents. She is beginning to initiate activities (Erikson, 1950) also. The social context becomes split between home and school. Reciprocity should be well formed in this stage. The child should be able to express wants, needs, and some emotions verbally. Gross motor skills are more developed and fine motor skills necessary for writing are beginning to develop. The child now learns to interact with groups of children. The rules for the group, as well as rewards and punishments, are still set by adults. Only minimal self-regulation is expected. Normative aggression should be declining as the socialization process proceeds.

The process that regulates aggression appears to be empathy or the ability to see things from another person's point of view. "Empathy comprises four components: perspective taking, fantasy, empathic concern, and personal distress" (Litvack-Miller, McDougall, & Romney, 1997). Empathy and modulation of aggression is learned through play, which only occurs in a safe, stable household with abundant parental involvement (Tremblay et al., 2005). Fear and states of deprivation eliminate play. Physical play attunes the child's body to that of another. More abstract play allows attunement to motivations and emotional states. Role play and fantasy create situations where the child can identify with an abstract entity, thus extending empathy to those as yet unknown. This process spans early and middle childhood. Without these experiences, empathy will not develop in a healthy age-appropriate manner.

A child should also gain skill in self-soothing at this stage. A youth who can self-soothe, regulate his emotions relatively well, and communicate his feelings to others is going to cope better who a child who has not developed these skills. For example, a child who gets upset over something in the classroom and continues to escalate may be seen as having serious behavior problems when compared with other children who get upset, but are able to calm down within a relatively short period of time. Traditionally, a child such as this may be treated with behavior management techniques, when what is really needed is family therapy.

Ez-Elarab, Sabbour, Gadallah, and Asaad (2007) studied the traits of aggressive elementary school children in Cairo. They found the following risk factors: absence of attachment figure, single parent, use of corporal punishment by caregivers, preference for violent video games, exposure to verbal aggression, aggressive peers, and victimization.

Middle Childhood

In middle childhood (ages 7–10 years), the child is expanding her ability to see things from another's point of view and to have empathy with someone who is in pain or having a hard time. Children are becoming more organized and less impulsive in this stage. The school age child continues to refine fine motor, social, self-management, and problem-solving skills. Self-regulation should be expanding slightly. Normative aggression should have disappeared by this stage due to socialization (Tremblay et al., 2005). Attention span lengthens during this level of development. The youth can become part of small social groups, usually at school or a community organization. The child who is developing in a healthy manner develops some empathy and concern for the feelings of others. However, children in this stage may still be impulsive. Reciprocity is continuing to develop, as well. This is the stage at which confidence can be built.

Preadolescence and Adolescence

As mentioned in Chapter 2, violence rises dramatically during the adolescent years for some youth, for a number of reasons, most of them due to the momentous physical and social changes that children undergo during this period.

> Developmentally, puberty is accompanied by major physical and emotional changes that alter a young person's relationships and patterns of interaction with others. The transition into adolescence begins the move toward independence from parents and the need to establish one's own values, personal and sexual identity, and the skills and competencies needed to compete in adult society. Independence requires young people to renegotiate family rules and degree of supervision by parents, a process that can generate conflict and withdrawal from parents. At the same time, social networks expand, and relationships with peers and adults in new social contexts equal or exceed in importance the relationships with parents. The criteria for success and acceptance among peers and adults change. Adapting to all of these changes in relationships, social contexts, status, and performance criteria can generate great stress, feelings of rejection, and anger at perceived or real failure. Young people may be attracted to violent behavior as a way of asserting their independence of the adult world and its rules, as a way of gaining the attention and respect of peers, as a way of compensating for limited personal competencies, or as a response to restricted opportunities for success at school or in the community. Good relationships with parents during childhood will help in a successful transition to adolescence, but they do not guarantee it.
>
> Youth Violence: A Report of the Surgeon General, 2001

During preadolescence, the peer group supplants the family as a dominant influence on behavior.

> Parents' direct influence on behavior is largely eclipsed by peer influence during adolescence. Not surprisingly, therefore, most family risk factors diminish in importance, including the influence of antisocial parents and low socioeconomic status, the most powerful early risk factors. There are no large or even moderate risk factors in the family domain in adolescence
>
> Youth Violence: A Report of the Surgeon General, 2001

Any trauma can interfere with the development of basic skills, leaving a child at a lower level of development (Van der Kolk, 2003). Poor affect regulation, early onset of puberty, and increased arousal patterns have also been associated with childhood exposure to violence. A youth who grows up in a chronically chaotic, conflicted, violent, or dangerous home can have the "set point" of their stress activation system set lower so they can act more quickly or always be alert for danger. These children react with a "hair trigger" when it comes to anything that might even remotely be seen as dangerous. Many everyday things can be interpreted as dangerous, even when they are not. It is a safety mechanism, which meant survival for that child when he was small. It should be recognized as a strength that kept him safe as a child, but that needs to be used more sparingly as one grows up by learning new ways to escape danger.

Behavior

Research into developmental trajectories (e.g., Moffitt, 2001) suggests that the greatest predictor of severe and chronic violent behavior problems is the early onset of behavior problems such as aggression, disregard for rules, delinquency, or substance abuse. "Analyses of predictors of violence among high school seniors and dropouts show that early deviant behavior, poor grades, weak elementary school bonds, and prodrug middle school environments fostered violent behavior several years later.... Coupled with poor grades, these deviant behaviors predicted relational and predatory violence, as well as overall violence" (Ellickson & McGuigan, 2000, p. 571).

Late onset adolescent antisocial behaviors tend to stop as the teen enters adulthood, whereas those with an early onset are more likely to be violent well into and throughout adulthood. "Adolescents who acted out by stealing or getting in trouble at school in grade 7 were significantly more likely to be violent 5 years later than those who did not" (Ellickson & McGuigan, 2000, p. 571). Those with severe and chronic preteen behavior problems need early intervention to prevent them from becoming aggressive or violent teens and adults.

However, the interventions for this group differs from that of traditional therapy. Very often, youth with early aggression are living in homes where aggression and violence are common. This becomes the model for how humans behave toward each other. Consequently, interventions *must* include an elimination of violence in the home. Therapy that includes families and reduces violence in the home has been found to be very effective with this group. Behavior modification in schools is generally not sufficient for significant change in conduct for youth with early behavior problems (Caspi, 2005; Seifert, 2007;

Tremblay, 2005). Later chapters in this book will describe successful violence prevention programs.

Temperament

Researchers have found linkages between a child's temperament and his or her likelihood to resort to violence.

> [T]emperament has been linked to both the expression of anger and anger coping. In the first case, participants with a more difficult temperament show greater externalized expression of state anger.... Thus, difficult temperament on the whole, as well as rhythmicity specifically, are associated with an increase in externalized anger: while the former affects state anger, the latter promotes both state and trait anger. With regards to coping, children who showed themselves to be less withdrawn and more oriented towards new situations and people coped with anger in a less internalized way, so that high temperament approach acted as an inhibitor of internalized coping.
>
> Ortiz and del Barrio Gandara, 2006

In his research on polyvictimization (children who experience multiple types of victimization), David Finkelhor (Finkelhor, Ormrod, Turner, & Holt, 2009, p. 317–318) suggests that poly-victimized children may

> have particular enduring behavioral patterns or emotional problems that make them victimization-prone (Bernstein & Watson, 1997). These patterns or problems, which may or may not be related to temperament, may make it hard for them to anticipate or protect themselves from dangerous people. They may also be widely perceived as annoying, frustrating, disruptive, passive, and difficult to relate to or weak—characteristics that may trigger victimization both in the family and outside the family, as well as compromise the likelihood that others will stand up on their behalf. The kinds of children discussed in the literature as attracting victimization include those who lack emotional self-control, who cry easily, who are ineffectually aggressive, disruptive, argumentative, or petulant, who are anxious or withdrawn, who behave submissively, have poor self-concepts, or who are depressed (Hodges & Perry, 1999). While such problems may also result from the experience of maltreatment, they may in some cases be features that precede such maltreatment. There may be other personal characteristics such as disabilities of certain types (Perry et al., 2001) or gender atypicality (Williams, Connolly, Pepler, & Craig, 2005) that also predispose children to victimization in a variety of contexts.

Mental Health

Twenty percent of youth are estimated to have some form of mental illness (Morrison & Anders, 1999; U.S. Department of Health and Human Services, 1999). Mental disorders common in youth will be discussed later in this section, but first, the link between disorders and violence must be addressed.

The MacArthur Study of psychiatric adult inpatients (Monahan et al., 2001) found that mental illness alone is not an accurate predictor of future violence. In fact, the study found that someone who is diagnosed as schizophrenic is even less likely to be violent than the average person in the community. This is not to say that mental illness and violence are completely unrelated, or that those who are diagnosed as mentally ill do not commit violent acts. However, adults with mental illness who do end up being violent tend to do so when they are off of their medications, avoiding treatment, abusing substances, and exhibiting other risk factors for violence.

They also tend to have additional diagnoses on Axis II, personality disorders. Personality disorders have been described by the *DSM-IV-TR* (2000) as personality patterns that are inflexible, inappropriate, and ineffective in coping with everyday life. This causes the interpersonal relationships of those with personality disorders to be chronically strained, difficult, and unstable. Because of poor interpersonal relationship skills, having a personality disorder places one at risk for interpersonal violence. Skill building through dialectical behavioral therapy, which involves skill building for coping with life problems and relationships, appears to be effective with some of those with personality disorders (Dziegelewski, 2010).

My own research on violence (Seifert, 2007) and the MacArthur Study (Monahan et al., 2001) have shown that psychiatric illness and symptomology alone are not sufficient to predict future violence. There is no simple construct. It takes a combination of risk factors and an absence of resiliency factors to predict future violence.

The following sections will address mental health diagnoses and disorders common in children and adolescents.

Depression
It is estimated that 2% to 6% of children and adolescents suffer from unipolar depression (Dziegelewski, 2010). Children who can be formally diagnosed with depression have five or more of the

following symptoms, including numbers 1 or 2: *DSM-IV-TR* (American Psychiatric Association [APA], 2000).

1. Depressed (very sad) mood (can be irritability in children and teens)
2. Loss of interest in regular activities
3. Large weight loss or gain
4. Sleeping too much or too little
5. Restless or agitated or greatly slowed down
6. Tiredness or loss of energy
7. Feeling worthless or guilty
8. Inability to concentrate or make decisions
9. Thinking of death or suicide

Youth with depression have a higher risk of suicide or suicide ideation, see the world in a negative light, and feel hopeless. These symptoms, compounded with a history of violence (as victim and/or perpetrator), poor coping skills, lack of success in school, deviant peers, substance abuse, and lack of treatment makes a child or adolescent at higher risk for aggressive acting out behaviors.

There are many different kinds of therapy for depression. Two that have shown efficacy are cognitive–behavioral therapy (CBT) and interpersonal psychotherapy (Martin & Volkmar, 2007). In general, medication coupled with therapy is more effective than either alone (Mayo Clinic, 2010).

Anxiety Disorders
Anxiety disorders are characterized by excessive worry, which interferes with functioning. Symptoms include irritability, anger, distress, sleep difficulties, poor concentration, disturbed sleep, palpitations, avoidance of interactions with others, and muscle tension. Panic attacks may or may not occur. Various types of anxiety disorders include generalized anxiety disorder, OCD, panic disorder, posttraumatic stress disorder, and social anxiety disorder. The National Institute of Mental Health estimates that about 25% of 13- to 18-year-olds will have an anxiety disorder at some point during their lifetimes; 5.9% have severe anxiety disorder. Mild-to-moderate anxiety may respond to either CBT, psychotherapy, or medication. Severe anxiety may respond to a treatment of both therapy and medication (Dziegelewski, 2010). Anxiety can be associated with depression and suicide attempts.

ADHD

Attention deficit hyperactivity disorder (ADHD) is characterized by higher than typical levels of distractibility, impulsivity, restlessness, and physical movement. Because of these symptoms, ADHD causes some children to do poorly in school. The prevalence of ADHD is estimated to be 5.5% among 4- to 10-year-olds, 8.6% among 11- to 14-year-olds, and 9.3% among 15- to 17-year-olds (Centers for Disease Control and Prevention [CDC], 2007).

The *DSM-IV-TR* (APA, 2000) lists the following criteria for ADHD. The child must have criteria for either A or B:

A. Six or more of the following symptoms of inattention for 6 months or more
  a. Does not give close attention to details and makes careless mistakes
  b. Often has difficulty keeping attention to tasks or activities
  c. Frequently does not appear to listen when someone speaks to the child directly
  d. Often does not follow directions and consequently fails to complete tasks
  e. Frequently has problems organizing work or tasks
  f. Often avoids activities that require mental effort, such as school work
  g. Frequently loses things needed to complete tasks
  h. Is often easily distracted
  i. Is frequently forgetful
B. Six or more of the following symptoms of hyperactivity/impulsivity for more than 6 months. Disruption caused by the behavior is not consistent with developmental level.
  a. Hyperactivity
    i. Often fidgets with hands or feet or squirms in seat
    ii. Frequently gets up from seat despite expectation to stay in seat
    iii. Often runs and climbs at inappropriate times and places
    iv. Frequently has difficulty enjoying amusement activities quietly
    v. Often is in motion
    vi. Frequently talks excessively
  b. Impulsivity
    i. Frequently blurts out answers before questions are completed

    ii. Often has trouble waiting his turn
   iii. Frequently interrupts or intrudes on others
   iv. Some symptoms causing impairment were present before
7 years of age
    v. Impairments present in two or more settings
   vi. There is significant impairment in functioning at home, at
school, or in the community
  vii. The symptoms are not better explained by another disorder

There are exercises that can help a child with ADHD organize and concentrate, but sometimes medication is needed. There is some controversy over the suspected overuse of the ADHD diagnosis. Some children, in particular boys, are naturally more active than others; thus, there is the suggestion that the sedentary nature of our educational system may be difficult for boys, who tend to be more active learners (Gurian, 2005). It is also believed that some hyperactive children may be showing symptoms of complex trauma (Van der Kolk, 2003). Children with ADHD behavior problems, who are in homes with poor parenting, can also be at higher risk for lifelong persistent antisocial behavior patterns, including delinquency, substance abuse, and violent behaviors (Lahey, Moffitt, & Caspi, 2003).

Psychosis

Until 20 to 30 years ago, child psychiatrists were reluctant to acknowledge or diagnose psychoses in children and adolescents, and various euphemistic terms tended to be used. Even at present, there may be a disinclination to do so because of fears about the potentially adverse consequences of diagnostic labeling.... Recent years, however, have witnessed a rebirth of interest in schizophrenia in children, especially in identifying continuities and discontinuities with the condition presenting in adolescents and adults.

Remschmidt, 2001, p. 1

According to the American Academy of Child and Adolescent Psychiatry (2004), the following symptoms and behaviors can occur in children or adolescents with schizophrenia:

▪ seeing things and hearing voices that are not real (hallucinations)
▪ odd and eccentric behavior and/or speech

- unusual or bizarre thoughts and ideas
- confusing television and dreams from reality
- confused thinking
- extreme moodiness
- ideas that people are out to get them or talking about them (paranoia)
- severe anxiety and fearfulness
- difficulty relating to peers and keeping friends
- withdrawn and increased isolation
- decline in personal hygiene

American Academy of Child and Adolescent Psychiatry, 2004

Estimates suggest that only 1 in 40,000 children can be diagnosed with schizophrenia, compared with 1 in 100 in adults. The disorder typically appears later in the life course; the average age of onset is 18 in men and 25 in women. Treatment includes medication, case management, therapy, and a supportive environment. A child or teen with psychotic or paranoid symptoms who is *not* being treated *may* be at risk for future violent behavior if he has other risk factors for violence.

Substance Abuse

Use and abuse of substances such as marijuana, cocaine, inhalants, ecstasy, and alcohol are highly prevalent among adolescents. Table 5.1 shows results from a CDC survey of high school seniors, 10th graders, and 8th graders from 1980 to 2009.

The connection between substance abuse and increased violence is well-known; among youth, the use of alcohol and other drugs has been linked to unintentional injuries, physical fights, academic and occupational problems, and illegal behavior. According to the National Survey on Drug Use and Health (2006):

- Youths aged 12 to 17 years who used an illicit drug in the past year were almost twice as likely to have engaged in a violent behavior as those who did not use an illicit drug (49.8% vs. 26.6%).
- Rates of past year violent behavior were higher among youths aged 13, 14, and 15 years than those younger or older.
- The likelihood of having engaged in violent behavior increased with the number of drugs used in the past year (i.e., 45.6% of youths who used one illicit drug engaged in violent behavior compared with 61.9% of youths who used three or more illicit drugs).

TABLE 5.1 Substance Abuse as Reported by Adolescents, 1980–2009

	1980	1990	2000	2009
Percentage reporting marijuana use in the past month				
High school seniors	33.7	14.0	21.6	20.6
10th graders	Not available	Not available	19.7	15.9
8th graders	Not available	Not available	9.1	6.5
Percentage reporting cocaine use in the past month				
High school seniors	5.2	1.9	2.1	1.3
10th graders	Not available	Not available	1.8	.9
8th graders	Not available	Not available	1.2	.8
Percentage reporting use of inhalants in the past month				
High school seniors	1.4	2.7	2.2	1.2
10th graders	Not available	Not available	2.6	2.2
8th graders	Not available	Not available	4.5	3.8
Percentage reporting use of ecstasy in the past month				
High school seniors	Not available	Not available	3.6	1.8
10th graders	Not available	Not available	2.6	1.3
8th graders	Not available	Not available	1.4	.6
Percentage reporting use of alcohol in the past month				
High school seniors	72.0	57.1	50.0	43.5
10th graders	Not available	Not available	41.0	30.4
8th graders	Not available	Not available	22.4	14.9
Percentage reporting binge drinking in the past month				
High school seniors	41.2	32.2	30.0	25.2
10th graders	Not available	Not available	24.1	17.5
8th graders	Not available	Not available	11.7	7.8

Other variables that impact the relationship between violence and substance abuse include the age of onset and perceptions of drug abuse among peers.

Two other drug-related variables, early use of drugs and perceived prevalence of drug use among one's middle school peers, affected the amount of violence in which teenagers subsequently engaged but did not predict its simple occurrence. The greater the frequency of one's own drug use during middle school and the higher the perceived level of drug use among one's peers, the greater the likelihood of frequent predatory violence.

Ellickson and McGuigan, 2000, p. 571

In summary, child and adolescent violence cannot be examined or treated without including its overlap with substance abuse. Substance abuse may be a part of a more complex picture; it can be related to other problems, such as mood disorders, family substance abuse, and trauma.

This also suggests that substance abuse prevention programs may have the added benefit of reducing violence, as well.

The link between exposure to pro-drug environments and subsequent violence for boys suggests that they may profit from extra training in how to resist social pressures that encourage deviant behavior.... [P]rograms aimed at preventing drug use may yield an added violence-reduction bonus. Because middle schools with high rates of drug use foster later violence, reducing overall levels of drug use in the middle school population might limit the subsequent contextual impact of "bad" school environments. Because exposure to drug offers increases the likelihood of more frequent relational or predatory violence, helping middle school children—particularly boys—learn how to resist such offers might have the added benefit of reducing levels of violence several years later. Future research is needed to determine whether drug prevention programs actually yield these added benefits.

Ellickson and McGuigan, 2000, p. 571

Sexual Behavior Problems and Violence

Sexual behavior problems (Association for the Treatment of Sexual Abusers [ATSA], 2006) and sexual offenses are a growing concern. Sexual behavior problems are defined as those that are developmentally or interpersonally inappropriate, but do not reach the level of a legal offense, such as two children with less than 5 years differences in their ages exploring each other's bodies sexually. These behaviors may have a reasonable explanation and fall with normal ranges of behavior, be time limited and respond to education or treatment, or may be behaviors that, if untreated, may lead to offending behavior, such as rape. Only the behaviors falling outside the researched developmental norms of sexual behavior are considered sexual behavior problems (ATSA, 2006). In order to address this problem, we must first understand it as behaviors outside of developmental norms.

There are no known population statistics on the prevalence of youth sexual behavior problems associated with child maltreatment or early exposure to pornography (ATSA, 2006). Youth with sexual behavior problems are primarily male. Treatment for this problem in childhood and adolescence appears to be effective if the family is included (ATSA, 2006). Some juvenile sex offenders are also violent offenders.

INDIVIDUAL RISK AND RESILIENCE FACTORS: A STUDY

The author's own research (unpublished study) into youth who demonstrate violent behaviors suggests that, as we would expect, they experience more significant stressors, and enjoy less resiliency factors, than those who do not perpetrate violent behaviors. The following study results, although not broad enough to generalize, highlight the author's own investigations into the importance of many of the risk and protective factors mentioned earlier in this chapter.

There were 1031 subjects in a study of child and adolescent behavior by Seifert. The group included 368 (36%) preadolescents, 638 (62%) adolescents (aged 13 years and older), and 25 missing data (2%). Six hundred and seventy-seven were male (66%) and 332 were female (32%). Twenty-two (2%) were missing this data. Ethnicity distribution for the group was 539 (52%) Caucasian, 381 African American (37%), 28 (3%) Hispanic, 7 (1%) Asian, 43 (4%) other ethnicity, and 33 (3%) unknown ethnicity. The majority of the sample (963 [93%]) came from the Mid-Atlantic and Northeastern regions of the United States. Sixty-eight (6%) came from the Central United States, Midwest, or were missing this data. At the time of testing, 742 (72%) youth were living at home with parents or relatives, 66 (6%) were in foster care, 65 (6%) were in detention or group homes, 18 (2%) were incarcerated, 74 (7%) were in residential treatment centers, 9 (1%) were psychiatrically hospitalized, 7 (1%) were living independently, and 50 (5%) were missing this data. Intelligence distribution was 191 (19%) below average IQ, 744 (72%) average IQ, 48 (5%) above average IQ, and 48 (5%) missing this data. One hundred and ninety-one (19%) had no or only mild behavior problems, 828 (80%) had moderate or more severe behavior problems, and 12 (1%) were missing this data. Four hundred and nine (40%) had never assaulted another person, 610 (59%) had histories of assaults on others, and 12 (1%) were missing this data.

Characteristics of chronically assaultive (more than three) compared with nonaggressive (no assaults) youth are

- 71% of the chronically (more than three assaults) violent group had delinquent acts and 58% lacked remorse, whereas 24% of the nonviolent youth had been involved in delinquency and 21% of nonviolent youth lacked remorse for their misdeeds.
- 53% of chronically aggressive youth had deviant peers (Mulder, Brand, Bullens, & van Marle, 2011) (21% of nonaggressive youth), 50% had attachment problems (28% of nonaggressive youth), and 58% of chronically aggressive youth believed in the legitimacy of aggression as a means to an end (20% of nonaggressive group).
- 59% of the group of chronically aggressive youth had learning problems, and 77% had school behavior problems, whereas 43% of the nonaggressive youth had learning problems, and 33% had school behavior problems.
- 73% of the aggressive youth had been traumatized by family violence (52% of nonaggressive youth), 71% aggressive youth had experienced childhood trauma (44% of nonaggressive youth), 74% had received inappropriate disciplinary practices (54% of nonaggressive youth), 73% had family members with untreated psychiatric or substance abuse problems (60% of nonaggressive), and 75% had at least one biological parent who was not involved in the child's life (61% of nonaggressive).
- 96% of chronically violent (assaultive) youth had anger management problems (67% of nonassaultive), 92% had poor problem-solving skills (66% of nonassaultive), 85% of assaultive and 82% of nonassaultive had psychiatric problems, and 55% of assaultive youth and 36% of nonassaultive youth had affect-management problems.
- In terms of resiliency, 61% of the aggressive group had average or above-average intelligence. However, more than 77% of the nonaggressive youth had average intelligence or higher; 21% of chronically aggressive youth and 40% of nonaggressive youth were involved in positive activities, 22% of assaultive youth and 48% of nonassaultive youth had caregivers with appropriate disciplinary practices, and 38% of assaultive and 60% of nonassaultive youth had supportive adults in their lives.

Traits of Violent Preadolescent Boys

The characteristics of 220 boys, aged 5 to 12 years, were assessed using the CARE2 assessment tool (Seifert, 2007; see the chapter on assessment for more information). In this study the author compared assaultive versus nonassaultive preadolescent boys. This is a subsample of the larger sample described earlier. Although we cannot draw global inferences from one such sample, the distinctions between the assaultive and nonassaultive boys found in this study do highlight the key findings of this chapter.

Of the entire sample:

- 11% were younger than 5 or 6 years; 44% were between the ages of 7 and 10 years, and 48% were aged 11 to 12 years.
- 98% was from the Mid-Atlantic region of the United States. This was primarily a rural/suburban sample; 2% from other areas of the country.
- 49% were Caucasian, 41% were African American, 3% were Hispanic, and 6% were other ethnicities.
- 94% were living at home or foster care and 4% were in the care of an agency.
- 55% had a history of assaulting others.
- 80% had a history of moderate-to-severe behavior problems.

There were characteristics of the families of the 123 assaultive boys that were more prevalent than among the families of nonassaultive preteens. There was a trend for more (68%) of the families of assaultive boys to have histories of family violence than the families of nonassaultive boys (56%, $P = .05$). A greater percentage of the group of assaultive preadolescent males had skill deficits when compared with the group of nonaggressive boys. More of the assaultive boys had deficits in problem solving (85% of assaultive boys; $P < .01$) and in anger management skills (93% of assaultive boys; $P = .00$).

The behaviors of the two groups of boys (assaultive and nonassaultive) were also compared. There were no differences in the percentage of the groups that abused substances (5% of assaultive and nonassaultive). The rates of the following for assaultive boys were roughly half the rates for nonassaultive boys, and differences were significant: harms animals (18% of assaultive; 8% of nonassaultive; $P < .05$), truant from school (9% of assaultive; 5% of nonassaultive; $P < .05$), fire setting (23% of assaultive; 11% of nonassaultive; $P < .05$), delinquency (38% of assaultive; 18% of nonassaultive; $P = .00$), and school behavior problems (67% of assaultive; 38% of nonassaultive boys; $P = .00$). There were larger differences between groups in the percentage of boys who engaged in bullying others (44% of assaultive; 15% of nonassaultive; $P = .00$). Almost twice as many of the assaultive group were identified as having attachment problems (57%) than the nonassaultive group (30%; $P = .00$) and the difference was significant.

In terms of resiliency factors, approximately 27% of the assaultive boys and 49% of the nonassaultive boys were engaged in some type of positive activity ($P = .00$).

There were no significant differences between groups on the rates of psychiatric (87% of assaultive; 89% of nonassaultive; no significant [ns]) or neurological problems (18% of assaultive; 11% of nonassaultive; ns) or distribution of IQ (70% of assaultive boys had average IQs or better; 76% of nonassaultive boys; ns). This study provides additional evidence of the risk and resiliency factors for violence discussed by other scientists (Caspi, 2005; Ellickson & McGuigan, 2000; Youth Violence: A Report of the Surgeon General, 2001).

Traits of Chronically Violent Teen Boys

This author undertook a study of 434 adolescent boys. Fifty-three percent (228) were Caucasian; 38% (163) were African American; 4% (17) were Hispanic; 4% (16) were other ethnicity; and 2% (10) were unknown ethnicity. Ninety percent (389) were from the Mid-Atlantic region of the United States; 10% (45) were from other parts of the country. Twenty-two percent (96) were below average IQ; 69% (300) were average IQ; and 4% (17) were above average IQ; 5% (21) were missing this data. Sixty-three percent were living in the community and 33% were living in facilities outside of the community. Eight percent (35) had no history of behavior problems or only mild behavior problems; 92% (399) had moderate-to-severe behavior problems.

The strongest correlates of chronic violent behavior among teen boys were history of assaults ($r = .39$; $P = .00$), assault with a weapon ($r = .39$, $P = .00$), delinquency ($r = .31$; $P = .00$), lack of remorse ($r = .30$; $P = .00$), assault of an authority figure ($r = .30$; $P = .00$), belief in the legitimacy of aggression as a means to an end ($r = .30$; $P = .00$), and moderate-to-severe behavior problems ($r = .19$, $P = .00$).

Ninety-nine percent (156) of 158 chronically violent teen males in the study had histories of moderate-to-severe behavior problems and 75% (119) had school behavior problems.

The family dynamics of chronically violent youth in this sample were also similar:

- For 73% (116), one or both parents were dead or uninvolved in the child's life
- 70% (111) used ineffective or inappropriate disciplinary methods
- 72% (113) had family members with psychological or substance abuse problems
- 64% (101) of families could be characterized as low warmth and high conflict
- 72% (113) of the young men had experienced childhood trauma

The psychological makeup and behavior of these youth were similar in many ways, but different from nonassaultive youth.

- 92% (146) were impulsive; 65% (76) of nonassaultive; $F = 35.38$, $P = .00$
- 84% (132) had moderate-to-severe behavior problems before age 13, 48% (56) of nonassaultive; $F = 46.32$, $P = .00$
- 89% (149) had poor problem-solving skills; 74% (87) of nonassaultive; $F = 7.85$, $P < .01$
- 75% (119) had chronic school behavior problems; 40% (47) of nonassaultive; $F = 30.54$, $P = .00$
- 61% (97) belonged to a deviant peer group; 34% (40) of nonassaultive; $F = 740$, $P < .01$

Protective factors found in this group included

- a supportive, nurturing caregiver (31% of group or 49 of chronically assaultive); 62% (73) of nonassaultive; $F = 17.85$, $P = .00$
- appropriate discipline by the caregiver (29% or 46); 49% (57) of nonassaultive; $F = 15.48$, $P = .00$
- the setting of appropriate and achievable future goals of the youth (23% or 36); 39% (46) of nonassaultive; $F = 3.95$, $P < .05$

These factors suggest rich and rewarding target areas for violence prevention programs.

Traits of Chronically Violent Preadolescent Girls

The individual and family characteristics of 117 preteen girls between the ages of 5 and 12 years were examined. Thirty percent of the sample were aged 5 to 7 years; 39% were aged 8 to 10 years; and 31% were aged 11 and 12 years. The girls underwent psychological evaluations for a variety of reasons, attended an outpatient mental health clinic, or were in a facility operated by a public agency. Forty-seven percent of the girls were Caucasian; 39% were African American; 2% were Hispanic; 12% were other ethnicity; 15% were missing this data. Ninety-seven percent of the sample came for the Mid-Atlantic United States; 3% came from other parts of the United States. Most (88%) lived at home; 6% were in foster care; 1% were in detention; and 5% were missing this data. Fourteen percent had below average intelligence; 80% had average intelligence; and 65% had above average intelligence. The majority of the sample (64%) had a history of moderate-to-severe behavior problems; 36% had less severe behavior problems. Most of the girls did not have histories of assaultiveness (62%; 38% had been assaultive in the past).

As mentioned in Chapter 2, gender has an influence on overall risk of violence as well as the types of violent behaviors used.

The following is a look at the picture of chronically (more than three assaults) violent preteen (5- to 12-year-old) girls.

These young girls

- had moderate-to-severe behavior problems (100%)
- had no remorse (67%)
- committed assault of an authority figure (44%)
- harm animals (39%)
- engage in bullying (78%)
- had poorly regulated emotions (83%)
- had enuresis (56%)
- had anger management problems (100%)
- had deficient problem-solving skills (100%)
- believed in the legitimacy of aggression (61%)
- were delinquents (56%)

- showed impulsivity (100%)
- had psychiatric problems (100%)
- showed psychosis, self-harm, or suicide attempts (44%)
- had chronic school behavior problems (61%)
- were truants (100%)
- had attachment problems (78%)

Among their families, I discovered the following commonalities:

- childhood trauma (78%)
- family violence (83%)
- inappropriate discipline (78%)
- low warmth and high conflict (83%)
- family psychiatric problems (78%)
- one parent dead or uninvolved (89%)

Some common risk factors among peers included being involved with a deviant peer group.

This group of girls did report some protective factors:

- 61% reported having a supportive adult in their lives.
- 44% were successful in school, and 50% were engaged in a positive activity.
- Most had an average or better IQ (83%).

Traits of Chronically Violent Teen Girls

The traits of 434 teen girls and their families were examined. Fifty-three percent were Caucasian; 38% were African American; 4% were Hispanic; 4% were other ethnicities; and 2% were missing this data. Ninety percent were from the Mid-Atlantic States of the United States; 10% were from other parts of the United States. The majority of these teen girls lived at home (61%); 4% were in foster care; 12% were in juvenile services detention or a group home; 19% were housed in a facility, 1% were living independently; 3.5% were missing this data. In terms of intelligence, 22% were below average intelligence; 69% were average intelligence; 4% were above average intelligence; 5% were missing this data. Most had moderate or severe behavior problems (92%) and 8% did not. Seventy-three percent had been assaultive and 27% had not. Twenty-four percent committed assaults that caused injury or death to the victim, and 36% of the girls had committed more than three assaults.

The traits most strongly correlated with chronic violence among the adolescent girls in this sample were any past assaults, severe and/or chronic behavior problems, lacking remorse, and delinquency. More specifically,

- a history of assaults that caused injury or death (32%),
- histories of moderate-to-severe behavior problems that began before the age of 13 years (82%),
- impulsivity (89%),
- anger management problems (89%),
- poor problem-solving skills (86%)
- history of delinquency (65%)
- psychiatric problems (78%)
- lack of appropriate social skills (71%)
- few prosocial peers (69%)
- school behavior problems (68%),

Family risk factors included

- history of family violence (65%)
- childhood trauma (69%)
- ineffective parenting by caregivers (78%)
- low family warmth and high conflict (67%)
- untreated or undertreated mental health or substance abuse problems among family members (76%)
- one or both parents dead or uninvolved in child's life (69%)

In terms of resiliency factors, this sample was low on nearly all:

- The majority of these teens had average IQ (62%).
- They did not have a supportive adult in their lives (60%).
- They were not successful in school (93%).
- They do not have appropriate future goals (69%).
- They do not have positive activities (84%).

REFERENCES

Ainsworth, M. D., Blehar, M. C., Waters, E., & Wall, S. (1978). *Patterns of attachment: A psychological study of the strange situation.* Hillsdale, NJ: Lawrence Erlbaum Associates.

Alia-Klein, N., Goldstein, R. Z., Kriplani, A., Logan, J., Tomasi, D., Williams, B., et al. (2008). Brain monoamine oxidase A activity predicts trait aggression. *Society for Neuroscience, 28*(19), 5099–5104.

American Academy of Child and Adolescent Psychiatry. (2004). *Schizophrenia in children.* Retrieved from http://aacap.org/page.ww?name=Schizophrenia+in+Children&section=Facts+for+Families

American Psychiatric Association. (2000). *Diagnostic and statistical manual of mental disorders, 4th ed., text revision (DSM-IV-TR).* Arlington, VA: American Psychiatric Association.

Archibald, S. L., Fennema-Notestine, C., Gamst, A., Riley, E. P., Mattson, S. N., & Jeringan, T. L. (2001). Brain dysmorphy in individuals with severe prenatal alcohol exposure. *Developmental Medicine and Child Neurology, 43,* 148–154.

Association for the Treatment of Sexual Abusers. (2006). *Report on the task force on children with sexual behavior problems.* Association for the Treatment of Sexual Abusers. Retrieved from www.atsa.com/pdfs/Report-TFCSBP.pdf

Berman, R. F., & Hannigan, J. H. (2000). Effects of prenatal alcohol exposure on the hippocampus: Special behavior, electrophysiciology, and neuroanatomy. *Hippocampus, 10*(1), 94–110.

Bernstein, J. Y., & Watson, M. V. (1997). Children who are targets of bullying: A victim pattern. *Journal of Interpersonal Violence, 12*(4), 483–498.

Borum, R. (2000), Assessing violence risk among youth. *Journal of Clinical Psychology, 56,* 1263–1288.

Bridges, K. M. (1933). A study of the social development in early infancy. *Child Development, 4,* 36–49.

Caspi, I. (2005). Life-course development: The interplay of social-selection and social-causation within and across generations. In E. L. Chase-Landsdale & K. Kiernan (Eds.), *Human development and the potential for change.* New York, NY: Cambridge University Press.

Centers for Disease Control and Prevention. (2007). *Attention deficit hyperactivity disorder (ADHD).* Retrieved from http://www.cdc.gov/ncbddd/adhd

Child Welfare Information Gateway. (2009). *Understanding the effects of maltreatment on brain development.* Retrieved from http://www.

childwelfare.gov/pubs/issue_briefs/brain_development/brain_development.
pdf

Dziegelewski, S. F. (2010). *DSM-IV-TR in action* (2nd ed.). Hoboken, NJ: John
Wiley and Sons.

Ellickson, P. L., & McGuigan, K. A. (2000). Early predictors of adolescent violence. *American Journal of Public Health, 90*(4), 566–572.

Erikson, E. H. (1950). *Childhood and society.* New York, NY: Norton.

Espelage, D. L., & Swearer, S. M. (2003). Research on school bullying and victimization: What have we learned and where do we go from here? *School
Psychology Review, 32,* 365–383.

Ez-Elarab, H. S., Sabbour, S. M., Gadallah, M. A., & Asaad, T. A. (2007).
Prevalence and risk factors of violence among elementary school children
in Cairo. *The Journal of the Egyptian Public Health Association, 82*(1–2),
127–146.

Finkelhor, D., Ormrod, R., Turner, H., & Holt, M. (2009). Pathways to poly-
victimization. *Child Maltreatment, 14*(4), 316–329.

Flannery, D. J., & Huff, C. R. (1999). *Youth violence: Prevention, intervention,
and social policy.* Washington, DC: American Psychiatric Press.

Frick, P. J., Cornell, A. H., Barry, C. T., Bodin, S. D., & Dane, H. E. (2003).
Callous-unemotional traits and conduct problems in the prediction of con-
duct problem severity, aggression, and self-report of delinquency. *Journal of
Abnormal Child Psychology, 31*(4), 457–470.

Gabel, S., & Shindledecker, R. (1991). Aggressive behavior in youth:
Characteristics, outcome, and psychiatric diagnoses. *Journal of the American
Academy of Child and Adolescent Psychiatry, 30,* 982–988.

Gurian, M. (2005). *The minds of boys: Saving our sons from falling behind in
school and life.* San Francisco, CA: Jossey-Bass.

Hahn, R., Fuqua-Whitley, D., Wethington, H., Lowy, J., Liberman, A.,
Crosby, A., et al. (2007, August 10). *The effectiveness of universal school-
based programs for the prevention of violent and aggressive behavior.*
Retrieved from http://www.cdc.gov/mmwr/preview/mmwrhtml/rr5607a1
.htm

Hay, D. (2005). The beginnings of aggression in infancy. In R. E. Tremblay
(Ed.), *Developmental origins of aggression* (pp. 107–132). New York, NY:
Guilford Press.

Herrenkohl, T. M., Maguin, E., Hill, K. G., Hawkins, J. D., Abbott, R. D., &
Catalano, R. F. (2000). Developmental risk factors for youth violence. *Journal
of Adolescent Health, 26,* 176–186.

Hodges, E. V. E., & Perry, D. G. (1999). Personal and interpersonal anteced-
ents and consequences of victimization by peers. *Journal of Personality and
Social Psychology, 76,* 677–685.

Hutman, T., & Dapretto, M. (2009). The emergence of empathy during infancy. *Cognitie, Creier, Comportament/Cognition, Brain, Behavior, 13*(4), 367.

Lahey, B. B., Moffitt, T. E., & Caspi, A. (2003). *Causes of conduct disorder and juvenile delinquency.* New York, NY: Guilford Press.

Leslie, A. M. (1987). Pretense and representation: The origins of "theory of mind." *Psychological Review, 94,* 412–426.

Levy, T., & Orlans, M. (1998). *Attachment, trauma, and healing: Understanding and treating attachment disorder in children and families.* Washington, DC: Child Welfare League of America.

Litvak-Miller, W., McDougall, D., & Romney, D. M. (1997). The structure of empathy during middle childhood and its relationship to prosocial behavior. *Genetic, Social, and General Psychology Monographs, 123,* 303–324.

Loeber, R. (1982). The stability of antisocial and delinquent child behavior: A review. *Child Development, 53,* 1431–1446.

Lyons-Ruth, K. (1996). Attachment relationships among children with aggressive behavior problems: The role of disorganized early attachment patterns. *Journal of Consulting and Clinical Psychology, 64,* 64–73.

Martin, A., & Volkmar, F. R. (2007). *Lewis's child and adolescent psychiatry: A comprehensive textbook* (4th ed.). Philadelphia, PA: Lippincott Williams & Wilkins.

McDermott, R., Tingley, D., Cowden, J., Frazzetto, G., & Johnson, D. D. P. (2009). Monoamine oxidase A gene (MAOA) predicts behavioral aggression following provocation. *Proceedings of the National Academy of Sciences, 106*(7), 2118–2123.

Mezzich, A. C., Tarter, R. E., Giancola, P. R., Lu, S., Kirisci, L., & Parks, S. (1997). Substance use and risky sexual behaviors in female adolescents. *Drug and Alcohol Dependence, 44,* 157–166.

Moffitt, T. (2001). Adolescence-limited and life course persistent antisocial behavior: A developmental taxonomy. In A. A. Piquero (Ed.), *Life-course criminology: Contemporary and classic readings.* Belmont, CA: Wadsworth.

Monahan, J., Steadman, H. J., Silver, E., Applebaum, P. S., Robbins, P. C., Mulvey, E. P., et al. (2001). *Rethinking risk assessment: The MacArthur Study of mental disorders and violence.* New York, NY: Oxford University Press.

Morris, C. M. (2007). *Psychopathic traits and social-cognitive processes in aggressive youth* (Dissertation). Ann Arbor, MI: ProQuest Information and Learning Co.

Morrison, J., & Anders, T. F. (1999). *Interviewing children and adolescents: Skills and strategies for effective DSM-IV diagnosis.* New York, NY: Guilford Press.

Mayo Clinic. (2010). *Depression (major depression): Treatment and drugs.* Retrieved May 4, 2011, from http://www.mayoclinic.com/health/depression/DS00175/DSECTION=treatments-and-drugs

Mulder, E., Brand, E., Bullens, R., van Marle, H. (2011). Toward a classification of juvenile offenders: Subgroups of serious juvenile offenders and severity of recidivism. *International Journal of Offender Therapy Comparative Criminology* [Epub ahead of print].

National Survey on Drug Use and Health. (2006). *Youth violence and illicit drug use.* Retrieved from http://www.oas.samhsa.gov/2k6/youthViolence/youthViolence.htm

Ortiz, M. A. C., & del Barrio Gandara, V. (2006). Study on the relations between temperament, aggression, and anger in children. *Aggressive Behavior, 32,* 207–215.

Perry, B. D. (1998). Homeostatsis, stress, trauma and adaption: A neurodevelopmental view of trauma. *Child and Adolescent Psychiatric Clinics of North America, 7,* 33–43.

Perry, B. D., & Pollard, R. (1998). Homeostasis, stress, trauma, and adaption: A neurodevelopmental view of childhood trauma. *Child and Adolescent Psychiatric Clinics of North America, 7*(1), 33–51.

Ramey, C. T., & Ramey S. L. (1998). Prevention of intellectual disabilities. *Preventive Medicine, 17,* 224–232.

Rand, M. L. (2002). Mirror neurons: Somatic empathy and countertransference. *Annals of the American Psychotherapy Association, 5*(3), 32.

Remschmidt, H. (Ed.). (2001). *Schizophrenia in children and adolescents.* Cambridge, UK: Cambridge University Press.

Sarchiapone, M., Jaussent, I., Roy, A., Carli, V., Guillaume, S., Jollant F., et al. (2009). Childhood trauma as a correlative factor of suicidal behavior—via aggression traits. Similar results in an Italian and in a French sample. *European Psychiatry: The Journal of the Association of European Psychiatrists, 24*(1), 57–62.

Seifert, K. (2006). *How children become violent: Keeping your kids out of gangs, terrorist organizations, and cults.* Boston, MA: Acanthus Publishing.

Seifert, M. K. (2007). *CARE 2: Chronic violent behavior risk and needs assessment manual.* Boston, MA: Acanthus.

Seligman, T. J. (2001). An IDEA schools can use: Lessons from special education legislation. *Fordham Urban Law Journal, 29,* 759–790.

Siegel, L. (2010). *Introduction to criminal justice* (12th ed.). Belmont, CA: Wadsworth.

Stickle, T. R., Kirkpatrick, N. M., & Brush, L. N. (2009). Callous unemotional traits and social information processing: Multiple risk factor models for understanding aggressive behavior in antisocial youth. *Law and Human Behavior, 33,* 515–529.

Tremblay, R. E. (2005). *Developmental origins of aggression.* New York, NY: Guilford Press.

Tremblay, R. E., Hartup, W. W., & Archer, J. (2005). *Developmental origins of aggression.* New York, NY: Guilford Press.

Tremblay, R. E., Mâsse, L. C., Pagani, L., & Vitaro, F. (1996). From childhood physical aggression to adolescent maladjustment: The Montréal prevention experiment. In R. D. Peters & R. J. McMahon (Eds.), *Preventing childhood disorders, substance abuse and delinquency* (pp. 268–298). Thousand Oaks, CA: Sage.

Turner, P. (1991). Relations between attachment, gender, and behavior with peers in the preschool. *Child Development, 62,* 1475–1488.

U.S. Department of Health and Human Services. (1999). *Mental health: A report of the surgeon general—Executive summary.* Rockville, MD: U.S. Department of Health and Human Services, Substance Abuse and Mental Health Services Administration, Center for Mental Health Services, National Institutes of Health, National Institute of Mental Health.

van der Kolk, B. A. (2003). The neurobiology of childhood trauma and abuse. *Child and Adolescent Psychiatric Clinics of North America, 12,* 293–317.

Weniger, G., Lange, C., Sachsse, U., & Irle, E. (2009). Reduced amygdala and hippocampus size in trauma-exposed women with borderline personality disorder and without posttraumatic stress disorder. *Journal of Psychiatry & Neuroscience, 34*(5), 383–388. Retrieved from http://goedoc.uni-goettingen.de/goescholar/bitstream/handle/1/5955/irle.pdf?sequence=1

Williams, T., Connolly, J., Pepler, D., & Craig, W. (2005). Peer victimization, social support, and psychosocial adjustment of sexual minority adolescents. *Journal of Youth and Adolescence, 34*(5), 471–482.

Youth Violence: A Report of the Surgeon General. (2001). Retrieved from http://www.surgeongeneral.gov/library/youthviolence/chapter4/sec3.html

Zimmermann, P., Mohr, C., & Spangler, G. (2009). Genetic and attachment influences on adolescents' regulation of autonomy and aggressiveness. *Journal of Child Psychology and Psychiatry, 50,* 1339–1347.

SIX

Environmental Factors That Impact Youth Violence

Chapter 5 looked at individual risk factors for youth violence. In this chapter, we will look at broader environmental influences that also have a significant impact. As with individual factors, environmental factors can either stress or support the health of a child; see Figure 6.1.

There is an optimal combination of individual and environmental factors that support healthy development in children. Some of the positive factors are as follows (Centre of Knowledge on Health Child Development, 2009).

For physical well-being, children need

- food security
- secure shelter
- good health behaviors

For development of good mental health, children need

- love, praise, and positive regard from trusted family members and other adults
- affection and loving attention, praise, and encouragement
- to have boundaries set on their behavior and to be monitored and supervised when at play or at leisure
- acceptance for who they are at home, school, and in the community
- encouragement and support to succeed at school and to develop their skills and talents
- a safe neighborhood in which to live and play
- loving guidance and discipline

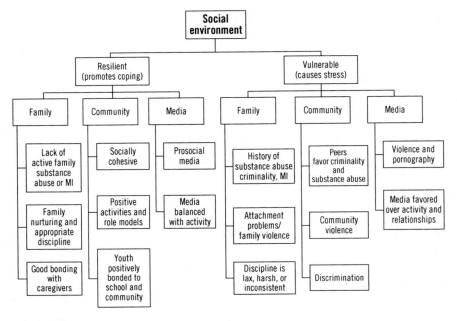

FIGURE 6.1 Environmental Factors.

On the other hand, there are common environmental factors associated with suboptimal development, including youth violence. Consider the following list (adapted from Moeller, 2001; Eliott, Hatot, Sirovatka, & Potter, 2001):

- Family stressors
  - violence in the household
  - parents who abuse substances and/or have mental health problems, particularly depression
  - parental behaviors that are intrusive, inconsistent, or do not meet child's needs
  - cold and hostile parental style
  - use of corporal punishment
  - failure to monitor and supervise children
  - lack of parental involvement with children's day-to-day activities
- School stressors
  - lack of school success; academic failure
  - attentional and behavioral problems treated as a disciplinary problem, rather than as a possible psychological issue needing treatment

- child's failure to receive appropriate services for learning problems
- school conflict
- school suspensions and expulsions without treatment
- poor physical condition of school
- aggression-prone children grouped together in lower academic tracks
- failure to provide interesting and relevant material in school that engages children in learning
- poor school climate
- adult indifference and lack of understanding the problems
- Community stressors
  - community disorganization
  - poverty
  - community unemployment
  - community disadvantage
  - high level of youth peer contact without adult supervision
  - community violence
  - availability of drugs and firearms
  - early youth substance abuse and peer substance abuse
  - easy access to guns
- Media stressors
  - violent TV
  - violent and antisocial video games
  - news

The remainder of this chapter will examine many of these environmental factors as they relate to youth violence.

FAMILY

A number of parental and familial issues can impact the development of violent behaviors in children. Parental behaviors that are intrusive, inconsistent, or insufficient can lead to delays in child development that result in youth violence. A cold and hostile parental style is associated with later youth violence (Eliott et al., 2001; Moeller, 2001). Children who do not have strong prosocial family attachments to their parents or caregivers do not internalize reciprocity, empathy, or the need to follow rules to be an effective member of a school or family group (Bowlby, 1980; Levy & Orlans, 1998; Seifert, 2007). If these are missing, they must be built in an appropriate developmental sequence (Braaten, 1998). Antisocial, substance abusing, and/or mentally ill parents who do not get treatment for their disorders can find it difficult to meet their children's needs, relate to their children in an adequate way, or model appropriate behavior for their children. Many of these factors will be discussed in more detail over the following pages.

Attachment

As discussed in Chapter 4, attachment is a key issue in infant development and highlights the importance of family influences to much of a child's later behavior. High conflict, low warmth, violence, and inappropriate discipline in the home can lead to attachment problems among children. These deficits can lead to significant behavioral issues later in life. "Abusive parenting in general and neglect in particular are predictors of later violence, but they have very small effect sizes. Neglect operates as a distinct risk factor, possibly because neglected children are less likely to be supervised or taught appropriate behavior. This is not to imply that child abuse and neglect do not cause serious problems in adolescence: Indeed, they have large effects on mental health problems, substance abuse, and poor school performance" (*Youth Violence: A Report of the Surgeon General*, 2001). Smith, Ireland, Thornberry, and Elwyn (2008) in a longitudinal study of 1,000 youth found that childhood maltreatment was significantly associated with later antisocial behavior.

Parental System

According to the Surgeon General's report on youth violence (2001), another childhood predictor of violence, albeit with a small effect size, are children who are raised by divorced, separated, or never-married parents. Separation from parents is also a small but distinct factor.

Socioeconomic Status

A family with a low socioeconomic status is a risk factor for youth violence, as discussed in Chapter 2. "Socioeconomic status generally refers to parents' education and occupation as well as their income. Poorly educated parents may be unable to help their children with schoolwork, for example, and children living in poor neighborhoods generally have less access to recreational and cultural opportunities. In addition, many poor families live in violent neighborhoods, and exposure to violence can adversely affect both parents and children" (*Youth Violence: A Report of the Surgeon General*, 2001).

Violent Behavior in the Home

Another familial factor is parents who routinely model violent behavior in their own lives. ".... children learn violent behavior by observing their parents rather than by inheriting a propensity for violence. In fact, attachment to parents, a possible protective factor, can have the opposite effect if the parents are violent" (*Youth Violence: A Report of the Surgeon General*, 2001).

Carlson (2000) estimated that 15 million children are exposed to intimate partner violence (IPV) each year in the United States and that children in homes with IPV are also more likely to be abused or neglected. Worldwide, it is estimated that 133 to 275 million children are exposed to IPV (Spilsbury et al., 2008). Witnessing family violence can be just as damaging as experiencing it (Carlson, 2000). As mentioned in Chapter 4, IPV between adults is significantly related to a child's violent behavior later on; Ireland and Smith (2009) reported that teens exposed to severe partner violence were more likely to engage in adult violent crime and domestic violence.

As hypothesized by the intergenerational theory (mentioned in Chapter 4), children who grow up in violent households may learn that violence is an acceptable way to solve problems and they may then use violence or aggression to get their own needs met. In addition, they may exhibit attachment disorders, substance abuse, criminality, poor performance in school or work, and mental health problems (Eliott et al., 2001).

Corporal Punishment

It used to be common and accepted practice for adults to use harsh physical punishment (such as spanking) at home and in schools to discipline children; such methods are now thought to be inappropriate and may possibly foster violence in children later on. "Although physical punishment may produce conformity in the immediate situation, in the longer run it tends to increase the probability of deviance, including delinquency in adolescence and violent crime inside and outside the family as an adult" (Straus, 1991, p. 133).

> ...if parents use negative forms of discipline (i.e., physical punishment), their children are more likely to use violence to resolve their own conflicts. Parents are the most influential people in their children's lives, and children's behaviors are often a reflection of their observations and imitation of parental behaviors. Children's early life experiences, which are in large part provided by their families, set the stage for how they will develop the ability to think, feel, trust, and relate to others. Particularly during the early years, when children have not fully developed the cognitive ability to understand and interpret their experiences, they are more vulnerable to violence exposure, and their early experiences may have long-term psychological impact
>
> Ohene, Ireland, McNeely, and Borowsky, 2006

Appropriate Parenting Skills and Supervision

Children learn to cope with stressors, solve problems, and interact with the world appropriately in an expected progression of developmental milestones that were described in the previous chapter. If the parents are unable to provide this necessary teaching and socializing, it must be taught by others: schools, churches, community organizations, mental health facilities, social service organizations, and so on. Alternately, parents may be taught the developmental skills that they have missed growing up, so that they can, in turn, parent appropriately and teach these skills to their children (Seifert, 2006).

Many studies suggest that parent's failure to monitor their children's whereabouts is related to youth delinquency and violence (such as Moeller, 2001). Adolescents need the guidance of adults, even though they are trying to find their place in the peer group and eventually individuate. Interestingly, the time period between 3 p.m. and 6 p.m.—when children are most likely to be unsupervised by either school or parents—is the time of day when most youth violence occurs (Eliott et al., 2001).

In summary, youth with violent behaviors require a multifaceted treatment plan that addresses the needs not only of the child but also of his/her family. Families must be included in the interventions for youth who are at risk for violent behaviors.

PEERS

Peers play an enormous influence in development, particularly during preadolescence and beyond. Peers have a major influence on the development of aggression or lack thereof in adolescence. This is also an interactive process: a youth affects his peer group and the group influences him. Positive interactions will support healthy development. The best way to encourage prosocial values is daily interactions with prosocial peers and adults in positive activities.

> Peer groups are all-important in adolescence. Adolescents who have weak social ties—that is, who are not involved in conventional social activities and are unpopular at school—are at high risk of becoming violent, as are adolescents with antisocial, delinquent peers. These two types of peer relationships often go together.... A third risk factor with a large effect size on violence is belonging to a gang. Gang membership increases the risk of violence above and beyond the risk posed by having delinquent peers (Thornberry, 1998). These three peer group factors appear to have independent effects, they sometimes cluster together, and they are all powerful late predictors of violence in adolescence.
>
> *Youth Violence: A Report of the Surgeon General*, 2001

Siblings play an important role in youth violence. "Farrington (1989) found that having delinquent siblings by age 10 predicted later convictions for violence.... antisocial siblings have a stronger negative influence during their sibling's adolescence than earlier in the child's development. Williams (1994) found that the influence of delinquent siblings was stronger on girls than on boys" (Hawkins et al., 2000, p. 5).

SCHOOL

According to the Surgeon General's report on youth violence (2001),

> the only early risk factor in the school domain is poor attitude toward
> and performance in school, and its effects are small. Numerous indi-
> vidual and family factors may contribute to poor performance, making it
> a fairly broad measure. For example, a child who is physically aggressive
> and is rejected by peers or who has difficulty concentrating or sitting
> still in class may understandably have difficulty performing academic
> tasks. Children who have been exposed to violence, as noted earlier,
> may also have trouble concentrating in school.

Many researchers (such as Maguin & Loeber, 1996; Denno, 1990)
have found that poor academic achievement consistently predicts
later delinquency. Academic failure in the elementary grades also
increases risk for later violent behavior (Farrington, 1989; Maguin
et al., 1995). Unfortunately, as mentioned in Chapter 4, early trauma
can impact a child's ability to pay attention and learn (Moeller, 2001;
Seifert, 2007). There is a strong tradition in the U.S. school system
to treat youthful misbehavior as disobedience and to use punishment, rather than appropriate treatment, to control the behavior.
Not providing treatment in the early stages of childhood problems
often leads to an increase in the severity and chronicity of those
problems (Eliott et al., 2001; Seifert, 2007). Schmidt, Seifert, Weist,
and Andrews (2009) conducted a 6-year survey of a school-based
mental heath program. Participants in the mental health program
showed reduced violence and disciplinary problems as compared
with the control group.

Poor performance in school can lead to truancy, another risk factor for youth violence. Farrington (1989) found that youth with high
truancy rates at ages 12 to 14 years were more likely to engage in
violence as adolescents and adults; leaving school before the age of 15
years also predicted later violence.

A healthy school environment supports child success, which in
turn promotes positive bonding to the school. All schools should be
violence-free and intolerant of bullying. Unfortunately, this is not
always the case. "Research on school violence indicates that a culture
of violence has arisen in some schools, adversely affecting not just

students but teachers and administrators as well.... Students exposed to violence at school may react by staying home to avoid the threat or by taking weapons to school in order to defend themselves...." (*Youth Violence: A Report of the Surgeon General*, 2001).

In a 2009 nationally representative sample of youth in grades 9 to 12 (Centers for Disease Control and Prevention, 2010)

- 31.5% reported being in a physical fight in the 12 months preceding the survey.
- 17.5% reported carrying a weapon (gun, knife, or club) on one or more days in the 30 days preceding the survey.
- 7.7% reported being threatened or injured by someone with a weapon on school property one or more times in the 12 months preceding the survey.
- 11.1% reported being in a physical fight on school property in the 12 months preceding the survey.
- 5% did not go to school on one or more days in the 30 days preceding the survey because they felt unsafe at school or on their way to or from school.

There is a school/community interaction, as well.

Schools located in socially disorganized neighborhoods are more likely to have a high rate of violence than schools in other neighborhoods.... however, researchers emphasize that most of the violence to which young people are exposed takes place in their home neighborhood or the neighborhood surrounding the school, not in the school itself (Laub & Lauritsen, 1998). Individual schools, like individual students, do not necessarily reflect the characteristics of the surrounding neighborhood. A stable, well-administered school in a violent neighborhood may function as a safe haven for students.

Youth Violence: A Report of the Surgeon General, 2001

Bullying in schools is another significant problem that, unfortunately due to a series of high-profile and tragic cases, may finally be getting the attention it deserves. In a survey of elementary school children (Tarshis, 2010), 90% indicated they had been bullied and 59% said they had bullied another child. Bullying will be discussed in more detail in Chapter 7.

COMMUNITY

I (KS) once went to consult in one of the persistently dangerous schools in Baltimore, Maryland. I had been warned that the neighborhood was dangerous. Driving to the school, I passed through a well-groomed middle class neighborhood, and I was puzzled about the warning. When I left the school, I turned left instead of right—and what a difference there was. Trash in the streets, houses boarded up, and gangs of older teens sporting gang colors hanging out in the streets. I realized that whereas I could quickly drive out, the children who lived in this neighborhood had little hope of ever getting out.

A healthy community environment contains access to positive activities, positive role models, opportunities for positive bonding to the community (Eliott et al., 2001; Hirschi, 1969), tolerance for differences and uniqueness, promotion of positive social environment and social cohesion. Prosocial groups and activities organized by prosocial role models can have a tremendous influence on children for positive development.

On the other hand, community factors that increase a youth's risk for violence include "... poverty, low neighborhood attachment, and community disorganization [defined as the presence of crime, drug-selling, gangs, and poor housing], the availability of drugs and firearms, exposure to violence and racial prejudice, laws and norms favorable to violence, and frequent media portrayals of violence" (Hawkins et al., 2000).

MEDIA

The Bobo experiments discussed in Chapter 4 spawned a tremendous amount of research over the potentially harmful effects of allowing children to watch violent content in the media—a debate that still rages to this day, and grows along with increasingly violent content in TV, movies, music lyrics, video games, and Web sites. Clearly it is an important area for research, given the amount of media most children consume. According to the American Academy of Pediatrics (2009, p. 1496),

> ... children between 8 and 18 years of age spend an average of 6 hours and 21 minutes each day using entertainment media (television, commercial

or self-recorded video, movies, video games, print, radio, recorded music, computers, and the Internet). Children between 0 and 6 years of age spend an average of almost 2 hours each day using screen media (television, movies, computers). Televisions are also commonly present in bedrooms, with 19% of infants, 29% of 2- to 3-year-olds, 43% of 4- to 6-year-olds, and 68% of children 8 years and older having a television in their bedrooms.

And much of this media consumption will include frequent portrayals of violence. "The typical American child will view more than 200,000 acts of violence, including more than 16,000 murders before the age of 18. Television programs display 812 violent acts per hour; children's programming, particularly cartoons, displays up to 20 violent acts hourly" (Beresin, 2010). Many critics note that this violence is often glamorized; violent protagonists are portrayed as attractive and heroic, and the physical and emotional consequences of violent behavior are underplayed or ignored.

There has been controversy (Moeller, 2001) about the role of violent media in modeling violent behaviors (specifically, physical aggression) in young people. Certainly, few would now argue that, say, listening to violent song lyrics alone will cause a child with no former history of behavioral problems to suddenly become violent; violent media is one factor among many. ".... [V]iolence is a complex interpersonal phenomenon that occurs when a host of contributing factors converge at the right (or wrong) time and place. The large number of contributing factors points to the complexities of understanding social and psychological causation in a context of human development" (Anderson et al., 2003, p. 105).

In a comprehensive study of nearly 30 years of research, Anderson et al. (2003, p. 86) summarize some of the findings:

In summary, many well-controlled, randomized experiments have examined how exposure to violent TV and film media affects aggression in youths of all ages. The evidence from these experiments is compelling. Brief exposure to violent dramatic presentations on TV or in films causes short-term increases in youths' aggressive thoughts, emotions, and behavior, including physically aggressive behavior serious enough to harm others. The effect sizes are moderate on the average but vary greatly depending on the outcome measure used; usually, effect sizes are smaller for more serious outcomes than for less serious outcomes. There is some evidence that youth who are predisposed to be aggressive or who recently have been aroused or provoked are somewhat more susceptible to these effects than other youngsters are, but there is no evidence of any totally immune group.

Put another way, as compared with our knowledge of other common health behaviors and their outcomes: "The strength of the association between media violence and aggressive behavior found in meta-analyses is greater than the association between calcium intake and bone mass, lead ingestion and lower intelligence quotient, and condom nonuse and sexually acquired HIV infection, and is nearly as strong as the association between cigarette smoking and lung cancer—associations that clinicians accept and on which preventive medicine is based without question" (American Academy of Pediatrics, 2009, p. 1497).

Fortunately, there are ways to counteract the impact of media violence: parents can limit and/or monitor children's overall media consumption and promote media literacy by encouraging children to think critically about what they watch.

REFERENCES

American Academy of Pediatrics. (2009). Council on Communications and Media. Policy statement—Media violence. *Pediatrics, 124*(5), 1495–1503.

Anderson, C. A., Berkowitz, L., Donnerstein, E., Huesmann, L. R., Johnson, J. D., Linz, D., et al. (2003). The influence of media violence on youth. *Psychological Science in the Public Interest, 4*(3), 81–110.

Beresin, E. V. (2010). *The impact of media violence on children and adolescents: Opportunities for clinical interventions.* American Academy of Child & Adolescent Psychiatry. Retrieved from http://www.aacap.org/cs/root/developmentor/the_impact_of_media_violence_on_children_and_adolescents_opportunities_for_clinical_interventions

Bowlby, J. (1980). *Attachment and loss: Vol. 3 loss, sadness, and depression.* New York, NY: Basic Books.

Braaten, S. (1998). *Behavioral objective sequence.* Champaign, IL: Research Press.

Carlson, B. E. (2000). Children exposed to intimate partner violence: Research findings and implications for intervention. *Trauma, Violence, and Abuse, 1*(4), 321–340.

Centre of Knowledge on Healthy Child Development. (2009). *What makes kids healthy, happy and well-adjusted?* Retrieved from http://www.knowledge. offordcentre.com/index.php?option=com_content&view=article&id=224&I temid=26

Centers for Disease Control and Prevention. (2010). Youth risk behavioral surveillance—United States, 2009. *MMWR, 59*(SS–5). Retrieved from http://www.cdc.gov/mmwr/pdf/ss/ss5905.pdf

Denno, D. W. (1990). *Biology and violence: From birth to adulthood.* Cambridge, UK: Cambridge University Press.

Eliott, D., Hatot, N. J., Sirovatka, P., & Potter, B. B. (2001). *Youth violence report of the Surgeon General.* Washington, DC: U.S. Department of Health and Human Services. Retrieved April 21, 2011, from http://www.surgeongeneral. gov/library/youthviolence/summary.htm#majorresearch

Farrington, D. P. (1989). Early predictors of adolescent aggression and adult violence. *Violence and Victims, 4,* 79–100.

Hawkins, J. D., Herrenkohl, T. I., Farrington, D. P., Brewer, D., Catalano, R. F., Harachi, T. W., et al. (2000). *Predictors of youth violence.* Office of Juvenile Justice and Delinquency Prevention. Retrieved from http://www.ncjrs.gov/ pdffiles1/ojjdp/179065.pdf

Hirschi, T. (1969). *Causes of delinquency.* Berkley, CA: University of California Press.

Ireland, T. O., & Smith, C. A. (2009). Living in partner-violent families: Developmental links to anti-social behavior and relationship violence. *Journal of Youth and Adolescence, 38*(3), 323–339.

Levy, T., & Orlans, M. (1998). *Attachment, trauma, and healing: Understanding and treating attachment disorder in children and families.* Washington, DC: Child Welfare League of America.

Maguin, E., Hawkins, J. D., Catalano, R. F., Hill, K., Abbott, R., & Herrenkohl, T. (1995, November). *Risk factors measured at three ages for violence at age 17–18.* Paper presented at the American Society of Criminology, Boston, MA.

Maguin, E., & Loeber, R. (1996). Academic performance and delinquency. In M. Tonry (Ed.), *Crime and justice: A review of research* (Vol. 20, pp. 145–264). Chicago, IL: University of Chicago Press.

Moeller, T. G. (2001). *Youthful aggression and violence: A psychological approach.* Mahwah, NJ: Lawrence Earlbaum Associates.

Ohene, S., Ireland, M., McNeely, C., & Borowsky, I. W. (2006). Parental expectations, physical punishment, and violence among adolescents who score positive on a psychosocial screening test in primary care. *Pediatrics, 117,* 441–447.

Schmidt, R., Seifert, K., Weist, M., & Andrews, C. (2009). Sustaining a school mental health program started through the safe schools/healthy students federal grant initiative. *Report on Emotional and Behavioral Disorders in Youth, 39–46*, 51.

Seifert, K. (2006). *How children become violent: Keeping your kids out of gangs, terrorist organizations, and cults.* Boston, MA: Acanthus Publishing.

Seifert, K. (2007). *CARE2 manual.* Boston MA: Acanthus.

Smith, C. A., Ireland, T. O., Thornberry, T. P., & Elwyn, L. (2008). Childhood maltreatment and antisocial behavior: Comparison of self-reported and substantiated maltreatment. *American Journal of Orthopsychiatry, 78*(2), 173–186.

Spilsbury, J. C., Kahana, S., Drotar, D., Creeden, R., Flannery, D. J., & Friedman, S. (2008). Profiles of behavioral problems in children who witness domestic violence. *Violence and Victims, 23*(1) 3–17.

Straus, M. (1991). Discipline and deviance: Physical punishment of children and violence and other crime in adulthood. *Social Problems, 38*(2), 101–123.

Tarshis, T. P. (2010). *Teens living with peer pressure and bullying.* New York, NY: Facts on File, Inc.

Youth Violence: A Report of the Surgeon General. (2001). Retrieved from http://www.surgeongeneral.gov/library/youthviolence/chapter4/sec3.html

Special Issues in Youth Violence

SEVEN

Bullying

Historically, bullying has been seen as a normal experience of childhood and adolescence with few, if any, lasting effects (Arseneault, Bowes, & Shakoor, 2010; Feinberg, 2003; & Lawrence, 1998). Many people have a story about a time when they were victims of a bully. Some of us have stories about how we *were* bullies, participating in what verges on a rite of passage in American culture (and in many other cultures).

More recently, experts have identified bullying as a significant problem with powerful impacts on victims, bullies, and bystanders. Consider the recent spate of suicides related to bullying (e.g., Tyler Clementi, age 18 years; Asher Brown, age 13 years; Seth Walsh, age 13 years; Justin Aaberg, age 15 years; Billy Lucas, age 15 years; Phoebe Prince, age 15 years; Alexis Pilkington, age 17 years; Bartoletti, 2010); the story of Tyler Clementi, a college student who committed suicide after a roommate videotaped him during a sexual encounter and broadcast it on the Web; and the involvement of bullying in critical incidents, such as the Columbine shootings. There are even movies with bullying as the topic (such as "Mean Girls"). In response, 45 states have enacted legislation to prevent and address bullying, and the Federal government held its first ever Federal Bullying Prevention Summit in August of 2010 (Duncan, 2010).

Bullying is a pervasive phenomena (Batsche & Knoff, 1994; Swearer, Espelage, Vaillancourt, & Hymel, 2010), found across countries, social economic statuses, and cultures. People tend to think of bullying as a normal experience of childhood and adolescence, but bullying extends to other locations as well, such as the workplace, college campuses, prisons (Ireland & Archer, 1996), and within families—although those issues will not be addressed in this chapter. It is complex, involving interactions of multiple people situated at different levels of ecological systems (Bronfenbrenner, 2005). Bullying damages everyone involved, including the victims, the bullies, and the bystanders who observe the interaction. Indeed, bullying is a "significant risk factor for mental health problems" (Arseneault et al., 2010, p. 719).

In this chapter, I will describe current definitions of bullying; its prevalence; person variables of the victim, the bully, and the bystander; characteristics of bullying interaction at the individual and microsystem levels; school and community influences on bullying; and potential interventions.

DEFINITION OF BULLYING

According to Olweus (1992) bullying consists of repeated, unwanted, aggressive actions between peers where there is an imbalance of power. Bullying may be classified as verbal, physical, or relational. Examples of verbal bullying include derogatory comments and name-calling. Physical bullying might involve hitting, kicking, shoving, spitting, repeated theft, damaging belongings, or forcing a person to do something he or she does not want to do. Relational bullying results in damage to relationships, either between two people or between the victim and a group of people; for example, spreading rumors about someone or excluding them socially from a group.

The differences between the categories should not be considered exclusive. For example, one episode of bullying may involve verbal harassment in a face-to-face encounter, which may later be continued with damages to the victim's relationships as the bully uses indirect and relational bullying.

Bullying may occur through electronic media (e.g., cyberbullying via cell phones or Internet) and/or may focus on the victim's perceived differences (Henderson, Hymel, Bonanno, & Davidson, 2002), such as weight (Lumeng et al., 2010), giftedness (Peterson & Ray, 2006a), disability (Flynt & Collins Morton, 2007), race/ethnicity, or sexual orientation.

Some children and adolescents are bullied and bully others; these are known as bully-victims. Bullying can be a solitary action by one person or can include bystanders in different roles. Some bystanders may observe and not be involved, some may support the bully, some may join in, and some may protect the victim.

PREVALENCE OF BULLYING

Bullying is indeed a common experience (Batsche & Knoff, 1994; Swearer et al., 2010), but the range of findings regarding prevalence varies widely. Some of these differences may be due to different operational definitions and measures of bullying (Espelage & Swearer, 2003). Other differences may be due to the fact that victims, peers, teachers, and parents tend to report different amounts of bullying for the same situations.

In a study of Midwestern students, Hoover, Oliver, and Hazler (1992) found that 77% reported being a victim of bullying. Duncan (1999) found that 28% of the subjects reported bullying others, whereas 25% of the subjects reported being bullied. In a large sample of U.S. youth, Nansel and colleagues (2001) found that 19.4% of the participants had bullied others "sometimes" or "frequently," whereas 16.9% of the participants had been bullied "sometimes" or "frequently." Henderson et al. (2002) found that 64% of their sample had been bullied at some time, and 12% were bullied at least once a week.

A cross-national study involving European countries, the United States, and Canada revealed rates of victimization from 5% in Sweden to 20% in Lithuania, with a variety of rates between those two results (Nansel et al., 2004). These are similar to studies from other countries, such as England and Germany (Wolfe, Woods, Stanford, & Schulz, 2001), Japan (Ando, Asakura, & Simons-Morton, 2005), and Norway (Olweus, 1994). In U.S. schools, bullying seems to increase through elementary school up to middle school and then decrease (Nansel et al., 2001; Peterson & Ray, 2006b).

THE EFFECTS OF BULLYING

Bullying has long been thought of as a "normal" activity of growing up with few ill effects, but the literature indicates that it is harmful and damages victims and bullies in a number of ways. Arseneault et al. (2006) conducted a nationally representative, prospective cohort study of children aged 5 to 7 years, $n = 2,232$, to examine the contribution of bullying to adjustment problems, while controlling for gender, previous adjustment problems, prosocial behavior at school, and happiness at school. They found that victims and bully/victims had significantly more internalizing problems than children who were not bullied while also exhibiting fewer prosocial behaviors. Students who were bullied were more apt to obtain D's or F's than students who were not bullied (DeVoe, Kaffenberger, & Chandler, 2005).

The researchers found some gender differences for victims and bully/victims. Boys who were victims developed internalizing problems, whereas boys who were bully/victims had internalizing and externalizing problems. Girls who were victims or bully/victims had both internalizing and externalizing problems. Another study found that girls who are bullied have greater depression and suicidal ideation than children who are not bullied (van der Wal, de Wit, & Hirasing, 2003).

In the study by Arseneault et al. (2006), victims did not have fewer prosocial behaviors at the beginning of the study, but victim/bullies had fewer prosocial behaviors at the beginning. Bully/victims had higher levels of behavioral and social adjustment problems, as well as academic problems, than did victims. Crick and Grotpeter (1995) found that relational victimization was more strongly correlated with depression and loneliness than direct victimization.

BULLYING: A BIOECOLOGICAL FRAMEWORK

Bullying is a complex phenomenon that, at the time of occurrence, involves the bully and the victim and often bystanders who are observing. Other levels of the social system are also involved, notably families, schools, and community. Bullying occurs within multiple systems and is an interactive and dynamic process. Bullying also serves various functions, and understanding those functions may lead to interventions to prevent bullying.

This section will review the individual as well as family, school, and community characteristics associated with bullying. That is an incomplete approach because of the interactive and ecological nature of bullying; therefore, the next section will address the function of bullying within a bioecological framework (Bronfenbrenner, 2005).

This framework postulates that people function within a microsystem (the immediate environment of family, neighborhood, and school), a mesosystem (the interactions between parts of the microsystem), exosystem (external environments not directly associated with an individual that still influence that person), and the macrosystem or larger sociocultural context (Bronfenbrenner, 2005).

For our discussion, an example of a child's microsystem would be the child's family, classroom, and home neighborhood. Those aspects of the microsystem interact, for example, when parents volunteer at school. Stressors at the parents' workplaces affect how the parents interact with the child and are an example of an exosystem interaction. Mass media coverage of local events, media depictions of violence, and legislation would be examples of the macrosystem affecting the child.

Individual Characteristics

Bullies

Common wisdom is that bullies use bullying because they are unhappy and lacking in social skills (Hymel & Swearer, 2008). But, bullying is not that simple. Bullying may have different functions, being a reaction to stressors in some cases and being instrumental in terms of helping bullies to achieve their goals in other cases (Aronson, 1992; Veenstra, Lindenberg, Munniksma, & Dijkstra, 2010). Recent research indicates that bullies may well be using high level skills to accomplish their own goals or to improve their social status.

In a Finnish study (Björkqvist, Österman, & Kaukiainen, 2000), researchers found that social intelligence was significantly correlated with aggression (including indirect, verbal, and physical), peaceful conflict resolution, and withdrawal from conflict. After the investigators controlled for empathy, the correlation of social intelligence with indirect aggression, verbal aggression, and physical aggression increased, whereas the correlation with peaceful conflict resolution and withdrawal from conflict decreased. This suggests that empathy may be a factor that could differentiate between people with good social skills who bully versus people with good social skills who do not. Examining the relationship between empathy and the same variables, with social intelligence controlled, resulted in significant correlations between empathy, peaceful conflict resolution, and withdrawal from conflict. Similarly, they found significant negative correlations between empathy and verbal, physical, and indirect aggression.

There are myths that bullies are rejected by their peers, have no friends, and have low self-esteem (Graham, 2011). It is true that sometimes bullies are rejected or disliked by their peers (Peeters, Cillessen, & Scholte, 2010), but the same study also found that some bullies were socially intelligent and popular. Other research indicates that bullies sometimes have high status in the classroom, have many friends, and are admired (Rodkin, Farmer, Pearl, & VanAcker, 2000). In one study, bullies were viewed by peers and teachers as having the highest status and victims the lowest status by many of the students in the study (Juvonen, Graham, & Schuster, 2003). Further, bullies may actually be well-liked by their peers (Rodkin et al., 2006; Veenstra et al., 2010). Research by Vaillancourt, Hymel, and McDougall (2003) found that most adolescent bullies are perceived by their peers as being attractive, popular, and leaders within their schools. One study found gender differences in expectations about bullying. Bullying by boys, at least at the preadolescent age, is more accepted than bullying by girls, whereas helping others is more acceptable for girls than for boys (Dijkstra, Lindenberg, & Veenstra, 2007).

Not all research finds bullies to have positive qualities. Bullies are more likely to bring a weapon to school and to be involved in fighting (Nansel, Overpeck, Haynie, Ruan, & Scheidt, 2003). This is similar to earlier findings by Olweus (1992), who found that 60% of former bullies had at least one conviction by age 24 years and 35% to 40% having at least three or more convictions. Nansel et al. (2003) also found that those who bullied had a higher correlation with other problematic behaviors, such as drinking alcohol and smoking. In this study, bullies also demonstrated worse adjustment to school in terms of academic achievement and perceptions of school climate. Bullies tend to have less success academically; lack empathy; be at greater risk for later substance abuse problems and criminal behavior; and have cognitive distortions related to perceived threats, how aggression is viewed, and problem solving (Merrell, Gueldner, Isava, & Ross, 2008).

Researchers have found a correlation between bullying and delinquency for both boys and girls; furthermore, the correlation is higher for those who use direct bullying than those who use indirect bullying (van der Wal et al., 2003). Some of these problems seem to be associated with early emotional dysregulation (Shields & Cicchetti, 2001), which is followed by development of bullying, suggesting that the bullying may serve to help regulate emotions.

In addition, explicit attitudes (van Goethem, Scholte, & Wiers, 2010) such as "It's fine to bully someone" and internal attributions (Crick, Grotpeter, & Bigbee, 2002) such as "He treated me badly so I can bully him" both seem to play a part in the mental world of some bullies.

There has been a significant amount of descriptive research about bullies, victims, bully/victims, and bystanders over the past 30 years (Merrell et al., 2008) but less research about how children are socialized into bullying. One qualitative study conducted in Hong Kong (Lam & Liu, 2007) using eight bullies as subjects found four phases of bullying: (a) rejecting phase, identifying with the victims; (b) performing phase, moving toward becoming a bully; (c) perpetuating phase, enjoying being a bully; and (d) withdrawing phase, moving away. In the first phase, all of the bullies reported observing others bullying and most sympathized with the victims. They moved through that to the performing stage when they began bullying others, perhaps timidly at first and with the support of others. The bullying functioned in different ways during this phase, to provide an emotional release, to avoid being victimized, to obtain a sense of power, or to obtain material rewards. The third phase involved enjoying being a bully, valuing the sense of power and prestige that came from bullying. Five of the participants moved on toward a withdrawing phase where they either reduced or eliminated their bullying. Police involvement in terms of harsh interrogations involving corporal methods seemed to propel some participants toward this phase. For others, "family acceptance, explanation, material support, and concern" (p. 68) assisted the bully to stop. Even this small study illustrates the complexity and variation involved in bullying and that bullying may be developmental in nature, with variations across time.

Another longitudinal study examined developmental trajectories more broadly and found four patterns of bullying (Pepler, Jiang, Craig, & Connolly, 2008). Participants varied in terms of amount of bullying as well as timing of bullying: 9.9% exhibited consistently high levels of bullying, 13.4% had early moderate levels but decreased to almost no bullying by the end of high school, 35.1% had moderate levels of bullying that stayed the same through high school, and 41.6% hardly ever reported any bullying behavior. The students who did bully had problems within themselves, with peers, and with parents. Understanding the patterns of bullying, when and how developmental changes occur, and how people are socialized into bullying or victim behavior would provide information useful for preventing bullying victimization.

Bullying also seems to fulfill multiple functions for the bully and for groups that the bully associates with. Children and adolescents may bully to reach or maintain status within a popular peer group (Dijkstra, Lindenberg, & Veenstra, 2008; Witvliet et al., 2009). When this is the case, the bullies are actually quite socially adept and popular, and bullying serves the function of maintaining that status. Further, when popular students engage in bullying behavior to maintain status, the bullying is not seen as negatively as when other students bully (Dijkstra et al., 2008). Pellegrini and colleagues have studied the interplay between bullying by young males as an agonistic strategy (i.e., adversarial) versus other strategies more affiliative in nature (i.e., maintaining social bonds) in relationship to dominance and found that there is a complex relationship. Bullying appears to be one of the strategies used to establish dominance within social groups, especially at times of transition (c.f., Long & Pellegrini, 2003; Pellegrini, 2002; Pellegrini & Bartini, 2001). Bullies use the agonistic strategies at that time to establish their own position within a group. Later, they are more apt to use affiliative strategies and become friendly with their victims. In a sense, bullying serves to help build the social structure of the group and that provides some security perhaps because it reduces competition for resources. We might think of bullying in this context as a tool, used when necessary and then set aside. In this type of situation, bullying is operating at the mesosystem level (Bronfenbrenner, 2005).

Victims

Victims tend to display lower levels of adjustment prior to bullying and also appear to be damaged by their victimization. Victims have difficulties with social relationships, reporting problems making friends, more loneliness, and poorer relationships with friends (Nansel et al., 2001). In the same study, victims also reported more depression and social anxiety. Perhaps the social isolation and lack of social skills make them more vulnerable to bullying, or perhaps they become more isolated and inept after the bullying occurs.

Victims tend to be smaller or weaker than the bully, anxious, depressed, have low self-esteem, and avoid school (Merrell et al., 2008) and have lower popularity than bullies (de Bruyn, Cillessen, & Wissink, 2009). In one study, victims had early problems with emotional dysregulation, similar to those of bullies (Shields & Cicchetti, 2001). Sometimes victims are negatively perceived by other students. Henderson et al. (2002) found that many students believed that victims deserved being bullied. In their study, 33% of students thought that "It's sometimes okay to bully others" and 25% thought that "It's sometimes okay to pick on losers."

Bully-victims

Those children and adolescents who are both bullies and victims share many of the characteristics described above but appear to experience the problems more strongly. In one study, bully-victims had poorer social and emotional adjustment and more problem behaviors than either bullies or victims (Nansel et al., 2001). The problems include social isolation, less success in school, depression, and anxiety. Carrie in Stephen King's movie of the same name is an extreme example of a victim who is bullied and then victimizes others in turn. Dylan Klebold and Eric Harris are real-life examples of victims who chose a violent reaction to their victimization.

The U.S. Secret Service and U.S. Department of Education commissioned a study of 37 incidents of school violence and found that 71% of the attackers felt bullied or persecuted (Vossekuil, Fein, Reddy, Borum, & Modzeleski, 2002). These are extreme examples and a more common presentation would be to be victimized and to victimize someone else with a similar degree of bullying. Cady Heron in the movie "Mean Girls," is an example of this, moving from being bullied to bullying her tormentor with rumors and verbal attacks.

Bystanders

Much bullying behavior occurs in the presence of other people or bystanders. They appear to adopt various roles in the process, such as *assistants* (those who help the bully), *reinforcers* (passive observers who do not take active action), *outsiders* (those who leave the area), and *defenders* (those who consoled the victim or intervened directly; Salmivalli, Lagerspetz, Björkqvist, Österman, & Kaukiainen, 1996). In one study (Trach, Hymel, Waterhouse, & Neale, 2010), younger students and girls were more apt to take positive action by directly intervening (*defenders*). The likelihood of taking action decreased as the participants got older. In another study (Pozzoli & Gini, 2010), older and more aggressive children were less likely to intervene to help a victim, taking on the *outsider* role. On the other hand, *defenders* were students who generally used a self-reliant problem-solving strategy. Distancing as a defense was associated with passive bystanding. Having a belief in personal responsibility as a moral stance was associated with intervening in bullying. Pro-victim attitudes were also associated with defending a victim. If participants perceived that peers expected them to intervene, there was more chance that they would. There is evidence that some bystander behavior, such as laughing and cheering the bully on appears to be damaging to the bystander (Frey, Hirschstein, Edstrom, & Snell, 2009). It appears that simply observing bullying at school increased the risk of mental health issues, such as anxiety or paranoid ideation, even after controlling for previous bully or victim status (Rivers, Poteat, Noret, & Ashurst, 2009). In addition, bullying by popular students may adversely affect other interactions in a classroom, decreasing peer acceptance and increasing peer rejection (Dijkstra et al., 2008). In some ways, bystanders may seem to be uninvolved in the bullying, but a systems approach suggests that their presence changes the situation and thus needs to be considered in prevention or intervention efforts.

Family Characteristics

Because bullying is often thought of as primarily a school issue, there is not as much research about family characteristics that may contribute to or reduce the prevalence of bullying. There are factors that have been identified as being associated with bullying; for instance, sibling violence is associated with peer and sibling bullying (Duncan, 1999). Other factors associated with bullying include parental physical discipline, lack of adult supervision, low warmth, and parents who permit children to act aggressively (Powell & Ladd, 2010). "Children who are early starters of aggressive behaviors have a higher risk of becoming delinquent or drug abusers. Hence, children manifesting aggressive behaviors should be referred for family-focused interventions" (Kumpfer & Alvarado, 2003, p. 458). Other risk factors may include lack of parent–child bonding, disorganization, ineffective parenting, stressors, and parental depression (Kumpfer & Alvarado, 2003). Parental maltreatment is associated with increased risk of both being a bully and being a victim (Shields & Cicchetti, 2001). This area remains under-researched in the bullying literature.

School Factors

There are some factors that can contribute to or reduce the amount of bullying that students experience. Two of those relate to school climate and school culture (Dessel, 2010). Glisson and colleagues (Glisson, 2007; Glisson & Green, 2006; Glisson & James, 2002) define *culture* as "the norms, expectations, and way things are done in the organization" (Glisson, 2007, p. 739).

Glisson and colleagues define *climate* as "the individual employees' perceptions of the psychological impact of their work environment on their own wellbeing" (Glisson, 2007, p. 739). Although their definitions refer to work settings, they can be applied to schools as well. Thus, matters of school organization, discipline, and teacher attitudes are matters of school culture, whereas perceptions of safety, affiliation with school, and desire to be at school are matters of school climate.

Prejudice may be a climate factor that leads to school harassment and bullying (Dessel, 2010). This concept arises from an understanding that prejudice is based on differences as bullying often is. "School is also a primary socializing force, providing an opportunity to learn about differences, conflict resolution, and peaceful coexistence" (Dessel, 2010). There is some research support for the correlation of bullying and the power imbalances based on ethnic differences (Graham & Juvonen, 2002), with a resulting contribution to poor learning, trauma, and potential violence in schools.

School staff members' conduct can contribute to or reduce the likelihood that bullying will occur. At the simplest level, there are teachers who bully other teachers or who bully students, with attendant negative effects (Tremlow & Fonagy, 2005). Schools with high levels of conflict (between students and teachers and/or between students and students) because teachers were not effectively maintaining order had higher levels of aggression (Kasen, Berenson, Cohen, & Johnson, 2004). On the other hand, when schools emphasize learning, aggression decreased. Positive school climates that produce a sense of connection between students and the school appear to buffer risk factors, such as reduced parental caring and poor peer influences (Espelage & Swearer, 2009).

The U.S. Secret Service and the U.S. Department of Education examined 37 instances of targeted school violence to develop a greater understanding of potential preventive factors. The authors noted that, although there was no common profile of characteristics or patterns of behavior among the attackers, 71% "of the attackers felt persecuted, bullied, threatened, attacked, or injured by others prior to the incident" (Vossekuil et al., 2002, p. 21). Reports of others in the school system verified that the attackers sometimes endured lengthy, severe bullying from a variety of other students in the school. These factors can be ameliorated (see the section on intervention in the schools). However, it is important to approach interventions from a relationship perspective, not at the individual level, and including multiple relationships. Craig and Pepler (in press) recommend using a broad-based approach that enhances relationships, promoting healthy relationships for all involved.

Community Factors—Bullying Within Ecological Systems

Bullying is embedded in interacting systems. As such, it is reasonable to expect that there are some interactive effects and that the bullying behavior serves a function within the system (Madanes, 1981). Madanes (2011) posits six universal human needs that can be satisfied in positive or negative ways: security, variety, love and connection, significance, and growth and contribution. Children and adolescents who come from violent neighborhoods or troubled families might be more likely to attempt to fulfill those needs in some indirect manner. But, people tend to focus on individual behavior rather than thinking in terms of systems and ecologies—and that omits critical information. Behaviors have a function, not only for individuals but also for the entire system. This seems like a difficult idea to apply to bullying because people's response to bullying is often so disapproving. Some creativity in thinking helps us see that bullying may serve to establish a hierarchy (c.f., Long & Pellegrini, 2003) and that structure within groups is helpful to group functioning. Bullying may serve to meet individual goals, such as security, variety, love and connection, significance, growth, or contribution (Madanes, 2011). I suspect that some people in society grant tacit approval of bullying because they do believe that victims do indeed "deserve it" or are "asking for it." Henderson et al. (2002) found this thinking among their participants. In that study, participants often agreed that victims either deserved it (68%) or brought it on themselves (56%). Some participants even rationalized bullying because it made people tougher (44%), could teach a lesson (52%), or could get kids to understand what is important in the group (33%).

Interaction Among Factors

There are limited studies that analyze these factors as they function together and affect each other. One study by Veenstra et al. (2005) had a large enough sample (n = 1,065) of preadolescents to use a multinomial logistic model of analysis, which is more suited to examine the complexities involved with bullying. These researchers first used univariate analyses and found similarities to previous studies: Bully/victims reported the most rejection at home and the highest family vulnerability for externalizing disorders. Bullies, victims, and bully/victims tended to have a more disadvantaged background than students not involved in bullying. Bullies and bully/victims had higher levels of aggression, and victims and bully/victims were more isolated. More boys were bullies or bully/victims than girls, and more girls were victims than boys.

However, when the authors conducted the multivariate analysis, they found that bully/victims and victims had more family vulnerability to externalizing and internalizing disorders. Bullies, bully/victims, and victims tended to have a lower socioeconomic status. Parental characteristics, such as emotional warmth, rejection, or overprotection, did not differentiate between the group. Bully/victims and bullies were more aggressive and victims were more isolated, whereas all three groups were more disliked than students not involved in bullying. This study suggests that bullying is a complex phenomena and that we would benefit from learning more about how the various aspects of bullying and victimization are related.

INTERVENTIONS

In this section, I will review a number of findings related to bullying prevention programs and concepts. For the sake of reporting the literature as it has developed, I will examine this area in terms of the levels presented above: individual, family, school, and community. However, it is important to bear in mind that bullying is a complex, systemic matter that needs to be addressed as a complex, systemic intervention. If we intend to reduce the amount of bullying our children and adolescents experience, it will not do to leave anyone out. Children, teens, and adults must contribute, as must families. Teachers, administrators, and schools need to be a part of the solution, which must also include total community support.

The Olweus Prevention Program was first used in Norway in response to student suicides following bullying episodes, and it had good results there (Olweus, 1994). Those results have not entirely generalized to populations in the United States. For example, in a trial with 10 public schools (7 intervention and 3 control schools) with outcome measures of relational victimization, physical victimization, attitude, students helping other students, and teachers helping students, the only variable that showed improvement across gender, ethnic, and grade levels was an increase in students helping other students (Bauer, Lozano, & Rivara, 2007). The authors speculated that possible reasons for the lack of generalization were the difference between the relatively homogeneous Norwegian society and the multiethnic society of the United States, the influence of the program's founder in Norway, or an increase in reported victimization after the program implementation rather than an increase in the victimization itself.

Individual Interventions

There are some interventions that are inexpensive, associated with positive outcomes, and not likely to cause negative effects. However, before choosing any intervention, it is important that providers undertake an accurate assessment of the person, such as whether that person is a bully, victim, bully/victim, or bystander. Then, interventions should be tailored to the assessment. Useful interventions may include emotional skills training, teaching children and adolescents how to recognize and regulate their own emotional states. After that, social skills training can be helpful, teaching participants about interactions, how to participate with others, how to share, and how to respond. These techniques would be good for victims and bullies with lower levels of social skills.

For those bullies with cognitive distortions, interventions that reduce prejudice and discrimination hold promise. For bullies who are angry or inept socially, learning how to problem-solve and how to manage their anger could give them alternatives to bullying. Resiliency and prosocial skills would be helpful for bullies, victims, and bystanders.

Frisén and Holmqvist (2010) undertook a study to ascertain ideas from students about interventions. Student responses included

- have a serious talk with the bully and victim oriented toward finding a solution, not toward blaming
- involve parents in the situation
- have school staff initiate action rather than waiting for students to ask for help
- action by other students to interfere with or report the bullying
- improve victims' coping strategies
- increase the bully's empathy for the victim
- separate the victim and bully, used as a last resort when other measures do not work
- prevention approaches

I interviewed a student who was a participant in our (Peterson & Ray, 2006b) qualitative study on bullying. One of the striking things that she said was "No one gets bullied around me." I asked why that was and she said, "Because they know not to bully around me." She attributed people's reactions to her decision and determination that bullying was unacceptable. I believe there is some merit in developing explicit attitudes like hers that are opposed to bullying because we have evidence that explicit attitudes are associated with behavior (van Goethem et al., 2010). In their study, explicit attitudes that bullying was positive were associated with bullying behavior. Thus, it would seem logical to help children and adolescents develop positive attitudes toward not bullying.

Another study (Black, Weinles, & Washington, 2010) that examined which strategies students found successful when dealing with bullying. The preferred strategies included fighting back (75%), making a safety plan (74%), telling a peer (71%), or telling an adult at home (71%).

Peterson and Ray (2006b) found that a number of former victims and their bullies had become friends once they became more acquainted with each other. As one urban student said: "If you actually get to know them, they're not really all that bad. When you give people the benefit of the doubt, they're not really so bad (p. 258)."

Family-Level Interventions

Family involvement in the treatment or prevention of bullying is crucial. As is true for individuals, an assessment of family needs and strengths is critical before undertaking an intervention. There are other interventions from related fields (e.g., substance abuse, violence, delinquency, and mental health prevention programs) that may also reduce bullying. Certain procedures may contribute to success with high-risk families. One of the necessary and early steps is to accurately identify families that need some kind of intervention in order to reduce their children's victimization or bullying. Implementing programs that address multiple problems is an efficient approach and reduces costs in terms of monetary outlay and staff support. "The major protective family factors for improving adolescent health behaviors include positive parent-child relationships, positive discipline methods, monitoring and supervision, and communication of prosocial and healthy family values and expectations" (Ary et al., 1999; Kumpfer & Alvarado, 2002, p. 458). Maternal and sibling warmth and a positive home atmosphere were all associated with resiliency to the negative effects of bullying (Bowes, Maughan, Caspi, Moffitt, & Arseneault, 2010). In addition, parental support that helps children achieve their dreams, goals, and purpose in life may be another protective factor (Kumpfer, 1999).

The question becomes, how do practitioners assist with the development of these factors when a child is in a family with multiple risk factors? Kumpfer and Alvarado (2003) examined pivotal studies and concluded that there were 13 principles of effective family-focused interventions:

- using a comprehensive approach
- using family-focused programs rather than child- or parent-focused programs
- improving family relations, communication, and parental monitoring
- choosing interventions that result in cognitive, affective, and behavioral changes in family dynamics
- increased dosage, meaning more time, with higher risk families

- using developmentally appropriate programming
- addressing risk and protective factors when participants are ready or need them
- if parents are more dysfunctional, begin interventions earlier in the life cycle of the child
- matching interventions to the family's cultural traditions
- using incentives such as food, child care, transportation, and rewards for homework completion, attendance, or graduation
- selecting trainers with personal efficacy and confidence as well as genuineness, warmth, humor, empathy, and the ability to structure sessions and be directive
- using interactive skills training methods, such as role plays, active modeling, family practice sessions, homework practice, and videos or CDs of effective and ineffective parenting skills
- collaborating with the clients so they identify their own solutions

School-Level Interventions

Because of the gravity of violence and bullying in public schools, a number of programs have been developed. Before choosing a specific program, undertaking a needs assessment to identify what problems with bullying are occurring would be helpful. The intervention for bullies who are maintaining social status is quite different than the intervention for a bully/victim who is reacting to multiple stressors, which in turn is different from the bullying that may occur related to a gang initiation.

Merrell et al. (2008) conducted a meta-analysis of bullying prevention research and identified approximately one-third of outcome variables as having positive effects, including enhanced social competence, self-esteem, peer acceptance, improving teachers' knowledge of effective practices and confidence about their intervention skills, and reducing student involvement in bully or victim roles.

Other programs also show some promise. For example, the *Steps to Respect* program demonstrated a decrease in school bullying, non-bullying aggression, and negative bystander behavior (Frey et al., 2009). The programs that are specific to bullying share some commonalities. One is that they raise awareness of the issue, giving actions a name, voicing an anti-bullying point of view, and giving students and staff ideas about actions they can take to avoid bullying.

School policies and procedures can provide important protective facts. For instance, schools that have clear policies against violence, positive relationships between teachers and students, and student participation in decision-making consistently had lower levels of a variety of victimization (Khoury-Kassanbri, Benbenishty, Astor, & Zeira, 2004). Improving relationships between teachers and students has a protective effect against bullying. Likewise, improving relationships between students serves to reduce victimization. Building awareness of issues connected with bullying and possible steps students can take has a beneficial effect. Building emotional and social skills also services to reduce bullying. For instance, there are novel ways to improve empathy, such as using infants to help students learn how to read other people's expressions and how to be open (Chetry & Garrett, 2010). Finally, efforts to pinpoint people who are already opposed to violence and increase their influence may be helpful. Madanes (2011) refers to the *third side,* meaning people who value peace and are likely to work to support outcomes that are conciliatory to all involved.

Community-Level Interventions

There are at least three possible ways for a community to be involved in bullying prevention programs. One, a community's norms affect the behavior of members of the community. If bullying is acceptable, we would expect to see more of it within such a community as opposed to seeing less bullying in a community that rejected such behavior. Norms are generally thought about as requirements for participating in a group or society that are often not verbalized but it is possible to bring them to consciousness and make deliberate decisions about what groups of people want. Madanes (2011) described the process of changing norms in a reciprocal manner: "People change when the social context changes and the social context changes when individuals change." There are programs available that deliberately promote changes in norms, such as Values in Education, Wise Skills, and I CAN Character Curriculum recommended by the Association of American Educators (2011) and Character Counts (Josephson Institute, 2011). These programs have research support as being effective at identifying laudable norms and then encouraging their development.

Two, communities can provide funding and leadership toward bullying prevention. It is helpful to have input from providers and people across a spectrum of the community: health care providers, business leaders, religious organizations, students, former victims, and former bullies. In these times of shrinking resources, coordination about prevention providers (substance abuse, mental health, medical health, and bullying) would provide the potential to avoid duplication of services and build on commonalities. At this time, the research on bullying prevention outcomes is sparse and conflicting.

Exploring other evidence-based prevention programs may help bullying prevention efforts avoid unneeded effort. Coordination of programs and providers is an essential component of valuable prevention programming in the future (Weissberg, Kumpfer, & Seligman, 2003). Further, programming should include remedial efforts for those children and adolescents who have either developed problems or are at risk for developing problems, and training and work to enhance lives and build positive life-skills.

Three, communities can establish and maintain policies and statutes that either contribute to an acceptance of bullying or a rejection of bullying. For example, as of the end of 2010, 45 states have enacted anti-bullying legislation (Patton, 2010). State laws provide a framework for local districts that guides decision making and action (Limber & Small, 2003). Laws may include a variety of provisions, such as statutes to forbid bullying, support for or encouragement of bullying prevention programs, requirements for employee training, reporting directives, disciplinary procedures for bullies, protection for victims, and/or address the importance of improved communication between staff and students.

Limber and Small provide recommendations for legislators to consider: (a) include a definition of bullying that does not equate bullying to harassment, (b) require local school districts to have bullying policies that are based on input from a number of stakeholders, (c) recommend adoption of research-based, comprehensive bullying prevention programs, (d) avoid using reporting of incidents of bullying as the primary intervention, (e) discourage policies that will exclude bullies from school, and (f) provide monetary support for program implementation. State legislation is an important piece of the solution but, without other coordination and changes, will not be sufficient to reduce bullying.

CONCLUSION

We have accumulated a large body of information about bullies, victims, and bystanders. We understand some of the interactions between multiple levels of a child's bioecological systems. What we do not yet understand is why does Baby Dale become a bully and Baby Alex does not. We are in need of research to explore and then explicate the processes that lead to being a bully and being a victim (Nansel et al., 2001). Developing a better understanding about what functions bullying serves for an individual and for a group would enhance our ability to identify better interventions to prevent bullying.

In addition, it is important to understand more about when underlying factors contribute to bullying versus other problematic behaviors. We do not yet know when bullying leads to other types of violence. Bullying behavior and its attendant victimization are complexly determined behavior and require complex solutions. It may be that there are different formative trajectories for various types of bullying, and that would indicate the need for different prevention and intervention strategies. That would indicate a need for targeted intervention strategies. However, it is also important strategically to integrate bullying prevention and intervention efforts with other prevention and intervention efforts to provide efficient and economical services, as well as to capitalize on any beneficial effects from other programs.

REFERENCES

Ando, M., Asakura, T., & Simons-Morton, B. (2005). Psychosocial influences on physical, verbal, and indirect bullying among Japanese early adolescents. *The Journal of Early Adolescence, 25,* 268–297.

Aronson, E. (1992). *The social animal.* New York, NY: Freeman.

Arseneault, L., Bowes, L., & Shakoor, S. (2010). Bullying victimization in youths and mental health problems: 'Much ado about nothing'? *Psychological Medicine, 40,* 717–729.

Arseneault, L., Walsh, E., Trzesniewski, K., & Newcombe, R., Caspi, A., & Moffitt, T. E. (2006). Bullying victimization uniquely contributes to adjustment problems in young children: A nationally representative cohort study. *Pediatrics, 118,* 130–138.

Ary, D., Duncan, T. E., Biglan, A., Metzler, C. W., Noell, J. W., & Smolkowski, K. (1999). Developmental model for adolescent problem behavior. *Journal of Abnormal Child Psychology, 27*, 141–150.

Association of American Educators. (2011). *Character Education Programs.* Retrieved from http://www.aaeteachers.org/index.php/character-education-programs

Bartoletti, J. D. (2010). *Stop the devastation of bullying.* Retrieved from http://www.njpsa.org/pubs/article.cfm?aid=1061.

Batsche, G. M., & Knoff, H. M. (1994). Bullies and their victims: Understanding a pervasive problem in the schools. *School Psychology Review, 23,* 165–175.

Bauer, N. S., Lozano, P., & Rivara, F. P. (2007). The effectiveness of the Olweus bullying prevention program in public middle schools: A controlled trial. *Journal of Adolescent Health, 40,* 266–274.

Björkqvist, K., Österman, K., & Kaukiainen, A. (2000). Social intelligence— empathy=aggression? *Aggression and Violent Behavior, 5,* 191–200.

Black, S., Weinles, D., & Washington, S. (2010). Victim strategies to stop bullying. *Youth Violence and Juvenile Justice, 8,* 138–147.

Bowes, L., Maughan, B., Caspi, A., Moffitt, T. E., & Arseneault, L. (2010). Families promote emotional and behavioral resilience to bullying: Evidence of an environmental effect. *Journal of Child Psychology and Psychiatry, 51,* 809–817.

Bronfenbrenner, U. (2005). The bioecological theory of human development. In U. Bronfenbrenner (Ed.), *Making human beings human: Bioecological perspectives on human development* (pp. 3–15). Thousand Oaks, CA: Sage.

Chetry, K., & Garrett, D. (2010, December 10). Babies go to school to teach. *CNN's American Morning.* Retrieved from http://articles.cnn.com/2010-12-10/living/babies.combating.bullying_1_indigo-anti-bullying-program-students-beam?_s=PM:LIVING

Craig, W. M. (2007). Bullying: A Relationship Problem. Strategies and Solutions to Stop Bullying. Education Letter, Faculty of Education and the Education Alumni Committee.

Crick, N. R., & Grotpeter, J. K. (1995). Relational aggression, gender, and social-psychological adjustment. *Child Development, 66,* 710–722.

Crick, N. R., Grotpeter, J. K., & Bigbee, M. A. (2002). Relationally and physically aggressive children's intent attributions and feelings of distress for relational and instrumental peer provocations. *Child Development, 73,* 1134–1142.

de Bruyn, E. H., Cillessen, A. H. N., & Wissink, I. B. (2009). Associations of peer acceptance and perceived popularity with bullying and victimization in early adolescence. *The Journal of Early Adolescence, 30,* 543–566.

Dessel, A. (2010). Prejudice in schools: Promotion of an inclusive culture and climate. *Education and Urban Society, 42,* 407–429.

DeVoe, J. F., Kaffenberger, S., & Chandler, K. (2005). *Student reports of bullying results from the 2001 school crime supplement to the National Crime Victimization Survey.* U.S. Department of Education Statistical Analysis Report. Washington, DC: U.S. Government Printing Office.

Dijkstra, J. K., Lindenberg, S., & Veenstra, R. (2007). Same-gender and cross-gender peer acceptance and peer rejection and their relation to bullying and helping among preadolescents: Comparing predictions from gender-homophily and goal-framing approaches. *Developmental Psychology, 43,* 1377–1389.

Dijkstra, J. K., Lindenberg, S., & Veenstra, R. (2008). Beyond the class norm: Bullying behavior of popular adolescents and its relation to peer acceptance and rejection. *Journal of Abnormal Child Psychology, 36,* 1289–1299.

Duncan, A. (2010). *Key policy letters from the education secretary and deputy secretary.* Retrieved from http://www2.ed.gov/policy/gen/guid/secletter/101215.html

Duncan, R. (1999). Peer and sibling aggression: An investigation of intra- and extra-familial bullying. *Journal of Interpersonal Violence, 14,* 871–886.

Espelage, D. L., & Swearer, S. M. (2003). Research on school bullying and victimization: What have we learned and where do we go from here? *School Psychology Review, 32,* 365–383.

Espelage, D. L., & Swearer, S. M. (2009). Contributions of three social theories to understanding bullying perpetration and victimization among school-aged youth. In M. J. Harris (Ed.), *Bullying, rejection, and peer victimization: A social cognitive neuroscience perspective* (pp. 151–170). New York, NY: Springer Publishing Company.

Feinberg, T. (2003). Bullying prevention and intervention. *Principal Leadership Magazine, 4,* Retrieved from http://www.nasponline.org/resources/principals/nassp_bullying.aspx

Flynt, S. W., & Collins Morton, R. (2007). Bullying prevention and students with disabilities. *National Forum of Special Education, 19,* 1–6.

Frey, K. S., Hirschstein, M. K., Edstrom, L. V., & Snell, J. L. (2009). Observed reductions in school bullying, nonbullying aggression and destructive bystander behavior: A longitudinal evaluation. *Journal of Educational Psychology, 101,* 466–481.

Frisén, A., & Holmqvist, K. (2010). Adolescents' own suggestions for bullying interventions at age 13 and 16. *Scandinavian Journal of Psychology, 51,* 123–131.

Glisson, C. (2007). Assessing and changing organizational culture and climate for effective services. *Research on Social Work Practice, 17,* 736–747.

Glisson, C., & Green. P. (2006). The effects of organizational culture and climate on the access to mental health care in child welfare and juvenile justice systems. *Administration and Policy in Mental Health and Mental Health Services Research, 33,* 433–448.

Glisson, C., & James, L. R. (2002). The cross-level effects of culture and climate in human service teams. *Journal of Organizational Behavior, 23,* 767–794.

Graham, S. (2011). *Bullying: A module for teachers.* http://www.apa.org/education/k12/bullying.aspx

Graham, S., & Juvonen, J. (2002). Ethnicity, peer harassment, and adjustment in middle school: An exploratory study. *Journal of Early Adolescence, 22,* 173–199.

Henderson, N. R., Hymel, S., Bonanno, R. A., & Davidson, K. (2002, February). *Bullying as a normal part of school life: Early adolescents' perspectives on bullying and peer harassment.* Poster session presented at the Safe Schools Safe Communities Conference, Vancouver, British Columbia.

Hoover, J. H., Oliver, R., & Hazler, R. J. (1992). Bullying: Perceptions of adolescent victims in the Midwestern USA. *School Psychology International, 13,* 5–16.

Hymel, S., & Swearer, S. M. (2008, November 10). Bullying: An age-old problem that needs new solutions. In S. Hymel, S. Swearer, & P. Gillette (Eds.), *Bullying at School and Online,* a special invited issue of Education.com. Retrieved from http://www.education.com/

Ireland, J., & Archer, J. (1996). Descriptive analysis of bullying in male and female adult prisoners. *Journal of Community and Applied Social Psychology, 6,* 35–47.

Josephson Institute. (2011). *Character counts.* Retrieved from http://charactercounts.org/

Juvonen, J., Graham, S., & Schuster, M. A. (2003). Bullying among young adolescents: The strong, the weak, and the troubled. *Pediatrics, 112,* 1231–1237.

Kasen, S., Berenson, K., Cohen, P., & Johnson, J. G. (2004). The effects of school climate on changes in aggressive and other behaviors related to bullying. In D. L. Espelage & S. M. Swearer (Eds.), *Bullying in American schools: A social-ecological perspective on prevention and intervention* (pp. 187–210). Mahwah, NJ: Lawrence Erlbaum Associates.

Khoury-Kassanbri, M., Benbenishty, R., Astor, R. A., & Zeira, A. (2004). The contributions of community, family, and school variables to student victimization. *American Journal of Community Psychology, 34,* 187–204.

Kumpfer, K. L. (1999). Factors and processes contributing to resilience: The resilience framework. In M. D. Glantz & J. L. Johnson (Eds.), *Resilience and development: Positive life adaptations* (pp. 179–224). New York, NY: Kluwer Academic/Plenum.

Kumpfer, K. L., & Alvarado, R. (2003). Family-strengthening approaches for the prevention of youth problem behaviors. *American Psychologist, 58,* 457–465.

Lam, D. O. B., & Liu, A. W. H. (2007). The path through bullying—A process model from the inside story of bullies in Hong Kong secondary schools. *Child and Adolescent Social Work Journal, 24,* 53–75.

Lawrence, R. (1998). *School crime and juvenile justice.* New York, NY: Oxford University Press.

Limber, S. P., & Small, M. A. (2003). State laws and policies to address bullying in schools. *School Psychology Review, 32,* 445–455.

Long, J. D., & Pellegrini, A. D. (2003). Bullying change in dominance and bullying with linear mixed models. *School Psychology Review, 32,* 401–417.

Lumeng, J. C., Forrest, P., Appugliese, D. P., Kaciroti, N., Corwyn, R. F., & Bradley, R. H. (2010). Weight status as a predictor of being bullied in third through sixth grades. *Pediatrics, 125,* 1301.

Madanes, C. (1981). *Strategic family therapy.* San Francisco, CA: Jossey-Bass.

Madanes, C. (2011). *Core beliefs.* Retrieved from http://www.cloemadanes.com/pages/core_beliefs.htm

Merrell, K. W., Gueldner, B. A., & Ross, S. W., & Isava, D. M. (2008). How effective are school bullying intervention programs? A meta-analysis of intervention research. *School Psychology Research, 23,* 26–42.

Nansel, T. R., Craig, W., Overpeck, M. D., Saluja, G., Ruan, W. J., & Health Behaviors in School-aged Children Bullying Analyses Working Group. (2004). Cross-national consistency in the relationship between bullying behaviors and psychosocial adjustment. *Archives Pediatrics and Adolescent Medicine, 158,* 730–736. doi: 10.1001/archpedi.158.8.730

Nansel, T. R., Overpeck, M., Pilla, R. S., Ruan, W. J., & Simons-Morton, B., & Scheidt, P. (2001). Bullying behaviors among US youth: Prevalence and association with psychosocial adjustment. *Journal of the American Medical Association, 285,* 2094–2100.

Nansel, T. R., Overpeck, M. D., Haynie, D. L., Ruan, W. J., & Scheidt, P.C. (2003). Relationships between bullying and violence among U.S. youth. *Archives of Pediatric Adolescent Medicine, 157,* 348–353.

Olweus, D. (1992). Bullying among school children: Intervention and prevention. In R. D. Peters, R. J. McMahan, & V. L. Quinsey (Eds.), *Aggression and violence throughout the life span* (pp. 100–125). London: Sage.

Olweus, D. (1994). Bullying at school: Basic facts and effects of a school based intervention program. *Journal of Psychology and Psychiatry, 35,* 1171–1190.

Patton, Z. (2010). *States get tough on bullies.* Retrieved from: http://www.governing.com/states-get-tough-bullies.html

Peeters, M., Cillessen, A. H. N., & Scholte, R. H. J. (2010). Clueless or powerful? Identifying subtypes of bullies. *Journal of Youth and Adolescence, 39,* 1041–1052.

Pellegrini, A. D. (2002). Bullying, victimization, and sexual harassment during the transition to middle school. *Educational Psychologist, 37,* 151–163.

Pellegrini, A. D., & Bartini, M. (2001). Dominance in early adolescent boys: Affiliative and aggressive dimensions and possible functions. *Merrill-Palmer Quarterly, 47,* 142–163.

Pepler, D., Jiang, D., Craig, W., & Connolly, J. (2008). Developmental trajectories of bullying and associated factors. *Child Development, 79,* 325–338.

Pepler, D. J., Craig, W. M., Connolly, J. A., Yuile, A., McMaster, L., & Jiang, D. (2006). A developmental perspective on bullying. *Aggressive Behavior, 32,* 376–384.

Peterson, J. S., & Ray, K. E. (2006a). Bullying and the gifted: Victims, perpetrators, prevalence, and effects. *Gifted Child Quarterly, 50,* 148–168.

Peterson, J. S., & Ray, K. E. (2006b). Bullying among the gifted: The subjective experience. *Gifted Child Quarterly, 50,* 252–269.

Powell, M. D., & Ladd, L. D. (2010). Bullying: A review of the literature and implications for family therapists. *The American Journal of Family Therapy, 38,* 189–206.

Pozzoli, T., & Gini, G. (2010). Active defending and passive bystanding behavior in bullying: The role of personal characteristics and perceived peer pressure. *Journal of Abnormal Child Psychology, 38,* 815–827.

Rivers, I., Poteat, V. P., Noret, N., & Ashurst, N. (2009). Observing bullying at school: The mental health implications of witness status. *School Psychology Quarterly, 24,* 211–223.

Rodkin, P. C., Farmer, T. W., Pearl, R., & Van Acker, R. (2006). They're cool: Ethnic and peer group supports for aggressive boys and girls. *Social Development, 36,* 14–24.

Salmivalli, C., Lagerspetz, K., Björkqvist, K., Österman, K., & Kaukiainen, A. (1996). Bullying as a group process: Participant roles and their relations to social status within the group. *Aggressive Behavior, 22,* 1–15.

Shields, A., & Cicchetti, D. (2001). Parental maltreatment and emotion dysregulation as risk factors for bullying and victimization in middle childhood. *Journal of Clinical Child and Adolescent Psychology, 30,* 349–363.

Swearer, S., Espelage, D. L., Vaillancourt, T., & Hymel, S. (2010). Challenges facing educators and researchers regarding school bullying: Linking research to educational practice. *Educational Researcher, 39,* 38–47.

Trach, J., Hymel, S., Waterhouse, T., & Neale, K. (2010). Bystander responses to school bullying: A cross-sectional investigation of grade and sex differences. *Canadian Journal of School Psychology, 25,* 114–130.

Tremlow, S. W., & Fonagy, P. (2005). The prevalence of teachers who bully students in schools with differing levels of behavioral problems. *American Journal of Psychiatry, 162,* 2387–2389.

Vaillancourt, T., Hymel, S., & McDougsall, P. (2003). Bullying is power: Implications for school-based intervention strategies. *Journal of Applied School Psychology, 19,* 157–176.

van der Wal, M. F., de Wit, C. A. M., & Hirasing, R. A. (2003). Psychosocial health among young victims and offenders of direct and indirect bullying. *Pediatrics, 111,* 1312–1317.

van Goethem, A. A. J., Scholte, R. H. J., & Wiers, R. W. (2010). Explicit- and implicit bullying attitudes in relation to bullying behavior. *Journal of Abnormal Child Psychology, 38,* 829–842.

Veenstra, R., Lindenberg, S., Munniksma, A., & Dijkstra, J. K. (2010). The complex relation between bullying, victimization, acceptance, and rejection: Giving special attention to status, affection, and sex differences. *Child Development, 81,* 480–486.

Veenstra, R., Lindenberg, S., Oldehinkel, A. J., DeWinter, A. F., Verhulst, F. C., & Ormel, J. (2005). Bullying and victimization in elementary schools: A comparison of bullies, victims, bully/victims, and uninvolved preadolescents. *Developmental Psychology, 41,* 672–682.

Vossekuil, B., Fein, R. A., Reddy, M., Borum, R., & Modzeleski, W. (2002). *The final report and findings of the safe school initiative: Implications for the prevention of school attacks in the United States.* Washington, DC: United States Secret Service and United States Department of Education.

Weissberg, R. P., Kumpfer, K. L., & Seligman, M. E. P. (2003). Prevention that works for children and youth: An introduction. *American Psychologist, 58,* 425–432.

Witvliet, M., Olthof, T., Hoeksma, J. B., Goossens, F. A., Smits, M. S. I., & Koot, H. M. (2009). Peer group affiliation of children: The role of perceived popularity, likeability, and behavioral similarity in bullying. *Social Development, 19,* 285–303.

Wolfe, D., Woods, S., Stanford, K., & Schulz, H. (2001). Bullying and victimization of primary school children in England and Germany: Prevalence and school factors. *British Journal of Psychology, 92,* 673–696.

EIGHT

Youth Suicide

The word suicide means to intentionally and deliberately kill oneself. Though the meaning and concept itself appear straightforward, how someone arrives at this point is quite complicated. How do the reasons to live become diminished by the reasons to die?

Suicide is a word typically not discussed due to the misconceptions and uneasiness it generates. However, a study from Columbia University (2005) found that talking about suicide actually helps by allowing our youth the opportunity to share their thoughts and to unburden themselves. By contrast, if we avoid this topic and discussion, we're sending the wrong message that we, as a society, don't care. The Columbia study reported that talking about suicide does not spur suicidal thoughts. Suicide needs to be discussed because so many precious lives are being lost to the silent darkness of pain. This chapter will review the prevalence, causes, and prevention of suicide in children and youth.

STATISTICAL REVIEW

Although it is important to review the data surrounding suicide, it is even more important that these data not be read as mere numbers. We can easily become desensitized or detached from the actual tragedies. We must remind ourselves that behind each number or statistic was once a hopeful and promising face.

According to the American Association of Suicidology, every 15 minutes, someone kills himself or herself. Every 38 seconds, someone attempts to kill himself or herself. Each completed suicide intimately

145

affects at least six other people. One in every 65 Americans knew someone who has committed suicide. The average annual number of suicides in the United States has increased from approximately 32,000 in 2006 to 34,598 in 2007. Overall, suicides outnumber homicides by almost two to one (McIntosh, 2010).

This chapter will focus on youth suicide. According to the Centers for Disease Control and Prevention (CDC), suicide is the third leading cause of death for youth between the ages 10 and 24 years. It results in approximately 4,400 lives lost each year (CDC, 2011). One young person kills him or herself every 2 hours and 7 minutes, and below age 15 years one suicide occurs every 2 hours (McIntosh, 2010).

Although research shows that rates of suicide increase with age, there are several specific characteristics pertaining to who is at most risk, including age, gender, sexual orientation, race, and ethnicity. The highest risk of suicide in the youth population is within the age 15 to 19 years compared with youth aged 10 to 14 years (Berman, Jobes, & Silverman, 2006). Gender appears to have a greater significance than race and ethnicity. Girls attempt suicide at three times the rate of boys; however, boys commit suicide at a rate of five times that of girls (Berman et al., 2006). Of the reported youth suicides in the 10- to 24-year-old age group, 83% were men and 17% were women (CDC, 2007).

Lesbian, gay, bisexual, and transgender/transsexual youth are at a much higher risk for suicide; some studies suggest that they may have an eightfold likelihood of attempted suicide compared with straight youth (Ryan et al., 2009).

In terms of race and ethnicity, the rates of attempted and completed suicides are highest among Native American populations, whereas the lowest are among Asian/Pacific Islanders. In general, White/Caucasian youth have had higher suicide rates than non-Whites; however, an alarming trend is emerging among African American males between the age 15 and 19 years. Within this age range, youth suicide has tripled increasing 234% between 1960 and 2000 (Berman et al., 2006).

The CDC's extensive Youth Risk Behavior Surveillance (YRBS) survey, a sampling of 16,410 high school students across 42 states in 2009, indicated that for an average classroom size of 25 students: 1 in 7 (13.8%) students thought about suicide; 1 in 8 (10.9%) students made a suicide plan; and 1.6 in 15 (6.3%) students made a suicide attempt during the year preceding the completion of the YRBS (CDC, 2009).

Further research on youth and suicide reveals

- 91% of teenagers surveyed indicated they would first tell a friend of their suicidal thoughts (Ross, 1985).
- 80% of suicidal individuals give verbal or behavioral clues of their intentions (Poland, 1989).
- In a research project reviewing 20 psychological autopsies from youth who committed suicide, aged 11 to 19 years, it was found that 85% of the suicide victims expressed suicide ideation at least once to parents, relatives, and, primarily, friends before they killed themselves; 80% verbalized their intention to kill themselves at least once during the previous days, weeks, or months before committing suicide; friends and peers were more aware of the victim's habits, behavior, suicidal ideation, threats, attempts, and drug and alcohol abuse than the parents, siblings, relatives, educators, or others (Pfeffer, 1989).
- Many experts believe that as many as nine of ten young people who commit suicide give clues as to their intentions well in advance (McEvoy & McEvoy, 2000).
- It is estimated that four of five suicide victims demonstrated identifiable warning signs before completing suicide.

Historically, funding designated to decrease and prevent suicide at both the national and state levels was almost nonexistent until the passage of the Garrett Lee Smith Memorial Act (PL 108–355) on September 9, 2004. This funding created a grant program at the Substance Abuse and Mental Health Services Administration (SAMHSA). This funding is to help states, tribes, and colleges/universities to develop, create, and implement a youth, adolescent, and college-age early intervention and prevention strategies to reduce suicide.

With great respect to all those working in the trenches to prevent suicide with limited or no resources, unless this type of funding that is specifically appropriated to establish preventative suicide programs and awareness at all levels continues, limited resources will limit the amount of effective programs in the future.

Joan Ryan, a writer for the San Francisco Chronicle, captured the essence of a family in mourning after losing a child to suicide. "When we think about protecting our children and keeping them safe, most of us think about things like drugs, cars, alcohol, and talking to strangers. We never thought about suicide. I often wonder how we keep our children safe when the greatest danger of all might come from within" (Ryan, 2006).

UNDERESTIMATING OFFICIAL SUICIDE DATA

In reviewing national suicide data and official statistics, there has been much debate about the classification of deaths by suicide. Many researchers have found that official annual suicide statistics are greatly underestimated due to misjudgments of cause of death by investigators and by classifications of the medical examiners (Pfeffer, 1989). Many suicides are intentionally intended to resemble accidents because the deceased do not want to be remembered as someone who committed suicide.

Without obvious evidence, a death may more likely be labeled a "suspicious death" versus a suicide (Granello & Granello, 2007). Researchers have called for the need to increase the accuracy in determining and classifying actual causes of death (Hawton, 1986; Shaffer & Fisher, 1981). Some have suggested that only one in five suicides is recorded as an actual suicide (Jobes, Berman, & Josselson, 1989). Many researchers agree that most suicides go unreported, are misclassified, or are labeled as suspicious. The gross underestimation of annual suicide data greatly suppresses the actual size and scope of the problem and, consequently, the availability of funding to develop, implement, and support effective programs to prevent suicide in both schools and communities.

As chilling as these statistics are, they cannot begin to measure the grief, anguish, confusion, guilt, and devastation felt by the family and friends of an adolescent who dies by suicide (Lester, 2000). A suicide leaves behind parents, friends, teachers, and mental health professionals searching for answers, trying to understand more fully why the suicide happened.

YOUTH SUICIDE: A CASE STUDY

It was 6:30 on a Friday evening when my phone rang. All I could hear were deep breaths and sobs, as the person calling was too upset to talk. Thinking this was a prank call, I started to hang up the phone but then heard a faint voice call my name. As she told me her name was "Allie," her face flashed in my mind. She was a 14-year-old girl I was counseling in school. Between deep breaths and sighs, Allie reported she had ingested half a bottle pills and was lying on the couch and beginning to feel "weird." No one was home. She said she wanted to die when she swallowed the pills, but now she was scared and realized she didn't want to die anymore.

She was reluctant to provide her address. In those days (prior to caller ID or cell phones), I had to coerce the address from her as her voice softened. She did not want to hang up the phone, even though I reassured her that I needed to be able to call for help. The police and fire department were dispatched to her home where they had to break down the front door.

Ultimately, Allie survived the attempt and later realized she almost made a fatal mistake. What drove Allie to the point of almost committing suicide was quite complicated. Allie just wanted to end her hidden pain—not her life.

How did she get to that point? Her story is a very rare case; that of a young girl who attempted suicide without telling friends or adults, or having previously exhibited any indicators of suicidal thoughts. However, Allie's actions were far from being an impulsive act. There was an event, "the straw that broke the camel's back," which made Allie feel that she couldn't take it anymore.

STRESSORS AND PROTECTIVE FACTORS

There is a complex procedure in the brain's attempts to decipher and shield itself from incoming stressors, events, or problems. As we attempt to cognitively process these elements, our success is based on our ability and skill to cope, adapt, react, and or respond. Hans Selye, known as the "father of stress research," documented the ways our stress responses can affect us both physiologically and mentally in his General Adaptation Syndrome model. When youth are unable to conquer stressors because of diminished or undeveloped adaptive skills, these stressors, and especially chronic or prolonged exposure to these stressors, can develop into physical or psychological illnesses (Selye, 1976).

The reasons a young person begins contemplating suicide are perplexing and elusive to even the experts. Why is Joey able to recover after being dumped by his girlfriend, whereas for the same reason, Allen attempts to hang himself? The integral elements that determine how a young person will respond to stress are related specifically to the youth's perception of the event/stressor, the social supports and resources that are readily accessible (Kirk, 1993), and the skills developed to cope with stress (Seifert, 2006). Having the youth identify and explore at least three protective factors, reasons for living, have been linked to reducing the risk of suicide attempts by 70% to 85% (Borowsky, Ireland, & Resnick, 2001).

These protective factors play a role in mitigating current and future suicidal risk in persons who are found to be moderate to low risk (Kavan, Guck, & Barone, 2006). What the youth identifies as his/her protective factors may buffer or reduce the impact of this perceived risk, interrupt a chain of risk factors, and prevent the possible onset of a risk factor (Jenson & Fraser, 2006).

Some of the stressors/variables that may contribute to suicidal thinking include dysfunctional families, alcohol or drug abuse, neighborhood problems, violence, parental divorce, physical or sexual abuse, experiencing loss, bullying, increased educational demands, violent games, depression or mental illness, and sexual orientation (McEvoy & McEvoy, 2000).

Youth are prone to exaggerate the importance or significance of their own thoughts, feelings, and perceptions (Fetsch, Collins, & Whitney, 2008). With this in mind, having the ability and flexibility to cope with life's challenges and changes is vital for survival through difficult and intense times.

One of the most interesting things I learned in my interviews and assessments of hundreds of youth for suicide was that most were unable to comprehend or correlate death to a permanent and irreversible final state. Again, it is this inability to think in terms of the future that becomes even more powerful when experiencing stressors and or problems.

What happens to these basic primal cognitive skills and abilities under exposure to stressors has become an intriguing mystery to researchers. The skills once used to decipher and interpret perceived threats while searching for solutions and resources in our children and youth seem to disintegrate under exposure to intense stressors.

These stressors do not have to be prolonged before the reality and decision-making skills become impaired and catapult a reaction that seems impulsive. These stressors also cause youth to feel helpless or defenseless (Kirk, 1993). Undeveloped or maladaptive coping skills coupled with poor interpersonal skills greatly decreases or limits the child's/adolescent's ability to problem solve and therefore increases the likelihood suicide will be considered the only solution (McBride & Siegel, 1997).

The intensity of this disintegration results in a young person quickly wanting to find an immediate solution to the problem, shutting down his or her own executive functioning ability to reason, rationalize, dissect the problem or problems, and seek help. This is especially true if the young people believe there is no one who understands them. During the interview phase of suicide assessment, I have never met any persons who wanted to kill themselves for no apparent reason. It always involved a precipitating element or a contributing factor to a preexisting psychological condition.

A precipitating factor or stressor may be an event that contributes to the youth's presenting problem while simultaneously being a catalyst to elicit some levels of adaptability. This may result in having the ability to cognitively process for the appropriate reaction to the stressor or may result in poor decision making or an impulsive choice.

These precipitating factors/stressors can be absorbed from an external source: parents separating, feeling bullied, breakup with boyfriend or girlfriend, rumors, etc. They can also develop internally from a biological/hereditary mental illness. Some examples are major depressive disorder, bipolar disorder, anxiety, learning disibility, or physical disability (U.S. Department of Health and Human Services, 2000).

Another risk factor is being exposed to traumatic events during infancy and/or childhood, such as neglect, physical or sexual abuse, isolation, and so on. The latent effects could be symptoms of post-traumatic stress disorder or developmental trauma disorder (Van der Kolk, Silberg, & Waters, 2003), such as anxiety, depression, and avoidance of events that would remind them of their trauma (Perry, 1994). They may have nightmares and be more susceptible to dissociate (Seifert, 2006).

Depending on a person's support systems, what might be a breaking point for some is not for others; hence, the mystery of why some choose to attempt or commit the ultimate act of violence, whereas others are able to cope or find mental health treatment or other supports.

With "Allie," the hidden problem of having been exposed to sexual abuse without supports or interventions was potentially catastrophic. She kept all the emotions, anger, and blame to herself; over time they manifested in a chronic state of hopelessness. She did not want to relive the memories repeatedly. Allie's hidden pain erupted and ultimately led to her suicide attempt.

THE WARNING SIGNS OF YOUTH SUICIDE

There are common behaviors or symptoms linked to youth who maybe either at risk for or experiencing suicidal thoughts. Risk factors and symptoms related to suicidal thinking among our youth are well documented and researched. Identified precipitating risk factors known to be associated with suicidal thoughts may include, but are not limited to, the following (Poland, 1989):

- experiencing family problems
- having a recent breakup with a boyfriend or girlfriend
- identifying as gay or lesbian
- experiencing a recent loss
- feeling bullied
- witnessing or being exposed to violence
- having a difficult relationship with parents
- a history of or experiencing physical, psychological, or sexual abuse
- parents' divorce or separation
- peer relational problems
- family financial difficulties
- school problems
- history of mental illness or depression
- knowing someone who died from suicide
- talking about death or dying
- self-drawings of death, hanging, shooting, or being shot
- learning or physical disability
- giving away prized possessions

- withdrawing
- chronic exposure to stress

Unless teachers, staff, parents, and community members are trained in recognizing these warning signs, youth at risk may not be identified as such. In a national sample of high school health teachers, only 9% believed they could recognize a student at risk for suicide (King, Price, Telljohann, & Wahl, 1999).

Research conducted by Ross (1985) found that 91% of teenagers surveyed indicated they would first tell a friend of their suicidal thoughts and that 80% of suicidal individuals give verbal or behavioral clues of their intentions (Poland, 1989). In a research project reviewing 20 psychological autopsies of victims from ages 11 to 19 years, it was found that 85% of the suicide victims expressed suicidal ideation at least once to parents, to relatives, and, primarily, to friends before they killed themselves. At least 80% verbalized their intention to kill themselves at least once during the previous days, weeks, or months before committing suicide. Friends and peers were more aware of the victim's habits, behavior, suicidal ideation, threats, attempts, drug, and alcohol abuse than the parents, siblings, relatives, educators, or others (Pfeffer, 1989). Many experts believe that as many as nine of ten young people who commit suicide give prior clues as to their intentions well in advance (McEvoy & McEvoy, 2000).

Some of the clues projected to parents, teachers, and peers are subtle and may be very easily overlooked. They can also become camouflaged within casual conversation, much like the student who tried to make weekend plans with her friend but who said casually, "Who knows, I might not be here." There are many clues given both verbally and behaviorally.

Examples of verbal clues include such statements as

1. The world would be better without me.
2. I can't do this anymore.
3. I can't go on without him/her.
4. You won't see me Monday.
5. Who would know if I even existed?
6. You won't see me again.
7. Please remember, I'll always love you very much.
8. I can't take it anymore.
9. Telling friends/family/teachers good-bye or thanking them

Examples of behavioral clues include

1. Giving away prized possessions
2. Writing poetry or drawing about death
3. Making final plans or arrangements as if going on a trip
4. Changes in school attendance or work
5. Decreased grades, increased suspensions, or disciplinary referrals
6. Withdrawal from activities
7. Change in physical appearance
8. Self-isolation or withdrawal from peers
9. Changes in mood

It is estimated that four of five suicide victims demonstrated identifiable warning signs before completing suicide (Poland & Lieberman, 2002). They are telling us of their intentions; reaching out to us. We need to listen.

PROGRAMS AND SUPPORTS FOR SUICIDAL YOUTH

To break the cycle of violence, including suicide, social disengagement, and psychological deterioration, effective prevention and intervention programs must be made readily available to children and youth (Schmidt, 2006). To accomplish this, it is the author's belief that there is no greater venue than the school system. Schools provide the unconditional support and structure for effective implementation and program monitoring.

In providing national technical support in building suicide prevention and school-based mental health programs to school districts, I have experienced more resistance and lack of follow through than I have for support in establishing self-sustainable and research-focused programs. There are some school administrators and community members who still believe that the discussion of suicide will make kids suicidal. Some believe suicide is not a problem in their district or community. There are many who avoid the issue within our communities but who are also charged to gatekeep the safety of our children. This is extremely alarming if the goal is to protect and prevent youth suicide. It is crucial to break the cycle of complacency concerning this issue because young lives are at stake. This is even more urgent for teenagers because thoughts of suicide and suicide attempts increase with age and peak during high school (Vega, Gil, Warheit, Apospori, & Zimmerman, 1993).

There are several reasons for this complacency, with fear, confidentiality, and liability being at the top. Of these, the major concern revolves around liability. Some schools are yet to realize that they are already liable for the safety and well being of their students during school hours. Schools have both an ethical and legal responsibility to establish clear, reasonable, and appropriate policies and procedures to prevent youth suicide (Jacob & Hartshorne, 2007). School personnel and mental health professionals alike must act when a child or adolescent is found to be presenting with suicidal thoughts or when the problems are brought to their attention.

There are several suicide prevention programs that are making a significant impact through educating staff, students, and community on the signs and symptoms of depression and suicide prevention. These programs can be incorporated within the school or community setting. They include the Yellow Ribbon Suicide Prevention Program (YRSPP), Applied Suicide Intervention Skills Training (ASIST), Signs of Suicide (SOS) Program, and the Suicide Risk Assessment and Management Training Program (QPRT). These programs have been recognized and listed in Section III of the Best Practices Registry (BPR) for addressing specific objectives of the National Strategy for Suicide Prevention. The BPR is a collaborative effort of the Suicide Prevention Resource Center (SPRC) and the American Foundation for Suicide Prevention. This project is funded by the SAMHSA. (To access the complete listing of the National Registry of Best and Promising Suicide Prevention Programs please visit the SPRC's Web site at www2.sprc.org.)

The YRSPP (www.yellowribbon.org) was founded in 1994 by the parents and friends of a bright, funny, loving teen, Mike Emme, who took his life because he did not know how to let someone know he was in trouble and needed help. As a result, Michael's parents and classmates developed a "Yellow Ribbon Card" to use as a resource if a student didn't know how to ask for help. The card contains simple instructions on what to do if a student or a friend is having thoughts of suicide and also provides crisis hotline phone numbers.

The YRSPP is a Gatekeeper Program that includes a standardized 2-day training that focuses on increasing peer help-seeking behaviors by sending the message, "It's OK to Ask 4 Help." The Gatekeeper Training Program is a community-based program developed to address youth/teen suicide through public awareness campaigns, education, and training, and by assisting communities to build capacity. It identifies known warning signs and risk factors for suicide, provides designated school staff or teacher training to "Be-A-Link & Save-A-Life," and empowers youth to Ask 4 Help. The training further provides participants with knowledge to help them identify youth at risk for suicide and refer them to appropriate help resources.

The YRSPP offers two trainings, including a high school curriculum-based training entitled "Ask 4 Help! Suicide Prevention for Youth" and "Be A Link! Suicide Prevention Gatekeeper Training." The key focus of the Ask 4 Help curriculum provides students with the knowledge to increase help-seeking behaviors for themselves or on behalf of others through the use of the Yellow Ribbon Suicide Prevention Card. This card provides three easy steps on how to help either themselves or others while providing immediate access to national hotline phone numbers listed in it.

The second training, "Be A Link! Suicide Prevention Gatekeeper Training" can be introduced into a variety of settings, including both in schools and within the community. The training offers participants knowledge to help identify youth at risk for suicide and how to refer to appropriate resources. Training includes information on

- Risk factors and suicide warning signs.
- School and community referral points for those who may need help.
- Crisis protocols for those who may be at risk, including the use of the National Suicide Prevention Lifeline phone number.

The ASIST (www.livingworks.net) is another standardized 2-day training that is designed for all caregiving professions. The central feature of ASIST emphasizes teaching the skills of suicide first aid to help a person who is at risk stay safe and to seek further help if necessary. This includes learning a suicide intervention model: identify persons with suicidal thoughts; increase understanding of reasons for living and dying; review risk and develop a safe plan; and to complete follow-up, including becoming involved in suicide-safer community networks. The key program objectives upon completing the ASIST training include

- Recognize that caregivers and persons at risk are affected by personal/societal attitudes about suicide.
- Discuss suicide in a direct manner with someone at risk.
- Identify risk alerts and develop related safe plans.
- Demonstrate skills required to intervene with a person at risk for suicide.
- List types of resources available to a person at risk, including themselves.
- Make a commitment to improving community resources.
- Recognize suicide prevention is broader than suicide first-aid and includes life promotion and self-care for caregivers.

The Signs of Suicide (SOS) Middle School Program (www.mental-healthscreening.org) offers a universal prevention approach to assist in the identification of at-risk youth by addressing issues of depression, suicide, and self-injury. School professionals show a video that teaches students how to identify symptoms of depression and suicidality in themselves or their friends. The SOS program also offers an optional student screening assessment for depression and suicide risk and identifies students to refer for professional help. The SOS program objectives include

- Increase awareness and knowledge of the symptoms of depression and suicide.
- Increase knowledge of how and where to seek help for themselves or peers.
- Decrease stigma related to mental illness.
- Increase identification of at-risk students (if screening option is used).

The QPRT Suicide Risk Assessment and Management Training Program (www.qprinstitute.com) was developed to reduce consumer morbidity and mortality by standardizing the detection, assessment, and management of patients at elevated risk for suicidal behaviors in all settings and across the age span. QPRT incorporates guided clinical interviews for suicide risk assessment and exploration of protective factors, suicidal ideation, desire, intent, planning, past attempts, and other self-reports of suicide propensity. The OPRT Program objectives include

- Competence/confidence in the assessment and management of those at risk for suicide.
- Ability to document suicide risk assessment and clinical decision making.
- Skills to conduct a suicide risk assessment.
- Ability to produce a standardized suicide risk assessment.

A Mid-Atlantic rural school district in Maryland, Talbot County Public Schools (TCPS), adopted the YRSPP in 2003. In 2002, a "suicide contagion" was uncovered within this district: 18 students in a single high school talking about acting on suicidal thoughts. (Further inquiry revealed that these students were classmates of a fellow student who committed suicide several years before.) While conducting teacher and staff training on the signs and symptoms of depression and suicidal ideation, TCPS decided to search for a suicide prevention program they could implement.

After reviewing nine nationally and internationally developed suicide prevention programs, they chose the YRSPP. Why was this program chosen over the others, especially since it wasn't research based or registered at the time as a Best Practice by the SAMHSA?

In reviewing research on youth and suicide, TCPS realized that difficulty in communicating suicidal intent was a key aspect that needed addressing, and the YRSPP addressed that issue. Since the adoption of the YRSPP in 2003, the district documented 39 school-aged youth using their Yellow Ribbon Card in asking for help.

In addition to the YRSPP, TCPS annually distributes Yellow Ribbon Cards, T-shirts with the Maryland Youth Crisis Hotline phone number (1-800-422-0009), and silicone wristbands that state "It's OK to Ask 4 Help," with the Maryland Youth Crisis Hotline phone number, and provides teacher training and an annual Pre/Post Knowledge Survey of 10 questions with parental permission.

Prior to the adoption of the YRSPP, TCPS was collecting data on youth suicidal ideation specific to their school district, which uses the data to allocate internal resources to prepare for each school year. The data continue to be collected, spanning 11 consecutive years (Schmidt, 2011). Some of the data are included below (see Table 8.1):

Between 1999 and 2010, based on 2,461 school-based mental health (SBMH) referrals

- an average of 224 unduplicated SBMH referrals occurred annually
- 37% (937) were generated by the school counselor
- grades 6 and 9 are the most referred (grade 9 the more frequent)
- chief complaints or reasons for referral were depressive type symptoms, family problems, behavior problems, symptoms of anxiety, grief or loss, suicidal ideation, and other
- two key spikes were seen in referrals, with October having the most, followed by February

Data on suicidal ideation indicate

- February had the most suicidal ideation referrals, 37, October followed with 22
- 9th grade had the greatest number of youth with suicidal ideation (32), followed by 7th grade (26), 6th grade (24), 8th grade (22), 10th grade (21), and 3rd grade (16).

The aforementioned Suicide Prevention Programs as well as SBMH Programs are becoming routinely adopted by school districts across the United States. Schools are realizing that in order for them to meet their increasing and demanding educational goals and objectives, they

TABLE 8.1 Reasons for Suicidal Ideation per Grade: 2007/2008 (TCPS)

Grade	Within Past Year (*n* = 153)	Past Few Days (*n* = 47)
6	Tied: family problems/grief, loss	Problems with peers—bullying
7	Stress	Stress
8	Family problems	Depressive symptoms
9	Family problems	Family problems
10	Family problems	Family problems
11	Family problems	Depressive symptoms
12	Breakup with boy/girlfriend	Tied: stress; family Breakup with boy/girlfriend

Source: Schmidt, 2011.
N = 200/1,767 (1,567 reported no SI). TCPS = Talbot County Public Schools.

must provide increasingly supportive programs for their students and families (Schmidt, 2006).

REFERENCES

American Association of Suicidology. (2006). *Youth suicide fact sheet*. Retrieved from http://www.sucidology.org

Berman, A. L., Jobes, D. A., & Silverman, M. M. (2006). *Adolescent suicide: Assessment and intervention*. Washington, DC: American Psychological Association.

Borowsky, I. W., Ireland, M., & Resnick, M. D. (2001). Adolescent suicide attempts: Risks and Protectors. *Pediatrics, 107,* 485–493.

CDC. (2007). *Web-based Injury Statistics Query and Reporting System (WISQARS™)*. Atlanta, GA: Author. Retrieved from http://www.cdc.gov/ncipc/wisqars/default.htm

Centers for Disease Control and Prevention. (2011). *Youth suicide*. Retrieved from http://www.cdc.gov/violenceprevention/pub/youth_suicide.html

Center for Disease Control and Prevention. (2010). Youth risk behavior surveillance, United States, 2009. *Morbidity and Mortality Weekly Report, 59,* SS-5.

Center for Disease Control and Prevention. (2007). Suicide trends among youths and adults aged 10–24 years—United States, 1990–2004. *Morbidity and Mortality Weekly Review, 56,* 905–908.

Emme, D., & Emme, D. (1994). Co-Founders—Yellow Ribbon Suicide Prevention Program. Light For Life Foundation, International/Executive & Deputy Director. PO Box 644 Westminster, Colorado 80036-0644; www.yellowribbon.org

Fetsch, J. R., Collins, L. C., & Whitney, D. (2008). *Preventing youth and adult suicide*. Colorado State University Extension, No. 10.213. Retrieved from http://www.ext.colostate.edu/pubs/consumer/10213.html.

Granello, D. & Granello, P. (2007). *Suicide: An essential guide for helping professionals and educators*. Stratford Publishing Services. Brattleboro, VT: Pearson Education, Inc.

Hawton, K. (1986). Suicide in adolescents. In A. Roy (Ed.), *Suicide* (pp. 135–150). Baltimore, MD: Williams & Wilkins.

Jacob, S., & Hartshorne, T. S. (2007). *Ethics & law for school psychologists* (5th ed.). Hoboken, NJ: John Wiley and Sons.

Jenson, J. M., & Fraser, M. W. (2006). A risk and resilience framework for child, youth and family policy. In J. M. Jenson & M. W. Fraser (Eds.), *Social policy for children and families. A risk and resilience perspective* (pp. 1–18). Thousand Oaks: Sage.

Jobes, D. A., Berman, A. L., & Josselson, A. R. (1989). Improving the validity and reliability of medical-legal certifications of suicide. *Suicide and Life-Threatening Behavior,* 31 (Suppl.), 106-121.

Kavan, M. J., Guck, T. P., & Barone, E. J. (2006). A practical guide to crisis management. *American Family Physician, 74,* 1159–1164.

King, K., Price, J., Telljohann, S., & Wahl, J. (1999). High school health teachers perceived self-efficacy in identifying students at risk for suicide. *Journal of School Health, 69*(5), 202–207.

Kirk, W. (1993). *Adolescent suicide.* Champaign, IL: Research Press.

Lester, D. (2000). *Suicide prevention: Resources for the millennium.* Ann Arbor, MI: Sheridan Books.

Linehan, M., Goodstein, J., Nielsen, S., & Chiles, J. (1983). Reasons for staying alive when you are thinking of killing yourself: The Reasons for Living Inventory. *Journal of Consulting and Clinical Psychology, 51*(92), 276–286.

McBride, H., & Siegel, S. (1997). Learning disabilities and adolescent suicide. *Journal of Learning Disabilities,* 30(6), 652–659.

McEvoy, L., & McEvoy, A. (2000). *Preventing youth suicide* (2nd ed.). Holmes Beach, FL: Learning Publications, Inc.

McIntosh, J. L. (for the American Association of Suicidology). (2010). *U.S.A. suicide 2007: Official final data.* Washington, DC: American Association of Suicidology. Retrieved from http://www.sucidology.org

Perry, B., & Murburg, M. (Eds.). (1994). Neurobiological sequel of childhood trauma: Post traumatic stress disorders in children. In M. Murburg (ed.), *Catecholamine function in posttraumatic stress disorder: Emerging concepts* (pp. 276–353). Washington, DC: American Psychiatric Press.

Pfeffer, C. R. (1989). *Suicide among youth: Perspectives on risk and prevention.* Washington, DC: American Psychiatric Press.

Poland, S. (1989). *Suicide prevention in the schools.* New York, NY: Guilford Press.

Poland, S., & Lieberman, R. (2002). Best practices in suicide intervention. In A. Thomas & J. Grimes (Eds.), *Best practices in school psychology IV* (pp. 1151–1165). Bethesda, MD: National Association of School Psychologists.

Ross, C. (1985). Teaching children the facts of life and death: Suicide prevention in the schools. In M. Peck, N. Farberow, & R. Litman (Eds.), *Youth suicide* (pp. 147–1690). New York, NY: Springer Publishing Company.

Ryan, C., Huebner, D., Diaz, R. M., & Sanchez, J. (2009). Family rejection as a predictor of negative health outcomes in white and Latino lesbian, gay, and bisexual young adults. *Pediatrics, 123*(1), 346–352.

Ryan, J. (2006). The Darkness Behind his Perfect Smile. *The San Francisco Chronicle.* January 15, 2006: B-1.

Schmidt, R. (2006). Chapter 12: A promising practice for the future; School-Based Mental Health. In K. Seifert (Ed.), *How children become violent* (pp. 223–236). Boston, MA: Acanthus Publishing.

Schmidt, R. (2011). *Lecture presentation on using the Risk Identification Suicide Kit (RISK).* Centreville, MD: Queen Anne's County Public Schools.

Seifert, K. (2006). *How children become violent.* Boston, MA: Acanthus.

Selye, H. (1976). *The stress of life* (2nd ed.). New York, NY: McGraw-Hill.

Shaffer, D., & Fisher, P. (1981). The epidemiology of suicide in children and young adolescents. *Journal of American Academy of Child Psychiatry, 20,* 545–565.

U.S. Department of Health and Human Services. (2000). *Mental health: A report of the surgeon general.* Washington, DC: Author.

Van der Kolk, B., Silberg, J., & Waters, F. (2003). *Complex PTSD in children.* Towson, MD: Sidran Institute.

Vega, W., Gil, A., Warheit, G., Apospori, E., & Zimmerman, R. (1993). The relationship of drug use to suicide ideation and attempts among African American, Hispanic, and White non-Hispanic male adolescents. *Journal of the American Association of Suicidology, 23*(2), 110–119.

Assessment, Prevention, and Intervention

NINE

Violence Risk Assessment for Children and Adolescents

Congresswoman Gabrielle Giffords was holding a "meet-and-greet" outside a Safeway in Tucson, Arizona when shots rang out. Tragically, 6 people were killed and 14 were injured. The 22-year-old suspect, Jared Lee Loughner, was tackled by bystanders when he attempted to reload his gun.

> Loughner reportedly had a troubled past, including drug use, multiple arrests, and incidents of vandalism. He was prone to outbursts in class; classmates described him as troubled and socially immature. His online writings and YouTube videos were rambling, delusional, and possibly psychotic. He may have associated with a white supremacist group. On his Facebook page, he listed "Mein Kampf" as one of his favorite books.
>
> Loughner was allegedly suspended from Pima Community College after posting a disturbing video and having several interactions with campus police. He was told he could not return to school unless he got a mental health clearance.

Jared Lee Loughner's case illustrates the importance of violence risk assessment. In many cases as extreme as his, there are warning signs long before any significant violence takes place. Violence risk and needs assessments are necessary in several contexts. Youth who demonstrate violent behaviors often have very complex sets of risk and resiliency factors. These factors need to be identified to develop an individualized treatment plan. They may influence placement decisions made by those in the juvenile justice, social services, and/or mental health systems. For youth who are likely to hurt themselves or another person, client and public safety must also be a consideration in the treatment plan.

Traditionally, these decisions have been made and are often still made by professionals using clinical judgment, which has a correct classification rate (dangerous vs. not dangerous) at chance levels (Rice, 2005). Risk and needs classification tools exceed clinical judgment in correctly determining which individual will most likely commit a violent act in the future and which will not.

Assessment for risk of violence is a relatively new field when applied to children and adolescents. Since children change rapidly, risk assessments can only be applied for very short periods of time (6 months) (Borum, Bartel, & Forth, 2002). In addition, Thornberry, Huizinga, and Loeber (2004) determined that violence occurs intermittently and may not occur at all for long periods of time for an individual youth. There is also some debate about unnecessarily stigmatizing children and teens, for example, by using the term psychopath.

There is also professional debate about the use of actuarial tools and risk assessments with juveniles. The argument for using actuarials is the research demonstrating that for adults, actuarials offer a better assessment of future risk than clinical judgment (Rice, 2005). Arguments against are typically based on fears of stigmatizing a child, and the inability of existing tools to take into account the plasticity of youth development.

This chapter proposes that violence is an interpersonal behavior that has a developmental trajectory and is influenced by environment, caregiver bonding, neurological development, and individual characteristics, such as temperament, genetics, and intelligence. A risk tool that measures dynamic factors that change over time, as well as historical factors, could capture a measure of risk at a particular point in time. A comprehensive risk assessment tool should present treatment and behavior management options, rather than just measuring risk.

This is in keeping with the general trend in violence risk assessments, which has shifted from a violence prediction model to a clinical model of risk assessment and management and evidence-based treatment. The task is to determine the nature and degree of risk an individual may pose, for whom, under what circumstances, and what preventive action to take.

Assessing for risk is the first step in preventing future violence, but we must understand that measuring risk is never 100% accurate. Risk means probability. There is an "X%" chance that someone will be violent in the future. This does not tell us when in the future, under what conditions, or to whom the violence will occur. However, it can inform suggestions for safety and treatment. Someone who is at high risk for future violence must be approached with caution and with safety in mind at all times, but we do not need to treat dangerous children or adolescents any differently than other clients in terms of emotional approach.

Violence risk assessments are extremely important and must include not only an individual child but also his or her family, school, peer group, and community. There are several tenets of systems that are useful in looking at children and families:

- Systems are made up of many interactive parts.
- The whole is more than the sum of its parts.
- Every part of a system can change and this will affect another part of the system.
- A well-functioning system will gather information from other systems and grow and learn from the interactions fairly easily.
- Closed systems will reject information and relationships from the outside and are more likely to be unhealthy.

With knowledge of how the child functions within his various systems and the impact of the systems on the child, an assessment and treatment plan can be multidimensional and more effective (Kashani, Jones, Bumby, & Thomas, 1999). To accomplish this, a professional must evaluate the youth and family, as well as school and community factors. This chapter will examine all aspects of violence risk assessment with children and adolescents.

ASSESSMENT OF YOUTH

Assessment of youth should include a minimum of the following topics gathered from multiple sources (the child, parents or guardians, family members, teachers, other service providers):

- neonatal and birth history
- developmental history
- school history, learning, and behavior
- family history

- any history of violence, trauma, or significant losses
- incidents of violence by the youth (with details)
- behavioral issues, if any
- intelligence quotient (IQ) levels
- level of development of life skills, such as executive functioning, regulation of emotions, adaptive abilities, interpersonal skills, and self-monitoring of behavior (Behavioral Objective Sequence; Braaten, 1998)
- history of court involvement, if any
- relationships to family members, peers, authority figures
- sexual development
- strengths
- results of any psychological evaluations
- physical and mental health
- history of illness, treatment, medication, and efficacy (physical and mental)
- important cultural ideas or influences
- awareness of emotional triggers
- history of substance use or abuse

Psychological testing should be a part of the youth assessment. Psychologists can assess IQ, personality, psychopathology, developmental maturity, trauma, strengths, and problems. Much of this can be done by standardized testing, such as the Wechsler Intelligence Scale for Children–IV (Wechsler, 2004) and the Millon Adolescent Clinical Inventory (MACI; Millon, 2006).

Self-report instruments, such as the MACI (Millon, 2006), alone, however, are insufficient for this population because there may be a great variance between what children and adolescents report versus their actual behavior. Therefore, for reliable assessment of this population, information must be taken from multiple informants: the youth, parents/caregivers, the school environment, peers, and the community.

ASSESSMENT OF PARENTS/CAREGIVERS

An evaluation of the parents/caregivers will give a picture of the home environment and dynamic, how the youth is affecting those in the home and how they are affecting the youth. Topics to explore include

- Attachment and trauma history
- Family of origin and functioning (genograms may help with this)
- Awareness of emotional and environmental triggers
- Parents' mental health and stability
- Relationships among siblings and between children and parents or caregivers
- Stressors
- Support systems
- Family dynamics and patterns
- Stress management effectiveness
- Rules, roles, and boundaries
- Parenting attitudes and competencies
    - Can they provide a loving nurturing home with affection, routine, structure, and boundaries?
    - What is their knowledge base and skill level in anger management, reframing the meaning of behavior, and teaching rather than punishing?
    - Do they have knowledge of attachment and trauma and how to help children heal?
- Health of the individuals and the marital dyad. Ability to communicate and problem solve
- History of substance abuse? History of violence? History of child abuse/neglect?

The health of the family will play an important part in helping children and teens gain healthy skills and functioning. Family therapy is an evidence-based practice for many youth at risk for violence. Caregivers may also need therapy for themselves.

ASSESSMENT OF THE SCHOOL ENVIRONMENT

It is important to know if the youth being assessed is successful in school, academically and socially. Talking to the youth, family, teachers, and school counselors can give the professional a picture of school life and whether it is a stressor, or is building strengths.

The school, in partnership with the youth, parents, and other professionals, can work to help a child or teen overcome any learning difficulties due to developmental, cognitive, mental health, family, or substance abuse problems.

As discussed in Chapter 7, bullying has become an epidemic in U.S. schools. If bullying is complicating the clinical picture, adults need to address this with the school and ensure that appropriate safeguards and services are in place. School-based mental health services address bullying problems very well, as do school-wide antibullying programs, such as Olweus (discussed in Chapter 10).

ASSESSMENT OF PEER RELATIONSHIPS

Research suggests that associating with a peer group that is also getting into trouble, engaging in delinquency, and using violence to get their needs met is strongly associated with youth violence (Welsh, Schmidt, McKinnon, Chattha, & Meyers, 2008). Having prosocial peers can be a protective factor against violent behavior. Peer relationships can best be assessed through interviews with the youth, family members, and school personnel. Although it may seem daunting to collect such massive amounts of information, each piece to the puzzle helps create a clearer picture of what is going on and what services are needed. The more people a youth has in his life who are pushing him in an antisocial direction, the harder the job of the professional becomes.

ASSESSMENT OF COMMUNITY ENVIRONMENT

As discussed in Chapter 6, community violence, easy access to guns and drugs, and a tacit or open approval of crime can greatly influence youth, especially if the community offers few positive outlets or opportunities. In some communities, gang membership offers the only opportunity for financial gain and security. If the community environment supports crime and gangs, there is little professionals can do to counteract that, especially in 1 hour per week in the therapist's office. A counter influence needs to be found within the community.

The community can be assessed by various socioeconomic indicators, such as levels of crime, substance abuse, and high school dropout rates. If the community is a significant negative influence, the community must change; this requires community action to rally neighbors to pull together to improve their neighborhood. The old-fashioned community worker/community organizer is needed as much as the teacher and the therapist.

RISK ASSESSMENT TOOLS

The risk factors used in most adult risk assessment tools have been clearly established in the literature, and most youth risk tools use many of the same items. The completion of any risk assessment tool first requires that the clinician gather a complete psychosocial history based on record review, direct interviews with the youth, and interviews with collateral informants such as parents, teachers, therapists, and so on.

Each risk assessment tool has unique characteristics. By comparing tools, practitioners can determine which tool(s) are best suited to their needs and their population(s). First, one must measure the approximate level of risk that a person poses for harm to self or others. Most violent risk assessment tools have receiver operating characteristics (ROCs; correct classification rates) from 60 to 93. A professional must carefully choose which risk assessment instrument best suits his or her needs based on population being assessed, population in the standardization sample, validity and reliability, and the presence of a manual to guide scoring. There should also be clinical guidance for treatment planning and need for structure.

The list of tools in this chapter is not exhaustive, but includes those most commonly used by practitioners.

The Centers for Disease Control and Prevention (CDC) has compiled a compendium of violence assessment tools (Dahlberg, Toal, Swahn, & Behrens, 2006) that includes more than 170 assessment tools, some of which have reliability statistics reported. The compendium can be found at http://www.cdc.gov/ncipc/pub-res/measure.htm.

Aside from the tools listed in the CDC compendium, there are several commercially available assessments for youth violence that are widely used and recognized. Some of these assessments have demonstrated reliability and validity; some have not been evaluated.

Thompson and Stewart (2006) described the necessary attributes of youth risk/needs assessments:

- Development must be through the use of empirical methods
- Tools must target reoffending
- Assessments should have solid theoretical underpinnings
- Static (unchanging) and dynamic (subject to change) factors should both be included
- Criminogenic risk, needs, and responsivity are important, such as the belief that the end (I get what I need) justifies the means (stealing)
- Items should cover multiple domains
- Instructions should include the need for information from multiple sources
- Use of actuarial decision making
- Provide for clinical overrides (this is controversial)
- Administration of the assessment according to its guidelines
- Good validity and reliability across populations
- User-friendly instrument
- Uses training to increase fidelity

The following section will review several assessment tools.

Structured Assessment of Violence Risk in Youth

The Structured Assessment of Violence Risk in Youth (SAVRY; Borum et al., 2002) is designed for ages 12 to 18 years and measures aggression and recidivism. It is composed of 24 risk items (historical, social/contextual, and individual) drawn from existing literature on adolescent development and aggression in youth. Six protective factors are also included.

Multiple studies have used the SAVRY. The AUCs (areas under the curve) indicate specificity and sensitivity characteristics of a test measuring a behavior that occurs infrequently. The ROCs are a statistical measure of the correct classification rate. If one uses this test on X number of students, what percentage of the classification decisions will be correct based on the actual criterion (in this case, actual violence). The AUCs and ROCs for this assessment are moderate to strong (total score ROC = .70; risk rating ROC = .89 with violence). Psychometrics are also good to very good (total score: r = .32 to .56 with violence; risk rating: r = .67 with violence; validity: r = .72 to .83). Reliability is .77 to .97 (Welsh et al., 2008).

The SAVRY is an empirically based, structured tool for guided clinical assessment. That is, the factors included in the tools are based on pertinent literature in the field, including published studies, and the instruments provide defined factors to be addressed and a specific structure to be followed by the clinician completing the evaluation. It is professionally scored. It does not recommend level or types of services. In addition, the developers of the SAVRY have included dynamic risk factors because personality and behavior traits are not stable in adolescence. For more information go to www.fmhi.usf.edu/mhlp/savry/statement.htm.

Child and Adolescent Risk/Needs Evaluation–2nd Version

The Child and Adolescent Risk/Needs Evaluation–2nd Version (CARE2; Seifert, 2007), created by the author of this volume, is for youth 6 to 19 years of age. It breaks out risk and resiliency that have been identified by a decade of research, by age and gender. There are suggestions for interventions that are evidence-based practice. Psychometrics are very good (ROC with violence = .88 to .91 for each age and gender group; correct classification rate is 88%–91%). This assessment is paper and pencil and is now available for online administration at http://care2systems.com. For more information on the paper and pencil version, go to http://drkathyseifert.com/book.html.

The CARE2 builds on its predecessor, the CARE, by refining the list used to identify dangerous behavior in children from ages 6 to 19 years. The evaluation tool takes into consideration a multitude of risk factors, which is clearly defined in the research on youth violence, including a youth's history of violence, severity of behavioral problems, substance abuse, impulsivity/attention deficit hyperactivity disorder, mental illness, abuse history, and family problems. Based on a scoring system of these in-depth risk factors, professionals can assess the best treatments and services to administer.

The CARE2 is based on the theory that the greater the number of risk factors and the fewer resiliency factors, the greater severity and chronicity of behavior problems (Welsh et al., 2008). The CARE2 assesses

- youth characteristics and behavior
- interaction with peers
- school/work behavior/success
- family characteristics
- protective factors

The CARE2 identifies "at-risk youth" as soon as possible. It has four scales, which differ by age and gender. It suggests treatment based on risk and resiliency factors. The validity association with violence in prepubescent males $r = .77$, ROC = .94; in teen males $r = .73$, ROC = .94; in preteen females $r = .73$, ROC = .98; in teen female $r = .72$, ROC = .93. It has a manual and peer review.

Youth Level of Service–Case Management Inventory

The LS-CMI (Hoge & Andrews, 2010b) is for youth 12 to 18 years of age. It has a very large sample and is widely used ($r = .26$ to .30, ROC = .40 to .67 for general recidivism; ROC for violence = .61 to .73; correct classification rate is 61%–73%). The LS-CMI is paper and pencil or on the Internet, and it recommends intensity of services necessary for optimal effectiveness. It includes a case management tool. Interrater reliability is .74 to .82. It has a manual and is peer reviewed with multiple studies. Information can be found at http://mhs.com/product.aspx?gr=saf&prod=yls-cmi&id=overview.

Positive Achievement Change Tool

This tool measures low, medium, and high risk for violent and non-violent recidivism. There are suggestions for interventions. The ROC with violent recidivism is .85 (correct classification rate is 85%, incorrect classification rate is 15%). The samples are very large, and this tool is widely accepted and used. More information can be found at www.assessments.com.

Psychopathic Checklist–Youth Version

The Psychopathic Checklist–Youth Version (PCL-YV; Forth, Kosson, & Hare, 2003) is a 20-item rating scale for the assessment of psychopathic traits in male and female offenders aged 12 to 18 years. Although Forth et al. (2003) believe that identifying youth with psychopathic traits is critical to understanding the factors that contribute to the development of adult psychopathy, the application of the concept of psychopathy to youth is very controversial. The youth PCL was adapted from the Hare Psychopathy Checklist–Revised (PCL-R), one of the most widely used measures of psychopathy in adults.

Using a semistructured interview and collateral information, the PCL-YV measures interpersonal, affective, and behavioral features related to the concept of psychopathy. The PCL-YV is professionally scored. Studies have found correlations with past violence to be good for males, but not females (ROC for male violence = .73; ROC for female violence = .50). Reliability is excellent. It does not recommend level or types of services. Information can be found at http://mhs.com/product.aspx?gr=saf&prod=pclyv&id=overview.

Early Assessment Risk Lists for Boys and Girls

The early assessment risk lists for boys and girls (EARL 20 B[oys] and 21G[irls]) (http://www.stopnowandplan.com/risk.php) is for ages 7 to 12 years. Research is still underway on this developing tool (Augimeri, Webster, Koegl, & Levene, 2001).

Comparison of Assessment Tools

Catchpole and Gretton (2003) compared the SAVRY, Youth Level of Service–Case Management Inventory (YLS-CMI), and PCL-YV for prediction of violent and general recidivism. The researchers used ROC analysis and "area under the curve" statistics. They found that all three instruments meaningfully distinguished youth at low or high risk for future violent offending, allowing the application of the most intensive services to the highest risk youth. Welsh et al. (2008) compared the validity of the SAVRY, PCL-YV and the YLS-CMI through a meta-analysis of 49 studies. They found that all three instruments

TABLE 9.1 Risk Assessment Comparison Chart

Instrument	Risk of violence—correct classification rate	Risk of recidivism/behavior problems—correct classification rate	Ages	Provides case management or interventions	Can be administered online with printed report
Unaided clinical judgment	50% (chance)	50% correct classification rate of recidivism (chance)	All	No	No
SAVRY	73% (moderate)	75% correct classification rate of recidivism (moderate)	12–18	No	No
CARE2	88%–95% (strong to very strong)	88%–95% correct classification rate of behavior problems (strong)	6–19	Yes	Yes
YLS-CMI	61%–73% (low to moderate)	61%–67% correct classification rate of recidivism (low)	12–18	Yes	Yes
MCASP/PACT/YASI	64% (low)	64% correct classification rate of recidivism (low)	12–18	Yes	Yes
PCL-YV	73% for males (moderate); 50% for females (chance levels)	63%–68% correct classification rate of recidivism—males (low); 50% recidivism—females (chance)	12–18	No	No

CARE2, The Child and Adolescent Risk/Needs Evaluation–2nd Version; MCASP, Maryland Comprehensive Assessment Service Planning; PACT, Positive Achievement Change Tool; PCL-YV, The Psychopathic Checklist–Youth Version; SAVRY, Structured Assessment of Violence Risk in Youth; YASI, Youth Assessment and Screening Instrument; YLS-CMI, Youth Level of Service–Case Management Inventory.

TABLE 9.2   ROC Comparison of the SAVRY and PCL-YV

	Violent recidivism	General recidivism
SAVRY-Total	.64	.69
SAVRY-Rating	.64	.69
PCL-YV	.54 (ns)	.60 (ns)

PCL-YV, The Psychopathic Checklist–Youth Version; ROC, receiver operating characteristics; SAVRY, Structured Assessment of Violence Risk in Youth.

TABLE 9.3   ROC Comparison of the SAVRY, PCL-YV, and YLS-CMI

	Violent recidivism	General recidivism
SAVRY	.81	.77
PCL-YV	.73	.74
YLS-CMI	.64	.60

PCL-YV, The Psychopathic Checklist–Youth Version; ROC, receiver operating characteristics; SAVRY, Structured Assessment of Violence Risk in Youth; YLS-CMI, Youth Level of Service–Case Management Inventory.

significantly and validly predicted future violent and nonviolent recidivism among juveniles. Thompson and Stewart's (2006) report found that the SAVRY, YLS-CMI, and the CARE had evidence of reliability, validity, use of risk and needs, and static and dynamic factors. Seifert (2007) compared the SAVRY, CARE2, and PCL-YV on a very small sample of youth (21). She found that all had acceptable validity and reliability in assessing risk for youth violence and the tools were highly correlated with each other. See Tables 9.1, 9.2, and 9.3.

MEASURING AND COMMUNICATING RISK IN A PROFESSIONAL SETTING

Many professionals work with clients who have the potential to be dangerous. Therefore, risk assessment and management is one of the keys to preventing dangerousness in any setting. Risk assessments are meant to make you, your clients, and your school or agency safe. There are safety precautions that one can take when working with dangerous clients. These involve the following:

- Being aware of where you are in relation to clients. Position yourself between the client and the door.
- If facing your client straight on is too threatening, move your body at an angle to the client. This is less threatening.
- Speak softly and reassuringly.
- Ask the client to take a deep breath.
- Help the client problem solve.
- Get rid of any peer audience. Remove a reason for a youth to put on a show to entertain his friends or save face in front of his friends.
- Ask the youth, "What is your goal?" and "How do you want this to turn out?" Get to the bottom of the cause of the upset.
- Motivational interview techniques can also be useful. "Do you want to be in and out of jail (rehab) for the rest of your life or do you want something different? What do you want? I can help you get something different for your life, if you want it. Let's make a plan together to make that happen."
- Research suggests (Borum et al., 2002; Seifert, 2006) that many dangerous clients have experienced trauma in the past. A threatening situation can resurrect feelings of the past trauma and generate fear and a defensive response. Trauma issues must be addressed in order to reduce the risk of future violence, suicidality, or sexual offending.

It is necessary to measure risk for the safety of all clients, coworkers, and one's self. If you are working with clients who have been referred by Parole and Probation or the Courts, public safety is also an issue. It is important to focus on risks as well as strengths in treatment planning, so that the mix of interventions is complete.

Once risk is measured, it is important to manage or eliminate any future risk. Level of risk should determine the intensity of services needed. Youth with the highest level risk need the highest variety and intensity of services. Types of services will be determined by the client's strengths, stressors, skills, and environment. It is important to use a holistic approach when working with high-risk clients. Intervention should be based on a triad created by the combination of biopsychosocial, developmental, and environmental approaches to treatment.

Part of managing risk is communicating level of risk to the client, the workplace, and other agencies appropriately. Risk of violence, suicidality, and sexual offending must be discussed with the client. It is preferred that rapport be established between the client and a professional before attempting to communicate risk to the client. However, this is not always possible in a crisis. The reason for discussing these topics preventively is to avoid the crisis. Risk is a tough topic for the client to discuss. It is important to be calm, self-assured, and supportive. However, pay attention to safety before you communicate risk to the client. The professional should be closer to the door than the client. Notify staff in advance if you think there will be trouble. Be aware of the client's body language, emotional tone, and words. Be alert.

When communicating risk to a client, be kind, but be frank. Be reassuring. Tell the client that you know he will be glad later if he allows you to help him now. Ask the client whether he thinks he is or is not dangerous to himself or others. Tell him what your assessment showed. If there are differences, discuss why they are different. Tell the client, "Remember, I've told you that there is no confidentiality if you are dangerous. I can't let you hurt yourself or anyone else." Make a plan together for the next 24 hours. If he cannot cooperate, you may have to send him to the hospital. Talk softly and be reassuring, but confident. Communicate probable risk to your employer and other agencies when needed. Use these techniques to increase safety in settings where professionals' work with clients that can be dangerous.

The goal in the above procedures is to reduce excitation, get the situation under control, and ensure that no one gets hurt. Once that is done, one must plan for next steps. Is this youth in the correct level of care for his/her degree of inability to self-manage behavior, problem solve, stay calm, sooth oneself, and refrain from using aggression to get his needs met? It has been repeatedly demonstrated that clinical judgment alone of a client's risk of future violence is only slightly better than chance (Lipsey, 2010).

Therefore, it is best practice to have evaluated risk and needs before a crisis erupts. The goal of the evaluation is to make sure that the program is applying the appropriate level of structure to compensate for the youth's lack of self-management skills. Youth that manage their behavior well may need very little structure and can be successfully treated in an outpatient setting. Those that have demonstrated in the past that their capacity for self-management and appropriate interpersonal skills are weak should have already been assessed to see if they are being treated in the setting that offers them the greatest safety for themselves and others. Youth with weak skills should be in highly structured setting with days highly structured and little unstructured time. Residential treatment centers are more appropriate for youth with a high risk of injuring themselves or others. The assessment should be done with one of the risk/needs assessments described earlier.

If a youth does not have sufficient internal controls to stay safe, the program needs to increase the routine. In other words, rules are few and clearly understood with natural consequences quickly applied without deviating from the rule. Appropriate behavior is constantly reinforced. There is a set schedule in writing that is never deviated from. Unstructured time is allowed in small time increments when good self-management is demonstrated. Positive alternatives to hitting, grabbing, shoving, yelling, and disrespect for others are prominently posted and referred to publicly and often. Problem solving, respect, and self-soothing are emphasized.

Another goal of the evaluation is to ensure that the youth's treatment needs are being met, hence the name "risk and needs." Youth at a high level of risk for aggressive acting out generally have very complex clinical pictures, and skills needed to succeed in the world are lower than their ages would indicate. They may also have violent chaotic families that need intervention, as well. Therefore, a risk and needs assessment should help a professional create an individualized plan that meets the youth's treatment needs and emphasizes his strengths. It is also important in times where there are heavy financial constraints to be able to effectively use the most intensive and costly services for those who will most benefit by it (Thompson & Stewart, 2006).

ADMISSIBILITY OF YOUTH RISK ASSESSMENTS IN COURTS

In order for risk and needs assessment to be used in the courts (often for sentencing), they must pass certain tests of the admissibility of expert scientific evidence. These tests are laid out in the decisions of *Daubert v. Merrell Dow Pharmaceuticals* (commonly known as Daubert) and *Frye v. United States* (Frye). Some states use the Daubert standard, some use the Frye standard, and some use both.

For both Daubert and Frye, testing techniques must be

- beyond the ken (knowledge) of the average person
- relevant to the case at hand
- more probative than prejudicial (explain more than lead to prejudice)
- may embrace the ultimate issue
- have general acceptance in the field

In addition, to meet the Daubert standard, tests must

- have testability or falsifiability
- have known error rates
- be subjected to peer review

Most existing adult assessment tests can potentially pass Daubert and Frye, except the newer tools without peer review, the clinical interview guides without psychometrics, and the self-report inventories. Many of the juvenile risk assessment tools are too early in development to pass Daubert, but may pass Frye and thus can be used in Court testimony.

REFERENCES

Augimeri, L. K., Webster, C. D., Koegl, C. J., & Levene, K. (2001). *Early assessment risk list for boys: EARL-20B, version 2.* Toronto, ON: Earlscourt Child and Family Centre (Child Development Institute).

Borum, R., Bartel, P., Forth, A. (2002). *Structured assessment of violence risk in youth (SAVRY).* Tampa, FL: University of South Florida.

Braaten, S. (1998). *Behavioral objective sequence.* Champaign, IL: Research Press.

Catchpole, R. E. H., & Gretton, H. M. (2003). Predictive validity of risk assessment with violent young offenders: A 1-year examination of criminal outcome. *Criminal Justice and Behavior, 30*(6), 688–708.

Dahlberg, L. L., Toal, S. B., Swahn, M. H., & Behrens, C. B. (2006). *Measuring violence-related attitudes, behaviors, and influences among youths: A compendium of asssessment tools, 2nd edition.* Retrieved from www.cdc.gov/ncipc/pub-res/pdf/YV/YV_Compendium.pdf

Daubert et ux., individually and as guardians Ad Litem For Daubert, et al. v. Merrell Dow Pharmaceuticals, INC., 92–102 (United States Supreme Court decided June 28, 1993).

Forth, A. E., Kosson, D. S., & Hare, R. D. (2003). *PCL-YV.* Tonawanda, NY: Multi-Health Systems.

Hoge, R., & Andrews, D. A. (2010a). *Evaluation for risk of violence in juveniles.* New York, NY: Oxford University Press.

Hoge, R. & Andrews, D. A. (2010b). *YLS/CMI™ Youth Level of Service/Case Management Inventory.* North Tonawanda, NY: Multi Health Systems.

Kashani, J. H., Jones, M. R., Bumby, K. M., Thomas, L. A. (1999). Youth violence: Psychosocial risk factors, treatment, prevention, and recommendations. *Journal of Emotional and Behavioral Disorders, 7*(4), 200–210.

Lipsey, M. W. (2010). *Improving the effectiveness of juvenile justice programs: A new perspective on evidence-based practice.* Washington, DC: Center for Juvenile Justice Reform.

Millon, T. (2006). *Millon adolescent clinical inventory.* London: Pearson.

Rice, H. Q. (2005). *Violent offenders: Appraising and managing risk* (2nd ed.). Washington, DC: American Psychological Association.

Seifert, K. (2006). *How children become violent.* Boston, MA: Acanthus.

Seifert, K. (2007). *CARE2 manual.* Boston, MA: Acanthus.

Thompson, C., & Stewart, A. (2006). *Comparative evaluation of youth justice risk/needs assessment tools.* Nathan, Qld, Australia: Griffith University. Retrieved from www.griffith.edu.au/.../208206/Review-of-empiricall-based-risk_needs-assessment-tools.pdf

Thornberry, T. P., Huizinga, D., & Loeber, R. (2004). The causes and correlates studies: Findings and policy implications. *Juvenile Justice, 9:*3–19.

Wechsler, D. (2004). *The Wechsler intelligence scale for children—fourth edition.* London: Pearson Assessment.

Welsh, J. L., Schmidt, F., McKinnon, L., Chattha, H. K., & Meyers, J. R. (2008). A comparative study of adolescent risk assessment instruments: predictive and incremental validity. *Assessment, 15,* 104–115.

TEN

Youth Violence Prevention Programs

Preventing youth violence should be a major objective of families, schools, child and family service organizations, communities, and all levels of government. Prevention is defined here as efforts that help youth avoid delinquent and violent behaviors, otherwise known as primary prevention. Secondary prevention focuses on treating the harm resulting from violent incidents, and tertiary prevention programs address the long-term effects of violence (such as therapy and rehabilitation). Secondary and tertiary prevention programs will not be addressed in this volume.

What are the components of an effective youth violence prevention program? Obviously, a program must have "demonstrated effects on youth violence and on the major risk factors for youth violence" (Youth Violence: A Report of the Surgeon General, Satcher, 2001). This sounds easy to determine, but unfortunately, many programs are not evaluated effectively—or at all—for us to be able to judge which programs actually help to change violent behaviors in youth. Even more difficult would be trying to compare programs to decide which work most efficiently, and most cost-effectively, for a given population in a given setting.

The Office of the Surgeon General (2001) describes in detail the necessary elements required to determine if a violence prevention program is actually effective. Some of those elements include the following:

- A statistically significant reduction in the onset or prevalence of violent behavior or individual rates of offending

- A reduction in delinquency and serious criminal acts, since those are closely correlated to violence. However, programs that show a direct reduction in violent behaviors are preferable.
- A reduction in the risk factors of violence. This is particularly true of programs aimed at children, since most violence begins in adolescence.
- Effects that are sustained in the long term. (Because it would be extremely difficult, not to mention expensive, to track program participants for a significant length of time, "long term" is defined by the Surgeon General as effects that last for at least 1 year after the program.)
- A program that can be implemented at the national level, with a demonstrated ability to be successfully repeated in a wide range of community settings. This is preferable to smaller programs that may not be as widely useful.

Fortunately, many organizations involved in the study of violence prevention—such as the Centers for Disease Control and Prevention (CDC), the Office of Juvenile Justice and Delinquency Prevention (OJJDP), the Office of the Surgeon General, and the Center for the Study and Prevention of Violence—have made efforts to systematically and rigorously evaluate various violence prevention programs around the country. This chapter will include many programs that have been acknowledged by at least one of these agencies for their effectiveness.

Kisiel et al. (2006) list four factors that should be included in all effective youth violence prevention programs:

- increasing awareness and knowledge among youth
- developing skills to help regulate behavior and emotions
- multiple opportunities for practice of skills and feedback
- social support for positive changes in multiple settings

In addition, most experts agree that what is needed is a full continuum of care from effective primary prevention to intervention (Lipsy, Howell, Kelly, Chapman, & Carver, 2010). Prevention programs can and should be cost-effective, as well. For example, one study (Webster-Stratton, 2001) found that new prison cells cost $100,000 each, but in contrast, the Incredible Years Program, aimed at increasing children's social and self-control skills, costs $5,200 per group and prevents delinquency.

Because there are multiple factors that contribute to the risk of and resiliency from violent behaviors, as discussed in Chapters 5 and 6, prevention, too, must address multiple factors. Services in the home, school, and community are needed. Factors to be addressed would include some or all of the following: preventing child maltreatment and exposure to violence, bullying, and stressors; improving youth and family health, skills, and school climate; and neighborhood stability.

In recognition of these multiple factors and settings, this chapter will divide programs into three categories: home-based programs, school-based programs, and community-based programs.

This chapter highlights several proven youth violence prevention programs, but there are many, many more to be considered. Resources at the end of this chapter will help readers locate additional programs.

HOME-BASED PROGRAMS

As all parents know, raising a family is challenging and can cause much financial and psychological stress. Parents who did not have good parental role models, or who experienced abuse and neglect as children, often need extra support, training, and assistance to help them avoid repeating the same mistakes. In recognition, many prevention programs seek to teach at-risk parents effective parenting strategies, in the hopes that these will strengthen the bonds between parents and children, promote family resilience, avoid child abuse and neglect, and thus, in the long term, prevent further violence.

Often, these programs occur in the home, since that is the most convenient way to reach at-risk families, and they frequently begin during pregnancy, so that mothers can begin adopting healthy behaviors that will have an immediate positive impact on them and their unborn children.

Research evidence in the late 1980s and early 1990s provided promising results for the effectiveness of home visiting programs. Such programs first received heightened national recognition in 1991 from the U.S. Advisory Board on Child Abuse and Neglect, which gave top priority to its recommendation for universal neonatal home visitation as a child abuse prevention strategy (U.S. Advisory Board on Child Abuse and Neglect, 1991). In 2003, the Centers for Disease Control's systematic review of the literature led them to conclude that home-visiting programs can be effective in reducing maltreatment (Centers for Disease Control and Prevention, 2003; Hahn, 2005).

FRIENDS National Resource Center for Community-Based
Child Abuse Prevention, 2007

This section will highlight several parental education programs that have proved effective in reducing child abuse and neglect—issues that are known risk factors for later violence.

Nurse–Family Partnership

The nurse–family partnership (NFP) originated in the work of Dr. David Olds and his early experiences working with troubled children in a day care center in inner-city Baltimore (Olds, 2002). Frustrated by the harm that had been done to the children, Olds gradually realized that the best way to help them would be to prevent their abuse and neglect in the first place. Over time, he devised a model in which at-risk first-time mothers would be visited in their homes by qualified nurses, who would teach them healthy behaviors and parenting techniques. The nurse visits would span from pregnancy through the baby's second birthday (Goodman, 2006).

The program proved remarkably successful when it was first tested with poor, rural white families in Elmira, New York; the results were later duplicated with African American families in Memphis and Hispanic families in Denver (Goodman, 2006). Today, the NFP now serves more than 22,000 families, with 1,152 home nurse visitors, in 32 states (NFP, 2011).

Among its many positive outcomes, the NFP has proved effective at reducing rates of child abuse and neglect—a significant risk factor in later violence.

In the Elmira trial (where families have been followed the longest), there were long-term effects on reducing state-verified rates of child abuse and neglect (a 48% reduction). Also in the Elmira trial, there was a 56% relative reduction in emergency department encounters for injuries and ingestions during the children's second year of life. In the Memphis trial, there was a 28% relative reduction in all types of health care encounters for injuries and ingestions, and a 79% relative reduction in the number of days that children were hospitalized with injuries and ingestions during children's first two years.

NFP, 2011

For its effectiveness and adaptability, the NFP was identified as a model program by Blueprints for Violence Prevention, a program at the Center for the Study and Prevention of Violence (CSPV) (2006), at the University of Colorado at Boulder.

The NFP program costs approximately $4,500 per family per year to fund. A RAND Corporation analysis, conducted in 2005, found a net benefit to society of $34,148 (NFP, 2011). For more information, go to www.nursefamilypartnership.org.

Healthy Families America

Healthy Families America (HFA) also targets at-risk families, particularly those who may have histories of trauma, intimate partner violence, or mental health and/or substance abuse issues. HFA services can last for as long as the families wish, up to 3 to 5 years after the birth of the baby. Services are provided by trained paraprofessionals (rather than nurses as in NFP). It currently operates in 35 states.

Program evaluations suggest that HFA is successful in the following areas (HFA, 2011):

- reduced child maltreatment
- increased utilization of prenatal care and decreased preterm, low weight babies
- improved parent–child interaction and school readiness
- decreased dependency on welfare and other social services
- increased access to primary care medical services
- increased immunization rates

Based on these results, HFA has been named a "proven program" by the RAND Corporation, and the OJJDP has rated HFA as effective. For more information, visit www.healthyfamiliesamerica.org.

The Parent–Child Home Program

Chapter 5 discussed the importance of cognitive and linguistic skills in a child's development and later social and educational success. The

Parent–Child Home Program helps foster verbal interaction between parents and their young children, by modeling reading, play, and conversation. These activities can both improve a child's cognitive development and strengthen bonds between parents and children. The Program offers home visits to at-risk families (low income, low education levels, language and literacy barriers) who have children between the ages of 2 and 4 years.

> An independent evaluation of Parent–Child Home Program replications in two Pennsylvania counties indicates that positive parenting behaviors increased dramatically as a result of program participation. Half of the children identified as "at risk" in their home environments at the start were found to be no longer at risk at the completion of the Program. The number of positive interactions between parent and child increased significantly during program participation, including instances of praise and/or encouragement observed; of parents showing warmth toward the child; and of parents giving their child directions and encouraging the child to follow them.
>
> Parent–Child Home Program, 2011

For more information, go to www.parent-child.org.

SCHOOL-BASED PROGRAMS

The school setting is an ideal one in which to teach children appropriate prosocial behavior and successful learning strategies. "Schools represent an ideal setting for influencing child behavior and development. Over the course of many years, most children attend school daily during a formative period in their development" (Task Force on Community Preventive Services, 2007).

School-based programs to reduce child and adolescent violence can take any number of approaches: they can address violent behaviors directly, or they can help students develop cognitive skills, prosocial behaviors, and self-esteem. In a report on the effectiveness of various school-based programs (Hahn et al., 2007), the Task Force on Community Preventive Services notes:

> Certain programs focus on providing information about the problem of violence and approaches to avoiding violence.... Other programs...

assume that self-concept and self-esteem derive from positive action and its rewards, so if children's behavior can be made more positive and sociable, they will develop better attitudes toward themselves and then continue to make positive choices.... Other programs are founded on the theory that they will be most effective if they modify the broader environment of the child.

Hahn et al. (2007) completed a meta-analysis of universal school-based prevention programs (i.e., programs that enroll every child in a particular school, district, or grade) that attempted to reduce school violence. Programs could use techniques of skill building, education, discussions, feedback, and/or reinforcement. The programs reviewed included the following:

- PATHS (Promoting Alternative Thinking Strategies; Greenberg, Kusché, & Mihalic, 1998); a social and emotional skill-building program to be used in the classroom
- Peace builders (Vazsonyi, Belliston, & Flannery, 2004); a program in which youth, parents, school, and community are involved in a campaign of rewarding the following of positive behavioral rules, such as "praise people" and "right wrongs"
- Second step (Grossman et al., 1997); a program that teaches through discussion and role playing
- Seattle Social Development Project (Hawkins, Catalano, Kosterman, Abbott, & Hill, 1999); a program that targets elementary schools in high crime areas; showed a 135% decrease in general crime
- Responding in peaceful and positive ways (Meyer, Farrell, Northup, Kung, & Plybon, 2000); a program based on social learning theory (see Chapter 4)
- Students for peace (Kelder et al., 1996); another program based on social learning theory

At the end of the study, universal programs such as these were "recommended" (meaning that the study found "strong or sufficient evidence that the intervention is effective") because they had positive effects on reducing school violence at all school levels and across populations. The study, and related materials, can be found at http://www.thecommunityguide.org/violence/school.html.

The following section will provide a brief sampling of successful school-based programs that attempt to reduce violence through a variety of means: by confronting aggressive behaviors, reducing bullying, improving student performance, and reducing substance abuse.

Antiaggression Programs

Aggressors, Victims, and Bystanders: Thinking and Acting to Prevent Violence

This curriculum is designed to prevent violence and inappropriate aggression among middle school children, particularly those living in environments with high rates of exposure to violence. Its key feature is a "Think-First Model of Conflict Resolution," which helps students find ways other than violence to respond to conflict. It was first published in 1994, has been implemented in more than 1,500 schools in 49 states, and has reached an estimated 275,000 students. Evaluations suggest that students who go through the program expressed a reduced belief that aggression is a legitimate response to conflict and a decreased intention to use aggression (NREPP, 2011). For more information see http://www.thtm.org/.

The Incredible Years

The Incredible Years (IYS) curricula targets problematic behaviors, such as aggressiveness, tantrums, and acting out behavior, in children from birth to 12 years of age. It teaches children how to manage their emotions and improve their social skills. There are school-based curricula for teachers, as well as materials that parents can use in the home. It can also be used with children who are diagnosed with oppositional defiant disorder/conduct disorder and attention deficit hyperactivity disorder.

IYS has earned many awards for its effectiveness; it has been elected by the U.S. OJJDP as an "exemplary" best practice program and as a "Blueprints" program, as well as a "Model" program by the Center for Substance Abuse Prevention (IYS, 2011). For more information, see www.incredibleyears.com.

Bullying Prevention Programs

As discussed in Chapter 7, bullying is a significant social problem that can have severe—sometimes tragic—consequences. Many recent cases have exposed a lack of planning on behalf of school teachers, staff, and administration, who are often unable and/or unwilling to identify bullying and intervene effectively. In a recent survey of school bullying prevention programs, Farrington and Ttofi (2009, p. 8) write:

> Given the serious short-term and long-term effects of bullying on children's physical and mental health (Ttofi & Farrington, 2008a) it is understandable why school bullying has increasingly become a topic of both public concern and research efforts. Research on school bullying has expanded worldwide (Smith, Morita, Junger-Tas, Olweus, Catalano & Slee, 1999), with a variety of intervention programs being implemented (Smith, Pepler, & Rigby, 2004a), and with some countries legally requiring schools to have an anti-bullying policy (Ananiadou & Smith, 2002). The cost of victimization in schools is considerable (Hawker & Boulton, 2000) and intervention strategies aiming at tackling school bullying and promoting safer school communities can be seen as a moral imperative (Smith, Ananiadou, & Cowie, 2003).

Olweus Bullying Prevention Program

This program is based on the work of Dr. Dan Olweus, a research professor of psychology in Norway who has been studying bullying since the 1970s and is often considered the "pioneer" of bullying research. The Olweus Bullying Prevention Program was created and instituted in Norway in 1983, after three adolescent Norwegian boys committed suicide, likely as a result of severe bullying. The program was successfully exported to other countries; today, hundreds of schools in nearly every state have implemented it (Olweus, 1999, 2011). It includes a bullying questionnaire, a Bullying Prevention Program Schoolwide Guide, a Bullying Prevention Program Teacher Guide, materials for classroom instruction as well as one-on-one sessions, and more.

Program evaluations in various American high schools reported significant decreases in being bullied, in bullying others, and in perceptions that adults within the school were not actively working to address bullying (Olweus, 1999, 2011). Olweus was identified as a Model Program by Blueprints for Violence Prevention, a program at the CSPV, at the University of Colorado at Boulder.

For more information, go to www.olweus.org.

Bully-Proofing Your School

Bully-Proofing Your School is a national school safety program that started in 1992. Interestingly, the program targets children who are neither bullies nor victims. It operates

> ...through the creation of a "caring majority" of students who take the lead in establishing and maintaining a safe and caring school community. The program focuses on converting the silent majority of students into a caring majority by teaching strategies that help them to avoid victimization and to take a stand for a bully-free school. In schools which have implemented the program, incidences of bullying behaviors have declined and feelings of safety among the students have increased

> The Partnership for Families and Children, 2011

For more information, go to http://www.pffac.org/index.php?s=120.

Improving Student Outcomes

Many programs focus on improving children's academic and social success and feelings of accomplishment in school, thus reducing the likelihood that frustration and alienation will contribute to future acts of violence by students.

Positive Behavioral Interventions and Supports

Positive Behavioral Interventions and Supports (PBIS) was established by the Office of Special Education Programs in the U.S. Department of Education. It emphasizes a full continuum of care based on the needs of youth, and helps schools to identify problem behaviors, intervene early, use multitiered models of service delivery to meet the needs of diverse students, use research-based interventions, use sophisticated assessments, and monitor youth for continuous progress. PBIS programs are associated with improved, more responsive learning environments (PBIS, 2011). For more information, go to www.pbis.org.

Promoting Alternative Thinking Strategies Program

PATHS helps students—including those who are at risk or with special needs—learn to better manage their classroom behavior by managing their feelings, their relationships, and their work. The program teaches emotional literacy, self-control, social competence, positive peer relations, and interpersonal problem-solving skills in three weekly 30-minute sessions. In studies, the PATHS program has been shown to

- reduce teachers' reports of students exhibiting aggressive behavior by 32%
- increase teachers' reports of students exhibiting self-control by 36%
- increase students' vocabulary for emotions by 68%
- increase students' scores on cognitive skills tests by 20%
- significantly improve students' ability to tolerate frustration plus their ability—and willingness—to use effective conflict-resolution strategies
- reduce behavior problems, such as aggression at school (for both regular and special-needs students)
- significantly decrease conduct problems and the percentage of aggressive/violent solutions to social problems
- reduce depression and sadness among special-needs students
- significantly increase teachers' reports of improved behavior in the classroom
- significantly increase teachers' reports of improved academic engagement
- significantly reduce students' reports of male students exhibiting aggressive behavior

PATHS Program, 2011

It has been identified as a Model Program by Blueprints for Violence Prevention, a program at the CSPV, at the University of Colorado at Boulder. For more information, see www.channing-bete.com/prevention-programs/paths/paths.html.

Substance Abuse Prevention

Because substance use and abuse is a significant risk factor for violence, programs that are aimed at reducing substance abuse often successfully reduce violence as well.

Botvin Life Skills Training Program

Developed by Dr. Gilbert J. Botvin (1998), *Life Skills Training* (LST) is a substance abuse prevention program that reduces alcohol, tobacco, drug abuse, and violence by targeting the factors that promote the initiation of substance use and other risky behaviors. It is intended to provide adolescents and young teens increased self-esteem, self-confidence, and the ability to successfully resist peer pressure.

LST has been identified as a Model Program by Blueprints for Violence Prevention, a program at the CSPV, at the University of Colorado at Boulder. For more information, go to www.lifeskill straining.com.

Project Toward No Drug Abuse (Project TND)

This drug abuse prevention program targets senior high schoolers. It was developed by Steve Sussman, PhD, and staff at the Institute for Health Promotion and Disease Prevention Research, in the Keck School of Medicine at the University of Southern California (Sussman, 2004). Research suggests that TND can reduce usage of tobacco, marijuana, and hard drugs. For more information, go to http://tnd.usc.edu.

COMMUNITY-BASED PROGRAMS

Head Start

Since 1965, Head Start (HS) has offered a wide variety of services—education, medical and mental health care, nutrition, and child development—to at-risk children and their families. It consists of two programs: HS, for preschool-age children and their families; and Early Head Start (EHS), serving children prenatal to age 3 years, pregnant women, and their families. It is a vast program; during 2009 to 2010, 1,117,687 children and pregnant women were served by HS (983,809 in HS and 133,878 in EHS) (HS, 2011).

A January 2010 report of the Department of Health and Human Services found that participation in HS had significant and beneficial short-term impacts; "Yet, by the end of 1st grade, there were few significant differences between the HS group as a whole and the control group as a whole for either cohort." For more information, go to www.nhsa.org.

Striving to Reduce Youth Violence Everywhere

The Striving to Reduce Youth Violence Everywhere Program from the Centers for Disease Control and Prevention is an online resource that uses a collaborative approach to help build strengths and safety among youth, families, communities, and society (CDC, 2010). For more information, go to www.safeyouth.gov/Pages/Home.aspx.

The Midwestern Prevention Project

The Midwestern Prevention Project is a substance abuse prevention program that uses community-wide strategies to help children avoid the pressure to use and abuse drugs: mass media programming, a school program and continuing school boosters, a parent education and organization program, community organization and training, and local policy change regarding tobacco, alcohol, and other drugs (Pentz, Mihalic, & Grotpeter, 1998). It is recognized as a Model Program by Blueprints. For more information, go to www.colorado.edu/cspv/blueprints/modelprograms/MPP.html.

Big Brothers and Sisters of America

Big Brothers and Sisters began in 1904, when a New York City court clerk realized that many of the troubled adolescent boys coming into the courtroom needed the guidance of caring adults (McGill, 1998).

A study of 950 boys and girls from eight Big Brothers Big Sisters agencies across the country, conducted in 1994 and 1995, found that after 18 months in the program, enrollees were

- 46% less likely to begin using illegal drugs
- 27% less likely to begin using alcohol
- 52% less likely to skip school
- 37% less likely to skip a class
- 33% less likely to hit someone

Big Brothers Big Sisters, 2011

For more information, visit www.bbbs.org.

The Adolescent Transition Program

Parenting programs can be very effective in reducing the aggressive and antisocial behaviors of children and adolescents. The Parent–Child Interaction Training and Adolescent Transition Program (ATP) has been cited as effective (Dishion, University of Oregon, http://

www.strengtheningfamilies.org/html/programs_1999/08_ATP.html).
ATP teaches parenting skills such as making neutral requests, making rules, effective consequences, monitoring youth behavior, active
listening, and rewarding positive behavior.

New Urbanism

Although not a violence prevention movement per se, New Urbanism
represents a new approach to urban planning that originated in the
1960s. The principles of New Urbanism involve preserving ecology,
creating walkable neighborhoods with pleasant central spaces for people to gather, and mixed use housing and jobs so that the poor and
disadvantaged are not segregated. New Urbanism promotes neighborhoods and communities that are self-governed, where gangs are less
likely to become established (NewUrbamism.org, 2011).

Scared Straight

For more than 25 years, the Scared Straight program has attempted to
shock at-risk teens out of bad behavior by bringing them face to face with
violent criminals in dangerous prisons. Prisoners describe their lives in
brutal and intimidating fashion, in the hopes of convincing teenagers
to choose a different path. Despite the good intentions of the program,
however, recent evaluations suggest that it simply does not work and may
in fact be harmful: "Meta-analysis results show the scared straight-type
intervention *increases* the odds of offending by between 1.6 and 1.7 to
1 compared to a no-treatment control group. These findings lead the
researchers to conclude that participating in the Scared Straight program
actually correlates with an increase in re-offending compared to a control
group of youth who received no intervention at all" (Schembri, n.d.).

FOR FURTHER INFORMATION

■ The Blueprints for Violence Prevention (http://www.colorado.edu/
cspv/blueprints/), assembled by the CSPV at the University of
Colorado, has collected and reviewed research on more than 900
violence prevention programs and identified those that meet certain standards and appear effective.

- The CDC maintains lists of effective and promising programs on its Web site (http://www.cdc.gov/ViolencePrevention/youthviolence/prevention.html)
- Best Practices of Youth Violence Prevention—A Sourcebook for Community Action is available at www.cdc.gov/violenceprevention/pub/YV_bestpractices.html (Thornton, 2000)
- SAMSHA's National Registry of Evidence-Based Programs and Practices (http://nrepp.samhsa.gov/) includes more than 190 interventions supporting mental health promotion, substance abuse prevention, and mental health and substance abuse treatment.
- Youth Violence: A Report of the Surgeon General is a 2001 report with a chapter on prevention and intervention, including programs that work and those that do not (or had not been studied) (http://www.surgeongeneral.gov/library/youthviolence/chapter5/sec1.html)

REFERENCES

Ananiadou, K., & Smith, P. K. (2002). Legal requirements and nationally circulated materials against school bullying in European countries. *Criminology and Criminal Justice, 2*, 471–491.

Big Brothers Big Sisters. (2011). Retrieved from www.bbbs.org

Botvin, G. H. (1998, Updated 2006). Life Skills Training: Blueprints for Violence Prevention, book five. In D. S. Elliott (Ed.), *Blueprints for Violence Prevention Series*. Boulder, CO: Center for the Study and Prevention of Violence, Institute of Behavioral Science, University of Colorado.

Center for the Study and Prevention of Violence. (2006). *Blueprints for violence prevention overview*, Boulder, CO: University of Colorado. Retrieved from http://www.colorado.edu/cspv/blueprints/

Centers for Disease Control and Prevention. (2010, September 28). *STRYVE: Striving to reduce youth violence everywhere*, Boulder, CO: University of Colorado. Retrieved from http://www.cdc.gov/violenceprevention/STRYVE/index.html

Department of Health and Human Services. (2010). *Head Start impact study: Final report*, Washington, DC: U.S. Department of Health and Human Services. Retrieved from http://www.acf.hhs.gov/programs/opre/hs/impact_study/reports/impact_study/executive_summary_final.pdf

Farrington, D. P., & Ttofi, M. M. (2009). School-based programs to reduce bullying and victimization. *Campbell Systematic Reviews, 6*, 5–148.

FRIENDS National Resource Center for Community-Based Child Abuse Prevention. (2007). *Home Visiting Programs: A Brief Overview of Selected Models*.

Goodman. (2006). *The story of David Olds and the nurse home visiting program*. Retrieved from http://www.rwjf.org/files/publications/other/DavidOldsSpecialReport0606.pdf

Greenberg, M. T., Kusché, C., & Mihalic, S. F. (1998, Updated 2006). Promoting Alternative Thinking Strategies (PATHS): Blueprints for Violence Prevention, book ten. In D. S. Elliott (Ed.), *Blueprints for Violence Prevention series*. Boulder, CO: Center for the Study and Prevention of Violence, Institute of Behavioral Science, University of Colorado.

Grossman, D. C., Neckerman, H. J., Koepsell, T. D., Asher, K., Liu, P. Y., Beland, K. N., et al. (1997). A randomized controlled trial of a violence prevention curriculum among elementary school children. *Journal of the American Medical Association, 277,* 1605–1611.

Hahn, R., Fuqua-Whitley, D., Wethington, H., Lowy, J., Liberman, A., Crosby, A., et al. (2007). The effectiveness of universal school-based programs for the prevention of violent and aggressive behavior. *Morbidity and Mortality Weekly Report, 56,* 1–12. Retrieved from http://www.cdc.gov/mmwr/preview/mmwrhtml/rr5607a1.htm

Hawkins, J. D., Catalano, R. F., Kosterman, R., Abbott, R. D., & Hill, K. G. (1999). Preventing adolescent health-risk behaviors by strengthening protection during childhood. *Archives of Pediatrics & Adolescent Medicine, 153*(3), 226–234.

Head Start. (2011). Retrieved from http://www.nhsa.org/

Healthy Families America. (2011). Retrieved from www.healthyfamiliesamerica.org

The Incredible Years. (2011). Retrieved from www.incredibleyears.com

Kelder, S. H., Orpinas, P., McAlister, A., Frankowski, R., Parcel, G. S., & Friday, J. (1996). The students for peace project: A comprehensive violence-prevention program for middle school students. *American Journal of Preventive Medicine, 12*(5), 22–30.

Kisiel, C., Blaustein, M., Spinazzola, J., Schmidt, C. S., Zucker, M., & van der Kolk, B. (2006). Evaluation of a theater-based youth violence prevention program for elementary school children. *Journal of School Violence, 5,* 19–36.

Lipsy, M. W., Howell, J. C., Kelly, M. R., Chapman, G., & Carver, D. (2010). *Improving the effectiveness of juvenile justice programs: A new perspective on evidence-based practice*. Washington, DC: Center for Juvenile Justice Reform.

McGill, D. M. (1998, Updated 2006). Big Brothers Big Sisters of America: Blueprints for Violence Prevention, book two. In D. S. Elliott (Ed.), *Blueprints for Violence Prevention series*. Boulder, CO: Center for the Study and Prevention of Violence, Institute of Behavioral Science, University of Colorado. Retrieved from http://www.colorado.edu/cspv/blueprints/model-programs/BBBS.html

Meyer, A., Farrell, A., Northup, W., Kung, E., & Plybon, L. (2000). *Promoting non-violence in early adolescence: Responding in peaceful and positive ways*. New York: Kluwer Academic/Plenum Publishers.

NREPP. (2011). Retrieved from http://www.nrepp.samhsa.gov/ViewIntervention .aspx?id=142

NewUrbanism.org. (2011). *New Urbanism*. Retrieved from http://www. newurbanism.org/

Nievar, A. M., Van Egeren, L. A., & Pollard, S. (2010). A Meta-analysis of Home Visiting Programs: Moderators of improvement in maternal behaviors. *Infant Mental Health Journal, 31*(5), 499–520.

Nurse–Family Partnership. (2011). Retrieved from http://www.nursefamily-partnership.org/assets/PDF/Fact-sheets/NFP_Snapshot

Olds, D. (2002). Home visiting by paraprofessionals and by nurses: A random-ized, controlled trial. *Pediatrics, 100*, 486–496.

Olweus, D. L. (1999, Updated 2006). Bullying prevention program: Blueprints for Violence Prevention, book nine. In D. S. Elliott (Ed.), *Blueprints for Violence Prevention series*. Boulder, CO: Center for the Study and Prevention of Violence, Institute of Behavioral Science, University of Colorado.

Olweus Bullying Prevention Program. (2011). Clemson, SC: Clemson University. Retrieved from http://www.olweus.org

Promoting Alternative Thinking Strategies Program. (2011). South Deerfield, MA: Channing Bete. Retrieved from www.channing-bete.com/prevention-programs/paths/paths.html

Partnership for Families and Children. (2011). Denver, CO: The Partnership for Families and Children. Retrieved from www.pffac.org

Pentz, M. A., Mihalic, S. F., & Grotpeter, J. K. (1998, updated August 2006). The Midwestern Prevention Project: Blueprints for Violence Prevention, book one. In D. S. Elliott (Ed.), *Blueprints for Violence Prevention series*. Boulder, CO: Center for the Study and Prevention of Violence, Institute of Behavioral Science, University of Colorado.

Positive Behavioral Interventions and Supports. (2011). *Positive behavioral interventions and supports*. Eugene, OR: University of Oregon, National Technical Assistance Center on Positive Behavioral Interventions and Supports. Retrieved from http://www.pbis.org/school/what_is_swpbs.aspx

Satcher, D. (2001). *Youth Violence: A Report of the Surgeon General*. Retrieved from http://www.surgeongeneral.gov/library/youthviolence/

Schembri, A. J. *Scared straight programs: Jail and detention tours*. FL: Florida Department of Juvenile Justice. Retrieved from http://www.djj.state.fl.us/ Research/Scared_Straight_Booklet_Version.pdf.

Smith, P., Morita, Y., Junger-Tas, J., Olweus, D., Catalano, R., & Slee, P. (Eds.). (1999). *The nature of school bullying: A crossnational perspective*. New York, NY: Routledge.

Smith, P. K., Pepler, D., & Rigby, K. (2004). *Bullying in schools: How successful can interventions be?* Cambridge, UK: Cambridge University Press.

Sussman, S. R. (2004). Blueprints for Violence Prevention, book twelve: Project towards no drug abuse. In D. S. Elliott (Ed.), *Blueprints for Violence*

Prevention series. Boulder, CO: Center for the Study and Prevention of Violence, Institute of Behavioral Science, University of Colorado.

Task Force on Community Preventive Services. A recommendation to reduce rates of violence among school-aged children and youth by means of universal school-based violence prevention programs. *American Journal of Preventive Medicine, 33*(2S), S112–113, 2007. Retrieved from http://www.thecommunityguide.org/violence/schoolbasedprograms.html

Thornton, T. N. (2000). *Best practices of youth violence prevention: A sourcebook for community action.* Atlanta, GA: Division of Violence Prevention, National Center for Injury Prevention and Control.

U.S. Advisory Board on Child Abuse and Neglect. (1991). *Creating caring communities: Blueprint for an effective federal policy on child abuse and neglect* [Annual Report]. Washington, DC: Administration for Children and Families, Department of Health and Human Services.

Vazsonyi, A. T., Belliston, L. M., & Flannery, D. J. (2004). Evaluation of a school-based, universal violence prevention program: Low, medium, and high risk children. *Youth Violence and Juvenile Justice, 2,* 185–206.

Webster-Stratton, C. M. (2001). The Incredible Years: Parent, teacher, and child training series: Blueprints for Violence Prevention, book eleven. In D. S. Elliott (Ed.), *Blueprints for Violence Prevention series.* Boulder, CO: Center for the Study and Prevention of Violence, Institute of Behavioral Science, University of Colorado.

ELEVEN

Interventions

The previous chapter discussed a number of effective prevention programs that can hopefully ward off aggressive or violent behavior in children and adolescents before it even starts. In this chapter, we will look at effective programs that can help treat youth who have already employed violent behavior to some degree, including those in the juvenile justice system. Interventions that take a positive approach toward rehabilitation are favored over those that feature punishment: in a meta-analysis of program effectiveness, Lipsey (2009) found "interventions that embodied 'therapeutic' philosophies, such as counseling and skills training, were more effective than those based on strategies of control or coercion—surveillance, deterrence, and discipline."

This chapter will include an overview of skills building, individual therapy, family therapy, multimodal treatment, and school-based mental health interventions. The chapter will end with interventions that can be employed for youth in the juvenile justice system, including those who have shown extremely violent behavior.

SKILLS-BUILDING PROGRAMS

Many youth who have issues with violence need to learn skills that will help them control their aggressive behavior and/or function more effectively in social environments. "Counselors, teachers, and others who deal with aggressive adolescents or juvenile delinquents understand that these youngsters often make use of high levels of acting-out behaviors in combination with substandard and deficient alternative prosocial behaviors. Many of these young people are skilled in fighting, bullying, intimidating, harassing, or manipulating others; however, they are frequently inadequate in more socially desirable behaviors, such as negotiating differences, dealing appropriately with accusations, and responding effectively to failure, teasing, rejection, or anger" (Goldstein & Glick, 1994).

To address these deficits, typical skill-building programs often include behavior management programs, cognitive-behavioral therapy, social skills training, "challenge" programs (i.e., wilderness therapy), academic training (GED programs, tutoring), and job-related skills (Lipsey, 2009). Teaching many of these skills is a long process; they must be presented in a developmentally appropriate and sequential fashion, and they must be practiced in some manner every day. It is also important that everyone significantly involved in the youth's life (parents, teachers, and agency staff) is aware and can offer the child opportunities to practice new skills.

The meta-analysis by Lipsey (2009) found that cognitive-behavioral approaches had the most significant effects on reducing recidivism (26%), followed by effects on behavior (22%), social skills building (13%), challenge (12%), academic skills (10%), and job skills (6%).

Botvin Life Skills Training

Botvin Life Skills Training (www.lifeskillstraining.com/), discussed in the previous chapter, has demonstrated success in reducing smoking, drug use, and aggression. It has programs for use in homes, schools, and communities. It has been endorsed by the U.S. Department of Education, Center for Substance Abuse Prevention, National Institute on Drug Abuse, U.S. Department of Justice OJJDP, American Medical Association, American Psychological Association, CDC, and Coalition for Evidence Based Practice.

Aggression Replacement Training

Aggression Replacement Training (Goldstein & Glick, 1994) is a 10-week, 30-hour program that focuses on three major components: skillstreaming, anger control training, and moral education. Skillstreaming teaches 50 prosocial behaviors, including beginning and advanced social skills, skills for dealing with feelings, alternatives to aggression, dealing with stress, and planning skills. Anger control training includes identifying anger triggers and cues, and using reminders and reducers to minimize aggressive responses. Finally, moral education helps children think about issues such as fairness and justice. In one evaluation, it was found to reduce recidivism an average of 7% when compared with other programs. The cost benefit is $11.66 saved for every $1 spent on the program (Justice Policy Institute, 2009).

Behavioral Objective Sequence

The Behavioral Objective Sequence (Braaten, 1998) includes a developmental sequence of skills in six domains:

- Adaptive
- Personal
- Task
- Interpersonal
- Self-management
- Communication

Most severely behaviorally disturbed youth have significant deficits in most or all of these domains. Once their deficits are measured, the necessary skills are taught in a developmentally appropriate and individualized sequence using behavior modification techniques.

In a variation of BOS implementation by Seifert, two skills per week are selected for practice. One skill is already being performed between 60% and 90% of the time by the youth (classified as an "often true level"); the other is only achieved 30% to 60% of the time (a "sometimes true level"). The "often true" skill is selected so that the child can feel competent about a skill he or she is already using and can reinforce its practice; the "sometimes true" skill will require more effort. Therapists, family, and other professionals provide frequent positive reinforcement when skills are rehearsed and mastered.

Every BOS skill is tracked with the youth and family, and the tracking of progress is another source of reinforcement. Each youth is presented with an age-appropriate certificate for the mastery of every eight skills and given a binder in which to keep all the certificates. The youth, family, therapist, teachers, and other professionals are encouraged to participate in selecting skills to be addressed and presenting opportunities for practice and reinforcement. Praise from the team is ongoing throughout the process.

INDIVIDUAL THERAPY

For some children, particularly those that have experienced trauma or have a co-occurring mental disorder, skill building alone may not be enough; they may require additional therapy.

As discussed in Chapter 4, many children who have experienced trauma in the past have a higher than normal arousal "set point" that must be addressed and lowered. Trauma-based therapy involves reducing the negative emotional and developmental impact of trauma on children and adolescents. It may utilize techniques such as psychodrama, mindfulness, relaxation and self-soothing techniques, exposure therapy or reducing emotional reactions to certain stimuli, story telling (Cohen, Mannario, & Deblinger, 1996), skill building, or other techniques.

There are techniques for reducing the emotional impact of traumatic memories and triggers, such as visualizing a "safe place" you can go to in your mind while using relaxation techniques. The most important element is for the therapist to be "present and aware" with the client when processing any part of the trauma experience or aftermath. Developing the capacity to tolerate the feelings associated with the trauma becomes part of the task. A client can "borrow strength" from the therapist until she can build a sufficient amount of inner strength and structure to master the traumatic experience, learn something from it, and "move on" (Shapiro, 2010).

The use of imagery can be very powerful in this type of work. The traumatic event is seen in the context of a story that may be spoken aloud, written, or acted out; however, in the therapy, the narrative is changed so that the child is the hero or heroine of the story. The hero or heroine overcomes the obstacles or solves the problem at hand, emphasizing her competence and strength. Trauma work can also involve working on trust and attachment. The process of developing healthy attachment patterns is often lengthy and difficult. It can involve corrective developmental experiences that go through stages of trust, parallel play, role play, rough and tumble play, reciprocity, empathy, and group membership.

FAMILY THERAPY

It is desirable and sometimes even essential to include family members in youth interventions. According to Lipsey (2000), programs using generic family therapy had the greatest effect size (.60) in reducing future violence. Programs following more specific treatments, notably "Functional Family Therapy" and "Multisystemic Therapy" (MST) had effect sizes from .1 to .2 in reducing recidivism.

Functional Family Therapy (www.fftinc.com) helps families find more effective ways of getting their needs met, change faulty attributions and expectations, and use more positive reinforcement with children (Kashani, Jones, Bumby, & Thomas, 1999). It is an 8- to 12-week program. It costs between $1,350 and $3,750 per family for 90 days. The program generates $10.69 in benefits for every dollar spent and reduces recidivism by an average of 16% when compared with other programs (Justice Policy Institute, 2009).

Parent training models teach caregivers communication skills, problem solving, and effective parenting techniques through direct teaching, modeling, and discussion groups. Although effective for many youth, their effectiveness with severely and chronically violent youth has not been demonstrated over the long term (Kashani, Jones, Bumby, & Thomas, 1999).

MULTIMODAL TREATMENT

As the name suggests, multimodal treatment involves a variety of approaches, including therapy with the youth (and possibly the family), skills building, case management, and other treatments as needed. With multimodal treatment, the practitioner has a complete picture of the youth's treatment and intervention needs. He or she can then put together a coordinated team that includes the youth, his or her family, teachers, social workers, and agency staff. Together they create a plan to decrease environmental stress and increase individual and family skills and strengths. In this way, the team can coordinate efforts and provide multiple interventions for the youth and the family.

Multisystemic Therapy

MST is "an intensive family- and community-based treatment program that focuses on the entire world of chronic and violent juvenile offenders—their homes and families, schools and teachers, neighborhoods and friends" (MST Services Web site, 2011).
MST interventions work to

- "increase the caregivers' parenting skills
- improve family relations
- involve the youth with friends who do not participate in criminal behavior
- help him or her get better grades or start to develop a vocation
- help the adolescent participate in positive activities, such as sports or school clubs
- create a support network of extended family, neighbors, and friends to help the caregivers maintain the changes" (MST Web site, 2011)

According to one study, MST reduces recidivism by an average of 10.5% when compared with other programs and yield benefits of $13 for every $1 spent on the program. Some MST programs have shown reductions in long-term recidivism rates from 25% to 70% (Justice Policy Institute, 2009); however, cross validation of these studies is still needed.

Multimodal Treatment Using the CARE2

Lipsey (2000) suggests that in order to be effective, interventions must be based on the needs of the particular youth and family. The CARE2 (Seifert, 2007), discussed in Chapter 9, was developed as a screening tool for the risk of chronic violence and a multimodal treatment planning instrument. The CARE2 contains 44 risk items, and each item is connected to a suggested intervention.

Multidimensional Treatment Foster Care

The Multidimensional Treatment Foster Care (MTFC) program was developed as an alternative to institutional, residential, and group care placements for adolescents with severe conduct disorders and delinquency. It typically lasts from 9 to 12 months and utilizes "intensive, well-coordinated, multimethod interventions conducted in the MTFC foster home, with the child's aftercare family, and with the child through skills coaching and academic support. A program supervisor (with a caseload of 10) oversees and coordinates the interventions that are implemented across multiple settings (e.g., home, school, community). Involvement of each child's family or aftercare resource is emphasized from the outset of treatment in an effort to maximize training and preparation for posttreatment care for youth and their families. Progress is tracked through daily phone calls with treatment of foster parents during which data is collected on the child's behavior" (MTFC Web site, 2011). Therapy is also provided. It costs $2,691 per youth per month (Heggeler, 1998/2006) and generates $11 in benefits for every $1 spent. Research by the Justice Policy Institute (2009) suggests that this program shows an average of 22% reduction in recidivism when compared with other programs.

SCHOOL-BASED MENTAL HEALTH SERVICES

According to the National Center for Education Statistics, 2010:

- there were 38 school-associated violent deaths in the 2008–2009 school year (24 homicides and 14 suicides)
- there were about 629,800 violent crimes among students aged 12 to 18 years in 2008
- 8% of students reported being threatened or injured by someone with a weapon on school property in 2009
- 75% of public schools recorded one or more violent incidents of crime during the 2007–2008 school year
- 25% of public schools reported that bullying occurred among students on a daily or weekly basis during the 2007–2008 school year
- 20% of public schools reported that gang activities had happened during 2007–2008

Based on statistics such as these, more and more schools are offering school-based mental health services to address mental and behavioral issues among students in schools. Quality school-based mental health services follow key principles:

1. Establishing a shared agenda involving school–family–community partnerships to provide a full continuum of mental health promotion and intervention both for youth in general and those in special education;
2. Assuring that programs are responsive to student, school, and community needs and built on strengths;
3. Focusing on reducing barriers to student learning through evidence-based programs and strategies;
4. Implementing systematic quality assessment and improvement and continuous student and program-level evaluation;
5. Hiring the right staff and providing them with ongoing training, coaching, and support for the delivery of high-quality and evidence-based services;
6. Assuring the developmental, cultural, and personal sensitivity of all efforts;
7. Building interdisciplinary teams and coordinating mechanisms;
8. Making strong connections between programs and resources within the school with programs and resources in other community settings (Andis et al., 2002; Weist & Murray, 2007; Weist, Paternite, & Adelsheim, 2005).

The Safe Schools/Healthy Students Initiative

The Safe Schools/Healthy Students (SS/HS) initiative is a prominent mechanism of federal support for school mental health programs and services (Schmidt, 2009). Grantees must propose an integrated and comprehensive plan to address problems of school violence and must address the following elements:

- SS environments and violence prevention activities;
- Alcohol and other drug-prevention activities;
- Student behavioral, social, and emotional supports;
- Mental health services;
- Early childhood social and emotional learning programs.

There is a limited published literature on experiences of SS/HS sites, and this literature generally presents anecdotal observations of program experiences (see Pollack & Sundermann, 2001), rather than empirical assessments of mental health services delivered through them. In one 3-year study at a single school (Schmidt, 2009), which compared students who accepted services versus those who declined services, there were notable differences between groups in key school indicators: attendance, suspensions, and disciplinary referrals. Attendance was improved and suspensions and discipline referrals were generally reduced for students who made use of the services.

TREATING MENTAL HEALTH AND FORENSIC POPULATIONS

Practitioners who treat clients who present with both mental health and forensic issues (such as legal infractions, violence, sexual behavior problems, delinquency, crime, and competency issues) must be well-versed in understanding the challenges presented by both. No longer is it possible to assess and/or treat a client with a mental health condition without also understanding the related forensic issues. Child and adolescent clients with mental health diagnoses (such as bipolar disorder, depression, posttraumatic stress disorder, or anxiety disorders) may require a variety of treatments, including medication and therapy, along with the skills training discussed earlier in the chapter.

GANG INTERVENTIONS

Interventions to reduce gang activity and involvement must take into account the complex relationships among gangs, gangs and communities, gangs and their members, gangs and organized crime, and gang members and their families (Duffy & Gillig, 2004). A better understanding of the impact of trauma on later violence is needed so preventive interventions can be created. Multiagency, multidisciplinary efforts in this arena to increase services to gang members in the community appear to be effective (Duffy & Gillig, 2004). Thus, integrating the efforts of departments of social services, juvenile justice, housing, mental health, somatic health, schools, families, communities, and the faith community will be important. Programs that bring gang members closer to their family members lead to members who are less involved in violent gang activity.

A number of creative and effective interventions work with former gang members. For example, Homeboy Industries was founded by Father Greg Boyle in East Los Angeles to increase job, education, and counseling resources for youth in East Los Angeles (see http://www.homeboy-industries.org/).

After the significant personal tragedy of losing 13 friends in gang wars, Aqueela Sherrills brokered a peace plan between the Crips and the Bloods in LA. He and his brother, Dahoud Sherrills, founded the Community Self-Development Institute in South Central LA (http://wn.com/Community_Self-Determination_Institute). Aqueela is now a consultant for the Urban Leadership Institute in Baltimore, MD. The mission of the institute is "shifting the commitment from youth problems to youth development" (http://www.urbanyouth.org/ourmission.htm).

In the San Fernando Valley, Blinky Rodriquez helped to create Community in the Schools to provide alternatives to joining gangs (see more here http://www.calwellness.org/leadership_recognition/sabbatical_program/2007/biographies.htm).

INTERVENTIONS WITHIN THE JUVENILE JUSTICE SYSTEM

Research demonstrates the effectiveness of certain programs for youth involved in the juvenile justice system. These programs offer a full continuum of care for all levels and types of youth and family needs (Lipsy, Wilson, & Cothern, 2000). Part of that continuum includes valid risk and needs assessments, which inform the level and types of interventions to be used to improve outcomes for these youth. Greater accountability of the juvenile justice systems is needed as well. Supervision and restriction of freedom should be proportionate to the risk to the community. The system should provide more structure and supervision when behavior worsens and less when behavior improves. Research (such as Lipsey, 2009) indicates that treatment that helps build skills reduces further recidivism, whereas punishment does not.

There have been three important findings in the literature (Chambers, 2010):

1. Juvenile justice supervisory systems, group homes, and correctional facilities have, at best, modest positive effects on recidivism.
2. Deterrence programs based on discipline or threat of punishment do not work (i.e., Scared Straight; see Chapter 10 for more on this program).
3. There are therapeutic programs aimed at changing behavior that have been very effective in reducing recidivism.

These findings have led to the following conclusions (Chambers, 2010):

1. Low-risk offenders should be diverted from the juvenile justice system.
2. Moderate- to high-risk offenders should have restrictions and supervision commensurate with the level of risk to public safety and should also be provided effective therapeutic interventions.
3. Punishment that exceeds the level needed for public safety is likely to increase recidivism.

Studies have identified evidence-based practices (EBPs). However, the outcomes of applying these EBPs to large-scale, real-life public programs have been uneven. In part, this reflects the difficulty of obtaining true fidelity when utilizing a program in larger, public system settings. There is also some evidence that "generic" forms of EBPs may be as effective as "brand name" programs, such as Functional Family Therapy and MST (Chambers, 2010).

There are three approaches to studying the outcomes of juvenile justice programs. Administrators can require that all programs within a system be evaluated, and if programs are found to be ineffective, improve or eliminate them. It might also identify groups of youth who respond best to a particular program. This method requires that multiple programs be compared with each other, which takes considerable expertise to implement.

Second, there are model programs that can be implemented with as much fidelity as possible. This is often difficult and fairly expensive.

Alternatively, "generic" evidence-based therapies, such as cognitive behavioral therapy and family therapy, can be implemented in a way that the program finds to be effective (Lipsey, 2000).

Lipsey (2000) found some commonalities among programs that were most effective. Reduction in recidivism of 10% to 13% was found for programs using restorative justice (RJ), skill building, counseling, and multiple services. Programs using disciplinary and deterrence methods (Scared Straight) increased recidivism, whereas those utilizing surveillance (intensive probation and parole) demonstrated a 6% reduction in recidivism. The authors of this study recommend the following guide for intervention programs in juvenile justice systems:

- Community primary prevention aimed at all students
- Focused secondary prevention for those at greatest risk but not involved in or diverted from juvenile justice
- Intervention programs tailored to an individual youth's risk and needs for those with first time minor offenses (diversion)
- For moderate offenders and nonserious repeat offenders, intermediate sanctions, such as regular probation plus effective treatment targeted to the needs of the juvenile and his family
- Intensive services geared toward risk and need factors for first time serious or violent offenders with stringent sanctions, intensive supervision, or residential placement
- Multiple interventions, intensive programs in secure correctional facilities for the most serious, chronic offenders
- Postrelease supervision and aftercare for youth released from a residential or correctional facility
- Use of a developmental perspective that can help create a full continuum of care over the life course of a serious delinquent trajectory of childhood through adulthood

Lipsey (2000) also found that interpersonal skill building and longer programs had better results for serious violent offenders being treated in the community. For institutionalized serious violent offenders, these researchers found that well-established programs run by mental health personnel, rather than juvenile justice personnel, using interpersonal skill building had significantly better results than other programs evaluated.

RJ is the general name given to a set of practices (notably victim–offender mediation, or VOM) that typically involve face-to-face meetings between victims and offenders; the benefits include the victim's ability to express his or her feelings about the crime, and the offender's ability to be confronted with the results of his or her actions and hopefully make amends for them. It is widely adopted nationally and internationally in many justice systems, as well as juvenile justice systems and even schools.

According to Abrams, Umbreit, and Gordon (2003) "A substantial body of research has considered the potential for VOM to prevent recidivism and results pertaining to juveniles are somewhat mixed. For example, Roy's (1993) study found no statistically significant difference in recidivism between youth who went through the VOM program and court imposed restitution program in Kalamazoo, Michigan. However, several recent studies found that youth who participated in VOM programs were less likely to re-offend than youth from a randomly selected comparison groups (Nugent, Umbreit, Winameki, & Paddock, 2001). Overall, the evidence from several empirical studies suggest that VOM can reduce recidivism rates, but the deeper question remains as to how and why this process works." Much more research remains to be done to understand the long-term results of RJ practices on youth in the juvenile justice system; however, it remains a promising approach for work with this population.

REFERENCES

Abrams, L. S., Umbreit, M., & Gordon, A. (2003). *Youthful offenders response to victim offender conferencing in Washington County, Minnesota.* Retrieved from http://www.cehd.umn.edu/ssw/rjp/resources/Research/Youthful_Offenders_Response_to_VOC.pdf

Andis, P., Cashman, J., Praschil, R., Oglesby, D., Adetman, H., Taylor, L., et al. (2002). A strategic and shared agenda to advance mental health in schools through family and shared partnerships. *International Journal of Mental Health Promotion, 4,* 28–35.

Braaten, S. (1998). *Behavioral objective sequence.* Champaign, IL: Research Press.

Chambers, B. (2010). *What works with serious juvenile offenders—Pathways to desistance study.* San Francisco, CA: Community Justice Network for Youth. Retrieved from http://www.cjny.org/index.php?option=com_content&view=article&id=359:benjamin-chambers-what-works-with-serious-juvenile-offenders-pathways-to-desistance-study&catid=6:news-and-updates

Cohen, J. A., Mannario, A. P., & Deblinger, E. (1996). *Treating trauma and traumatic grief in children and adolescents.* New York, NY: The Guilford Press.

Duffy, M. P., & Gillig, S. E. (Eds.). (2004). *Teen gangs: A global view*. Westport, CT: Greenwood Press.

Goldstein, A. P., & Glick, B. (1994). Aggression replacement training: Curriculum and evaluation. *Simulation and Gaming*, 25(1), 9–26.

Heggeler, S. W.-M. (1998/2006). Multisystemic therapy: Blueprints for violenceprevention, book six. In D. S. Elliott (Ed.), *Blueprints for Violence Prevention series*. Boulder, CO: Center for the Study and Prevention of Violence, Institute of Behavioral Science, University of Colorado.

Justice Policy Institute. (2009). *The costs of confinement: Why good juvenile justice policies make good fiscal sense*. Washington, DC: Justice Policy Institute.

Kashani, J. H., Jones, M. R., Bumby, K. M, & Thomas, LA. (1999). Youth violence: Psychosocial risk factors, treatment, prevention, and recommendations. *Journal of Emotional and Behavioral Disorders*, 7(4), 200–210.

Lipsey, M. W. (2000). *Effective intervention for serious juvenile offenders*. Washington, DC: Office of Juvenile Justice and Delinquency Prevention.

Lipsey, M.W. (2009). The primary factors that characterize effective interventions with juvenile offenders: A meta-analytic overview, *Victims and Offenders* 4(2): 124–147.

Multidimensional Treatment Foster Care Web site. http://www.mtfc.com/

Multisystemic Therapy Web site. http://mstservices.com/

National Center for Education Statistics. (2010). *Indicators of school crime and safety*. Retrieved from http://nces.ed.gov/programs/crimeindicators/crimeindicators2010/key.asp

Nugent, W., Umbreit, M., Winamaki, L., & Paddock, J. (2001). Participation in victim-offender mediation and re-offense: Successful replications? *Journal of Research in Social Work Practice*, 11(1), 5–23.

Pollack, I., & Sundermann, C. (2001/. Creating safe schools: A comprehensive approach. *Juvenile Justice*, 8, 13–20.

Roy, S. (1993). Two types of juvenile restitution programs in two Midwestern counties: A comparative study. *Federal Probation*, 57, 48–53.

Schmidt, R. C. (2009). Sustaining a School Mental Health Program started through the safe schools/healthy students federal grant initiative. *Report on Emotional and Behavioral Disorders in Youth*, 51, 39–46.

Seifert, K. (2007). *CARE2 Manual*. Boston, MA: Acanthus.

Shapiro, R. (2010). *The trauma treatment handbook: Protocols across the spectrum*. New York, NY: Norton.

Weist, M. D., & Murray, M. (2007). Advancing school mental health promotion globally. *Advances in School Mental Health Promotion*, 1, 2–12.

Weist, M. D., Paternite, C. E., & Adelsheim, S. (2005). *School-based mental health services*. Commissioned report for the Institute of Medicine, Board of Health Care Services, Crossing the Quality Chasm: Adaptation to Mental Health and Addictive Disorders Committee. Washington, DC.

TWELVE

Youth Violence: Policy Implications

The juvenile justice system has always struggled to balance its perceived roles in punishing offenders and bringing about constructive behavioral change among violent youth, while ensuring public safety. There is now a movement to abandon the punitive measures of the juvenile justice system and instead concentrate on treatment and rehabilitative efforts. Lipsey, Howell, Kelly, Chapman, and Carver (2010) have proposed that the two goals of juvenile justice should be protecting the public from harm and changing the life trajectories of violent youth, so they can become productive citizens. There is a large body of research, much of it cited in the preceding chapters, outlining what works and what does not work to help youth with violent behaviors. The goal now is to apply that knowledge to the juvenile justice system.

Lipsey et al. (2010) recommends that the juvenile justice system should use validated risk and needs assessment tools and treatment programs to individualize interventions, reduce risk, and meet the treatment needs of young offenders. They also recommend providing increased structure and supervision when a youth's behavior worsens and reduced structure when it improves.

The remainder of this chapter will examine various policy initiatives and their potential impact on youth violence.

COLLABORATION AMONG PUBLIC AGENCIES

Agencies most often accessed for youth with problems are (1) mental health (93%), (2) juvenile justice (80%), (3) school-based educational services (71%), and (4) child welfare (69%) (Howell, Kelly, Palmer, & Magnum, 2004). To effectively help this group with very complex and chronic problems across multiple agencies, public and private organizational coordination is essential.

For example, it has been estimated that two-thirds of juveniles in the juvenile justice system have mental health or substance abuse problems (Justice Policy Institute, 2009). Estimates of youth with trauma histories in the juvenile justice system are also high (Seifert, 2006). In general, treatment for these conditions is presently insufficient in the juvenile justice system. One solution might be to create joint (mental health and juvenile services) funding of services for youth in juvenile services that need mental health treatment.

Howell et al. (2004) describe an interagency collaborative system for high-risk youth. They make a strong case for the fact that high-risk youth have problems in multiple domains and are often served by multiple public agencies. For more effective services, a collaborative model of multiple agencies working together is needed (Howell et al., 2004; Tuell, 2002). In the Howell et al. model, there is a list of necessary components for such a system and a model for constructing it. Key features of a comprehensive system include the following:

- Support and strengthen families to give support and guidance to their children
- Adequately support youth and family serving agencies, faith-based programs, and community organizations in developing capable, responsible youth; support coordination of agencies that work with the same families
- Prevent delinquency as a very efficient and cost-effective approach to lowering the rate of juvenile delinquency
- Provide services immediately and effectively the first time delinquent behavior occurs to prevent future offending
- Identify and provide structure for serious, violent, chronic, high-risk juvenile offenders who have failed to respond to intervention in nonsecure community-based treatment programs
- Use a continuum of prevention programs, interventions, and sanctions. Ensure that youth can move up and down the continuum of structure and intensity, as needed, based on their ability to self-manage their own behavior. Follow this with aftercare
- Reduce risk and enhance protection

- Provide early intervention with predelinquent and delinquent children and their families, especially for children younger than 13 years, as this is a sign of Moffitt's lifelong trajectory of violence
- Place the most serious, violent, and chronic offenders in secure correctional type facilities

The Center for Juvenile Justice Reform is working on a project to train professionals in the integration of services from multiple agencies, particularly social services and juvenile services. More information can be found at http://cjjr.georgetown.edu/certprogs/public/capstonepublic.html.

IMPROVED SCHOOL SERVICES

Many youth who demonstrate assaultive behaviors also have learning problems and are failing in school. They may be rejected by their peers. They may be bullies, or bullied, or both. They may eventually drop out of school or get expelled.

Many school systems offer services for these youth, which are often run as a disciplinary alternative to the regular classroom. These programs may include intensive school-based mental health and skill building programs (Schmidt, 2009). For example, PBIS (Positive Behavioral Interventions and Supports, www.pbis.org) classifies students with moderate to severe behavior problems into "yellow zones" and "red zones," respectively. It uses a system of evidence-based behavioral interventions to increase positive behaviors and reduce negative behaviors among students. For example, Red Zone children need intensive services that are given on an individual basis.

IMPROVED JUVENILE JUSTICE FACILITIES

"Juvenile justice facilities across the nation are in a dangerously advanced state of disarray, with violence an almost everyday occurrence and rehabilitation the exception rather than the rule. Abuse of juvenile inmates by staff is routine" (Cannon, 2004, in Abrams 2005).

Unfortunately, enacting change among the juvenile justice facilities can be difficult if not impossible. According to Tim Decker, the reform-oriented Director of Missouri Division of Youth Services: "Across the system there were entrenched organizational cultures. We protected both turf and the status quo instead of shared values and communication. Misperceptions related to the service offerings and strengths of others in the system were common. Both efforts faced a prevalent status quo bias and little faith in the possibility of a different approach to serving the youth" (Decker, 2010, in Lipsey et al. 2010).

In 2008, the Office of Juvenile Justice and Delinquency Prevention reported that approximately 93,000 youth were placed in juvenile justice facilities. Seventy percent were in state funded, post-disposition residential facilities at an average cost of $241 per youth per day. The Justice Policy Institute (May, 2009) reported that the United States spends $5.7 billion yearly in the confinement of delinquent youth. These placements are intended to protect public safety, but do they? The Institute proposes that the majority of these youth can be managed in the community without substantial risk to others and that funding could be more appropriately used on community services. The Institute offers several reasons why residential placements are ineffective for some youth:

- Negative conditions in large, overcrowded facilities have been the cause of multimillion dollar lawsuits, poor outcomes for youth, and a focus on punishment, which is ineffective in changing behavior.
- Confinement reduces young people's ability to gain experience and skills in the work world, school, and community, thus reducing their future opportunities.
- Research has demonstrated that states that increased the number of youth in residential facilities did not see a concomitant reduction in community crime and thus public safety.

The need for public safety is an important factor to consider in the issue of juvenile confinement. Another aspect is the need for more widespread use of valid and reliable tools to determine risk of dangerousness when determining need for confinement.

The conclusions derived from a meta-analysis of the effectiveness of juvenile justice programs by the Center for Juvenile Justice Reform (Lipsey et al., 2010) determined that successful programs demonstrated the following factors:

- Risk management and reduction through reduced recidivism
- Evidence-based practices based on research that reduce criminogenic risk and increase adaptive functioning
- Use of empirically based risk assessment and management tools and individualized treatment plans
- A diverse array of services that can meet individual juvenile treatment needs
- Graduated levels of supervision and control that allow more structure and control when youth are less able to exert self-management and less structure when they demonstrate more self-management and good choices
- Improve future behavior rather than punish past behavior
- Programs with higher intensity and longer lengths of time should be reserved for high-risk cases
- Program effectiveness is related to the following:
  - principles of family therapy, multisystemic, and developmentally appropriate approaches
  - a program does not necessarily have to be "brand name," but must be high quality and monitored for effectiveness
  - quality services and intensity and length of services matched with risk
- Standardized program assessment based on meta-analysis, such as the Standardized Program Evaluation Protocol for Assessing Juvenile Justice Programs

Several cost-effective community programs have proven effectiveness in reducing juvenile recidivism.

For example, RECLAIM Ohio (Reasoned and Equitable Community and Local Alternatives to the Incarceration of Minors) is a funding initiative that encourages local juvenile courts to develop or contract for a range of community-based sanctions options. The program, which was implemented statewide in 1995, has reduced juvenile confinement by 42% from 1992 to 2009. Every Reclaim dollar spent for community services saves from $11 to $45 in commitment and processing costs. Similarly, Redeploy Illinois has reduced juvenile commitment by 51% by financially incentivizing local jurisdictions to create and support community services as a diversion from confinement. New York, Pennsylvania, California, and Wisconsin have had similar results.

If violent juveniles cannot be safely housed in the juvenile system and effective treatments are not available, alternatives must be found. Some states are experimenting with hybrid solutions that allow homicidal adolescents to be exempt from the adult system and be released after receiving appropriate treatment.

IMPROVED ASSESSMENT AND INTERVENTION OF CHILD MALTREATMENT

As discussed in Chapter 6, maltreatment in childhood increases the risk of imprisonment 59% in adolescence and 28% in adulthood; 70% of child victims report engaging in violent behaviors at some time. In one study (Hosser, Raddatz, & Windzio, 2007), 46% of those maltreated in childhood displayed violent behaviors later in their lives. Thirty percent of those who were not maltreated engaged in later violence.

At an International Conference on Children and the Law in Prato, Italy (September 7–10, 2009), many presenters stated that in their countries, the child welfare/protective services systems "feed" the juvenile justice systems. Children who grow up in violent homes tend to perpetrate violence as they grow older. The research is clear on the connection between child maltreatment and later delinquency, criminal acts, and violence (Tuell, 2002). Because departments of social and juvenile services tend to be understaffed, overworked, underpaid, lack resources, and serve many of the same families, some countries, such as Scotland (McGhee & Waterhouse, 2009), are examining the advantages of combining departments of social and juvenile services for better efficiency and effectiveness.

There is some controversy about classifying exposure to domestic violence as child abuse or neglect; therefore, the policies of departments of social services in this area are slow to change to include treatment for the child victims of domestic violence as well (Jouriles, McDonald, Slep, Heyman, & Garrido, 2008). However, the research is clear that exposure to domestic violence is also associated with later violence perpetrated by juveniles (Hosser, Raddatz, & Windzio, 2007; Jouriles, McDonald, Slep, Heyman, & Garrido, 2008; Seifert, 2006).

ADOLESCENT VERSUS ADULT COMPETENCE TO STAND TRIAL

The 1960 *Milton Dusky v. United States Supreme Court* hearing held that for adults to be competent, they must be able

> to consult with one's attorney with a reasonable degree of rational understanding." and a "rational as well as factual understanding of the proceedings against him."

> Chief Justice Earl Warren, April 18, 1960

There is some controversy about whether the *Dusky* standard for competency should apply to juveniles, and under what circumstances. Because juveniles in juvenile court have been afforded the legal rights given to any adult defendant, they also have the right to be competent to stand trial. States vary on their application of this principle (Sanborn, 2009). In general, the majority of youth aged 13 years and over are found competent to stand trial, whereas those younger than 13 years are generally not found competent. In some states, a youth can be civilly committed until he is restored to competence. What to do when a youth is found not competent in juvenile court is also under debate. Alternatives include educating the youth until he or she is competent, or allowing the Court to proceed.

Although there are no universal standards for measuring competence, cognitive approaches generally find that adults and juveniles over the age of roughly 13 years are very similar in this regard (Sanborn, 2009). Twelve- to fourteen-year-olds are generally able to understand rights and the roles of judges and attorneys. Juvenile decision making may be very similar to adult decision making by 14 or 15 years of age. By age 15, most youth are adequately able to assist their attorneys and can think in hypothetical situations. Teens are generally able to reason, understand, act responsibly, and understand court proceedings (Sanborn, 2009). The literature suggests the following:

- Teens are not incompetent by virtue of their age alone.
- Competency as defined by Dusky applies to both the adult and juvenile Courts.

YOUTH TRIED AS ADULTS

The Campaign for Youth Justice (2010) recently issued a report on reductions in prosecution of juveniles in adult court. The report found that states are increasingly removing juveniles from their adult correctional systems; they are raising the age of juvenile court jurisdiction; transfer laws have been changed in some states to make it easier to keep juveniles in the juvenile system; and sentencing laws are being examined.

Juveniles typically are incarcerated equal amounts of time for equivalent crimes, whether they are prosecuted through the juvenile or adult systems. Youth prosecuted as adults recidivate more quickly than those processed through the adult system, but after 6 years, the recidivism rates are the same (Snyder, Sickmund, & Poe-Yamagata, 2000). Another problem arises when juveniles must be released from the juvenile system when they reach (in most cases) the age of 21 years, whether they are still in need of more structure, support, and services or not. Some states have experimented with a hybrid system that keeps juveniles in juvenile facilities until they are 21 years of age and then they are transferred to an adult facility if that is needed, or they can be continued in community treatment if that is needed. This is called blended sentencing and can be found in Colorado and Michigan (Redding & Howell, 2000).

A hybrid system is described by Bill Sturgeon on The University of Cincinnati's School of Criminal Justice Web site at Corrections.com (http://www.corrections.com/bill_sturgeon/?tag=outdated-juvenile-justice-systems). He proposes that for very chronic and dangerous young offenders between the ages of 12 and 18 years, a new type of facility be created that provides both safety and security as you would find in an adult jail and the intensive treatment you would find in a juvenile facility. The staff would be highly trained, professional, and able to meet the needs of this particular group of youth. Perhaps this would give them a chance to become productive adults.

CONCLUSION: MEASURES TO PREVENT YOUTH VIOLENCE

Youth who are at risk for aggression typically have multiple complex problems. One key to helping them is to provide services for all family members and to coordinate those services for efficiency and better outcomes. Outcomes for this population can be improved by supporting families, coordination of care among agencies and community groups, offering prevention services, providing services at the time of the first delinquent act, and providing a continuum of care from light services to intensive services for severely and chronically aggressive youth.

Changes are also needed in the individual agencies that serve this population. The juvenile justice system needs to emphasize treatment and rehabilitation more strongly, and should use empirically based risk assessments and evidence-based practice. The social services system needs to look at addressing the needs of maltreated children and those exposed to domestic violence.

Schools typically fail to meet the needs of at-risk youth. The educational system still leans in the direction of punishment (suspension and expulsion) rather than treatment, even though suspension and expulsion usually leads to more problems for the child. School-based mental health can be an important treatment option.

The legal system continues to grapple with the concept of whether youth from the ages of 13 to 18 years are juveniles or adults. Some have proposed a third category of youthful offenders that are managed in a separate system that combines treatment and security for high-risk offenders and hybrid sentencing that can hold a youth beyond his 21st birthday when needed.

As repeatedly discussed throughout this volume, many violent children and youth have histories of neglect, abuse, and/or trauma. Improvements in public agencies might better serve these children and their families before they commit acts of violence:

■ Increased screening of foster parents and their ability to care for children, particularly special needs children

- Stringent monitoring of children in homes with ongoing domestic violence
- Decreased caseloads of Child Protective Services (CPS) workers
- More involvement of law enforcement investigative departments when children are harmed or killed by caregivers
- Increased services to abusive and neglectful families
- Increased funding of family and child services agencies
- Use of highly qualified child and family experts to determine child and family needs
- Increased educational requirements for case workers in public agencies
- Ongoing education and consultation of public agency staff on family functioning, counseling, child development, trauma, sexual offending, violence, case management, substance abuse, forensics, and other topics
- Mental health services for all youth and families that need it

REFERENCES

Abrams, D. E. (2005). Reforming juvenile delinquency treatment to enhance rehabilitation, personal accountability, and public safety. *Oregon Law Review, 84,* 1001–1092.

Campaign for Youth Justice. (2010). *State trends: Legislative victories from 2005 to 2010 removing youth from the adult criminal justice system.* Retrieved from http://www.campaignforyouthjustice.org/documents/CFYJ_State_Trends_Report.pdf

Hosser, D., Raddatz, S., & Windzio, M. (2007). Child maltreatment, revictimization and violent behavior. *Violence and Victims, 22*(3), 318–333.

Howell, J. C., Kelly, M. R., Palmer, J., & Magnum, R. L. (2004). Integrating child welfare, juvenile justice and other agencies in a continuum of services. *Child Welfare, 83*(2), 143.

Jouriles, E. N., McDonald, R. Slep, A. M. S., Heyman, R. E., & Garrido, E. (2008). Child abuse in the context of domestic violence: Prevalence, explanations and practice implications. *Violence & Victims, 23,* 221–234.

Justice Policy Institute. (2009, May). *The costs of confinement: Why good juvenile justice policies make good fiscal sense.* Washington, DC: Justice Policy Institute.

Lipsey, M. W., Howell, J. C., Kelly, M. R., Chapman, G., & Carver, D. (2010, December). *Improving the effectiveness of juvenile justice programs: A new perspective on evidence-based practice.* Washington, DC: Center for Juvenile Justice Reform.

McGhee, J., & Waterhouse, L. (2009, September 7). *Youth justice and child welfare: Unraveling a paradox within state intervention in children's lives.* Retrived from www.med.monash.edu.au/socialwork/conference09/finalprogram.pdf

Redding, R. E., & Howell, J. C. (2000). The blended sentencing in American juvenile courts, NCJ 192953. In: J. Fagan & F. Zimring (Eds.), *The changing borders of juvenile justice: Transfer of adolescents to the criminal court* (pp. 145–180). See NCJ-192949. Retrieved from http://www.ncjrs.gov/App/publications/Abstract.aspx?id=192953

Sanborn, J. B. (2009). Juveniles competency to stand trial: Wading through the rhetoric and the evidence. *Journal of Criminal Law and Criminology, 99*(1), 135.

Schmidt, R. C. (2009, Spring). Sustaining a school mental health program started through the safe schools/healthy students federal grant initiative. *Report on Emotional and Behavioral Disorders in Youth, 8,* 39–46, 51.

Seifert, K. (2006). *How children become violent.* Boston, MA: Acanthus.

Snyder, H. N., Sickmund, M., & Poe-Yamagata, E. (2000). *Juvenile transfers to criminal court in the 1990's: Lessons learned from four studies.* Washington, DC: Office of Juvenile Justice and Delinquency Prevention.

Tuell, J. A. (2002). *Child maltreatment and juvenile delinquency: Raising the level of awareness.* Washington, DC: Child Welfare League of America Press.

Index

CPSIA information can be obtained
at www.ICGtesting.com
Printed in the USA
FFOW03n0935281214
9877FF